CUISINES OF THE CAUCASUS MOUNTAINS

The Hippocrene Cookbook library

AFRICA AND OCEANIA
Best of Regional African Cooking
Traditional South African Cookery
Taste of Eritrea
Good Food from Australia

ASIA AND MIDDLE EAST
The Best of Taiwanese Cuisine
Imperial Mongolian Cooking
The Best of Regional Thai Cuisine
Japanese Home Cooking
The Best of Korean Cuisine
Egyptian Cooking
Sephardic Israeli Cuisine
Healthy South Indian Cooking
The Indian Spice Kitchen
Cuisines of the Caucasus Mountains
Afghan Food and Cookery
The Art of Persian Cooking
The Art of Turkish Cooking
The Art of Uzbek Cooking

MEDITERRANEAN
Best of Greek Cuisine,
   Expanded Edition
Taste of Malta
A Spanish Family Cookbook
Tastes of North Africa

WESTERN EUROPE
Art of Dutch Cooking, Expanded
   Edition
A Belgian Cookbook
Cooking in the French Fashion (bilingual)
Cuisines of Portuguese Encounters
The Swiss Cookbook
The Art of Irish Cooking
Feasting Galore Irish-Style
Traditional Food from Scotland
Traditional Food from Wales
The Scottish-Irish Pub and
   Hearth Cookbook
A Treasury of Italian Cuisine (bilingual)

SCANDINAVIA
Best of Scandinavian Cooking
The Best of Finnish Cooking
The Best of Smorgasbord Cooking
Tastes & Tales of Norway
Icelandic Food & Cookery

CENTRAL EUROPE
All Along the Rhine
All Along the Danube
Best of Austrian Cuisine
Bavarian Cooking
The Best of Czech Cooking
The Best of Slovak Cooking
The Art of Hungarian Cooking
Hungarian Cookbook
Polish Heritage Cookery
The Best of Polish Cooking
Old Warsaw Cookbook
Old Polish Traditions
Treasury of Polish Cuisine (bilingual)
Poland's Gourmet Cuisine
The Polish Country Kitchen Cookbook

EASTERN EUROPE
Art of Lithuanian Cooking
Best of Albanian Cooking
Traditional Bulgarian Cooking
Best of Croatian Cooking
Taste of Romania
Taste of Latvia
The Best of Russian Cooking
The Best of Ukrainian Cuisine

AMERICAS
Argentina Cooks
A Taste of Haiti
A Taste of Quebec
Cooking With Cajun Women
French Caribbean Cuisine
Mayan Cooking
The Art of Brazilian Cookery
The Art of South American Cookery
Old Havana Cookbook (bilingual)

CUISINES OF THE CAUCASUS MOUNTAINS

RECIPES, DRINKS, AND LORE FROM ARMENIA, AZERBAIJAN, GEORGIA, AND RUSSIA

Kay Shaw Nelson

HIPPOCRENE BOOKS, INC.

NEW YORK

Also by Kay Shaw Nelson:

TABLE OF CONTENTS

ACKNOWLEDGMENTS. vii

PREFACE xi

INTRODUCTION. 1

APPETIZERS 21

SOUPS. 49

DAIRY DISHES 73

FISH 99

MEAT, POULTRY, AND GAME 121

VEGETABLES AND SALADS 151

GRAINS AND LEGUMES 177

BREADS, PASTAS, AND SAVORY PASTRIES 197

DESSERTS AND SWEETS 225

BEVERAGES, DRINKS, AND WINES 249

BIBLIOGRAPHY 257

RECIPE INDEX 259

SUBJECT INDEX. 269

ACKNOWLEDGMENTS

For this book I am especially grateful to the publisher, George Blagowidow, and my editors, Carol Chitnis and Anne McBride, of Hippocrene Books.

As always I wish to thank my daughter, Rae, for her continual support and editorial assistance while writing the book.

Over the years, beginning at Syracuse University while majoring in Russian Studies and Journalism, and later living in Washington, D.C., Turkey, Greece, and Germany I met many people who shared their special knowledge, folklore, culinary traditions, and recipes with generosity. I thank them all, especially those who spent hours with me in markets, kitchens, and providing hospitality with friendly conversations, enjoying libations and dining on fine fare.

Among those who helped me recently with information, books, and recipes I wish to thank the Armenian Embassy of Washington D.C., Claudia Kousoulas, Fran MacLean, Jane Mengenhauser, Elisavietta Ritchie, and Rose Balian, Thelma Kostegian and other members of The Ladies Guild of Soorp Khatch Armenian Apostolic Church, Bethesda, Maryland.

To the memory of Dr. Warren B. Walsh and Dr. Geoge B. Cressy, my professors at Syracuse University's Maxwell School of Citizenship and Public Affairs, who introduced me to the history and geography of the Caucasus Mountains, the Caucasian lands, and people.

PREFACE

"At last I'll find out if Georgia is the real Garden of Eden," I jokingly remarked to a traveling companion as we disembarked from an Aeroflot plane in Tbilisi, the capital city of the fabled country in the Transcaucasus region between the Black and Caspian Seas. In the distance I glimpsed the towering Caucasus Mountains, one of the world's great mountain chains. My spirits were high. I was looking forward to tasting the spicy exotic Georgian culinary specialties, enjoying their reputed "hot hospitality," and discovering why the Georgians are among the longest-lived people in the world.

I had flown from Leningrad, now St. Petersburg, to Tbilisi, once a famous trading center, during a two-week, 3,500-mile late-summer tour with other members of the National Press Club. It was my first time in the pic-turesque Caucasus region about which I had acquired considerable knowl-edge while majoring in Russian Studies and Journalism at Syracuse University several years before. Meanwhile, I'd became a devotee of the distinctive Georgian cuisine, described by one writer as "a love poem to the culinary arts." Little wonder it has achieved worldwide fame.

Wedged in between the southern slopes of the majestic Caucasus Mountains and the Black Sea with Russia to the north, Azerbaijan to the east, and Armenia and Turkey to the south, Georgia is a legendary land that traces its origins back for millennia. If it is not the actual biblical Garden of Eden, as my Georgian friend had boasted, it was one of the cradles of civilization.

Long ago, the country was called Iveria, renamed by the Greeks *Georgiana*, meaning "Promised Land." According to Greek mythology Prometheus, chained to a rock for stealing fire from heaven for the mor-tals, suffered in the rugged mountains. And, on the coast of the Black Sea in western Georgia, lies the ancient land of Colchis to which Jason and his Argonauts sailed in search of the Golden Fleece.

An intensely captivating and beautiful country with a wealth of scenic delights, natural resources, and native foods, Georgia endured scores of invasions from Mongols, Persians, Romans, and Ottoman Turks who dev-astated the land. But through the centuries of turmoil, as well as years of Russian domination, the proud and spirited people managed to preserve themselves as a distinctive and colorful country with their own language, culture, cuisine, and generous hospitality, as well as a strong tradition of nationalistic sentiment.

Known for its variety of landscapes and climates, the country has manifold tourist attractions, ranging from northern snow-capped Caucasus peaks for mountaineers and skiers to the southwestern subtropical Black Sea resorts of Sukhumi and Batumi. One can enjoy mineral spas in Borzhomi and Central Georgia, or visit age-old vineyards in the eastern province of Kakheti. The Georgian Military Highway, an ancient caravan route sometimes called "Poet's Road" because of those who traveled over it, offers a spectacular tour of the northern mountain region, past turbulent rivers, deep gorges, fertile valleys, and the ancient capital of Mtskheta.

I, however, began my sightseeing in Tbilisi, one of the world's oldest surviving cities, located along the banks of the Kura River and founded on a site chosen because of healing sulfur springs which flow beneath it. During Georgia's flourishing Golden Age, as the capital of an independent kingdom, it was known as Tiflis. A lively metropolis with tree-lined boulevards and a cosmopolitan atmosphere bustling with animation, Tbilisi prides itself on being the home city of Georgian poets, writers, artists, musicians, and sculptors. I would find it to be a great city for artistic, historic, and culinary explorations.

Believing that a traveler in a new place should visit a marketplace to view the country's foods, I strolled down *Rustaveli Prospekt*, a nineteenth-century avenue linking the two main squares and named for Georgia's national poet, Shota Rustaveli, to the enormous farmers' market. A colorful and vibrant maze of produce stands and small shops, it was alive with the shouting and cajoling of vendors, reminiscent of a Near Eastern bazaar. Passing the counters of meat and poultry, I was excited to find a wondrous cornucopia of fresh, luscious fruits, ranging from apricots and many-seeded pomegranates to several kinds of plums and cherries, arranged artistically next to a great variety of vegetables. I tasted a soft goat's milk cheese called *suluguni*; passed tubs of creamy yogurt; plate-size wild mushrooms; rows of nuts, notably almonds, walnuts, and hazelnuts; and mounds of ground spices. Colorful spice ladies hawked their own blends of a wonderfully fragrant specialty called *khmeli-suneli*, meaning "mixed smell," made from various combinations of dried herbs and spices.

Because Georgians love aromatics and have a particular flair for seasoning their dishes with intense flavorings, I was fascinated with the marvelous array of leafy bunches of herbs (including the ubiquitous coriander and opal basil), wild greens, all kinds of onions, strings of garlic and hot peppers, pickled acacias, and an uncommon variety of fenugreek, as well as fragrant flower blossoms like marigolds. Also of great interest were heaps of dried fruits, cultivated grains, and ground corn that Georgians use to make several dishes, including breads.

It doesn't take long to become friendly with the vivacious dark-eyed Georgians who love to communicate with visitors, either by sign language or perhaps a few words of English. They are also celebrated traders. Out of the blue, a loquacious woman pointed to her basket of peaches, indicating with her fingers that she would like to exchange them for a lipstick. I gladly obliged; we both smiled, and parted with friendly nods. An elderly man, however, just handed my friend a beautiful bouquet of fresh herbs, waving her away when she offered a coin. And food, I learned that morning in the market, and later along the streets, is an esteemed and valuable prize that Georgians like to share with others for them to enjoy.

For our first meal, a luncheon in a modern hotel, the menu was a typical Georgian repast featuring favorite traditional dishes, beginning with a splendid selection of appetizers, and an array of dishes placed along the center of the table. We tasted fresh and pickled vegetables, a spinach purée known as *pkhali*, slices of air-dried beef called *basturma*, and a beloved favorite, *lobio*, made of highly seasoned red beans. After a bowl of spicy beef soup, we continued with a local version of beef stroganoff that was cooked in a saffron-tomato sauce, *khachapuri* (cheese-stuffed bread), and then fresh fruits and a honey-walnut sweet, along with glasses of a fruity white *Tsinandali* and robust red *Mukuzani* wines.

As I knew from previous dining experiences with high-spirited Georgians in other locales, they love the pleasures of the table, not just to enjoy their treasured dishes and wines, but also the companionship of family and friends. Tradition demands that all guests be given a banquet, as bountiful as the host can provide, and during our visit we dined regally from the country's cornucopia in atmospheric restaurants and homes. Meanwhile, I was learning more about the cuisine with great pleasure.

Although Georgians have a healthy diet based on vegetable oils, nuts, whole grains, grilled lamb and chicken, greens, cheeses, and yogurt, all their specialties have tantalizing flavors due to their exquisite and spicy seasonings. While some gastronomes have compared the Georgian cuisine to those of the Mediterranean countries or India, I believe that it is unique. And because of the harmonious blending of unusual ingredients with marvelous fresh foods and intense flavorings, the dishes are extremely tasty, and sometimes difficult to describe and duplicate elsewhere. The people, men as well as women, are instinctive cooks who take time and pleasure in creating dishes for themselves and, hopefully, to share with others. Their inventiveness is incredible.

From Tbilisi our small group of journalists traveled by bus to the eastern wine-growing region of Kakheti where, in the capital of Telavi ("place of trees") at the foothills of the Caucasus Mountains, we spent a few days and met with several Georgians. There we also visited ancient monasteries, a former prince's family estate, and wine cellars. Believed to be one of the world's original wine-producing areas, Georgia is proud of its reputable reds and whites and, if Georgians did not really discover the pleasure of drinking wine, as they like to say, the drink is an integral part of everyday life. No occasion is complete without a little or a lot of the local wine.

A highlight of our trip was a late-afternoon visit to the nearby 200-year-old village of Saniore, surrounded by vineyards, where, in the home of a cooperative farm family, we enjoyed a ceremonial feast based on the traditional ritual called *supra*. It holds a special place in the culture of these ancient people and observes, along with eating and drinking, a fixed pattern of toasting in which participants pay tribute to just about anything and everything, past as well as present. After cordial introductions, our small group gathered around a festive table and the feasting began with a welcome drink of wine, absolutely essential to the supra, and not drunk without a toast.

Earlier in Leningrad, our guide had laughingly, but appearing serious, warned us that it was "dangerous" to go to Georgia where, she said, we should be aware of the "hot hospitality." "They give you too much wine to drink and are offended if you don't drink a whole horn at once. Remember what I've said, watch out," she chided.

As our *tamada*, or toastmaster, seated at the head of the table, raised a glass to celebrate the arrival of the Americans, I thought briefly about the guide's counsel. But, after the traditional friendship welcome, sprinkling salt on a chunk of bread broken from a long crusty loaf, the procession of ceremonial drinks and orations began. First, we drank to peace, then to our political leaders, families, ancestors, the arts, holidays, beautiful women,

September's harvest, and a happy future, with five kinds of wine as well as several sips from a small, clay friendship bowl. Our host kept filling and refilling the glasses. Then came the ornate ibex horn filled with wine. Bottoms up, our host proclaimed. I opted for a sip of wine. He was not offended, explaining that ladies may be excused from drinking bottoms-up, but men are not.

Meanwhile, women in flowered dresses kept bringing plates of appetizers: eggplant in walnut sauce, smoked sturgeon, red caviar with buttered bread, rice-stuffed peppers, cheeses, pickled garlic cloves, meat-filled dumplings, spicy green and red pepper mixtures. Then came chunks of a glorious skewered lamb, or *shashlyk*, accompanied by *tkemali*, a spicy sour-plum sauce, and a superb loaf known as *deda's puri* (mother's bread), baked in an outdoor round clay oven called a *toné*. Traditionally, Georgians eat fruit for dessert but on this occasion there were cakes and pastries, as well as more drinks. A young girl played spirited Georgian songs on the piano. We had dancing and singing, and lots of conversing and conviviality.

At one point during the meal our congenial host, enjoying every minute of the celebration while trying to explain some Georgian traditions, turned to me and said, "I want you to know that my father is over 90 years old and is in perfect health. He drinks over four bottles of our local wine every day. Let's have a toast to our parents."

I had imbibed slowly and, like my companions, was not overwhelmed by the consumption of wine. We were, though, mellow and pleased with our festive meal. Now is the time to ask about the elusive secret of their longevity, I mused. For centuries, the Georgians and other Caucasians have been mentioned by travelers amazed at their good health at an old age, 100 years or over, even, as one said, as old as Moses (120 years). Could it be the wine, which one man called "life giving"? Was it their love of vegetables and fruits? Perhaps it was the yogurt, the garlic, or the onions? Or some people say, because the Georgians do not overeat, but enjoy food and wine leisurely and with convivial companions, rarely dining alone? They, I knew, are born optimists, always looking at the bright side of life. As for my query, our *tamada* shrugged and replied, "I've heard that the experts are studying why Georgia has so many centenarians. I tell them it's because we have such fun living." So we drank to that.

As we were leaving Georgia I recalled a tale that I'd heard years before from a former Georgian princess living in Istanbul, Turkey, and was repeated by the toastmaster at our recent banquet. When God was creating the earth and had finished dividing it into nations, he had saved one special place for himself: paradise. It was where everything was beautiful, a land of milk and honey with all the best foods and wines. But, on his way home, passing some Georgians, sitting in an arbor dining and drinking, God noticed what a good time they were having. Pleased that they were so happy, he decided to give them his prized corner of the world to use in the best way possible. So, ever since, Georgians have thought of their small country as the Garden of Eden.

Surely, this remembrance would call for another Georgian toast that translates: "Here's to whatever you believe."

For me, my sojourn in Georgia had been a great and rewarding experience, fulfilling a dream of many years. Not only had I learned more about the creative cuisine, but I'd had the opportunity to dine with the vibrant people who enjoy life with a rare enthusiasm. Fortunately, the love of good eating and drinking continues in all the regions of the Caucasus as it has for centuries.

INTRODUCTION

The cookery of the Caucasus, a picturesque ancient region of great natural and cultural diversity, between the Black Sea in the west and the Caspian Sea in the east, is as fascinating to explore as it is delightful to savor. For it includes a marvelous collection of healthful and inviting traditional dishes that were evolved over the centuries by creative cooks from different nationalities. Such gastronomic specialties, which are challenging and rewarding to prepare, are marvelous additions to the culinary repertoire, either for everyday dining or for special occasions.

Dominated by the towering Caucasus Mountains, one of the world's great mountain systems, the area called the Caucasus traditionally has been a world in itself, remote and intriguing where human history is old. To the

© RFE/RL

ancient Babylonians, the Caucasus Range was part of a mountainous chain that separated the world into lands of light and dark. Serving both as a bridge and as a barrier to migration and invasion, this historically complex crossroads has witnessed continuous political revolts and changes.

Following the 1991 collapse of the United Soviet Socialist Republic, the North Caucasus area, stretching across the south of the Russian Federation, is bounded by the Black Sea and Sea of Azov to the west and the Caspian Sea to the east. It includes the autonomous republics of Dagestan, Chechnya, Ingushetia, North Ossetia, Kabardino-Balkaria, Karachay-Cherkessia, Krasnodar, and the Stavropol territory. In the southern region called the Transcaucasus or Transcaucasia, meaning "across the Caucasus," there are three independent countries, former republics of the U.S.S.R. Grouped around the Caucasus mountain range east of the Black Sea they are Georgia, Armenia, and Azerbaijan. Here national and regional cooking traditions are deeply respected and passed on to succeeding generations.

The Caucasus Mountains, extending about 750 miles between Russia in the north and Georgia and Azerbaijan in the south, from the Black Sea in the west to the Caspian Sea in the east, form what is considered by some geographers to be a natural border between Europe and Asia. Presenting great topographic variety where climate and vegetation change abruptly with altitude and exposure, the mountains were formed near the edge of the Alpine Geosyncline about 25 million years ago. Now they include three ranges and rise to a maximum elevation of 18,510 feet in Mt. Elbrus.

The Greater Caucasus, the main range of the mountain system, separating temperate and subtropical climate zones, extends northwest-southeast from the Taman Peninsula, between the Black Sea and the Sea of Azov, to the Apsheron Peninsula on the Caspian Sea. It has low hills at two extremities and exceeds the highest Alpine peaks in its central section, rising at ten points above the elevation of Mt. Blanc. Many of the major ones, notably Mt. Elbrus, the highest point of the Caucasus and Europe at the western end of the high peaks, lie in these lateral ranges. Others are Ushba (over 15,403 feet), Dykh-Tau (over 17,070 feet), Shkhara (over 16,594 feet), and, on the east, Kazbek (over 16,558 feet). Considerable areas are above the snow line, and there are well over a thousand glaciers. The topography is superbly rugged and beautiful.

South of the central ranges are the Lesser Caucasus, a longitudinal depression made up of a series of river valleys that begins in the northwest on the Black Sea in the lowlands known as Kolkhida, ancient Colchis celebrated in mythology as the special domain of sorcery. It continues eastward along the valley of the Kura River to the broad Kura-Aras plain on the Caspian Sea. A block-faulted highland with numerous dormant volcanoes, generally from 6,000 to 10,000 feet, the range includes part of the high Armenian Plateau. The crests nowhere reach the snow line and the highest point is Mt. Aragats, rising to 13,418 feet. The famous Mt. Ararat, an extinct volcanic massif in eastern Turkey overlooking the point at which the frontiers of Turkey, Iran, and Armenia converge, is 16,916 feet, and in the east, the dominant feature is a high mountain lake surrounded by mountains. Lake Sevan, the largest lake of the Caucasus region, lies at 6,250 feet, while the surrounding mountains soar to 11,800 feet.

In the center of the Greater and Lesser Caucasus is the low Surami range, a granite massif oriented north and south, and forming the watershed between the Rioni and Kura rivers. Here are passes as low as 3,280 feet.

Since ancient times the Caucasus has served as a refuge for persecuted peoples who fled to the mountain valleys for protection from potential enemies. Wave after wave of settlement resulted in a complex ethnic pattern and entangled melange of nationalities throughout the area. The princely fourteenth-century historian Abu al-Fida called the Caucasus region *jabal al-alsun*, "The Mountain of Tongues," for there he counted more than 300 languages, remarkable not only because of their number and diversity but individual linguistic structures.

In *Highlanders: A Journey to the Caucasus,* the author, Yo'av Karny, offers a colorful explanation for the multitude of languages. He writes that, "An Arab legend ascribed it all to the narrowness of mountain passages. God's mule, which was carrying a pouch of languages to be distributed worldwide, stumbled on one of those treacherous paths, the sack opened wide, and the languages were scattered all over and remained there for posterity." But, Karny continues, "A likelier explanation for the diversity is that the impassable terrain and harsh climate kept small communities free from external influence. Because mighty empires rarely bothered with mountaintops, no centralizing cultural influence forced the fragments together. Elsewhere, archaic languages evolved toward simplicity of use and broad literacy, but in the Caucasus they remained in their pristine stage—unwritten, unread, and helpfully uncontested."

Although the regions of the North Caucasus within the Russian Federation include a predominance of Russians who settled there beginning in the eighteenth century, there are also a number of minorities. Among these are the colorful Circassians who live in scattered areas; the peoples of Dagestan, a conglomerate of several ethnic groups; and those of the other autonomous republics who maintain their individual traditions as well as languages. The Ossetians, for example, are the only surviving people to speak the language of the ancient Scythians, and, in the southeastern country of Azerbaijan, the official language is Azeri of Turkic derivation that in modern times has been written variously in the Arabic, Cyrillic, and Latin alphabets.

The three nations of Transcaucasia, a vibrant and diverse area, have a population belonging to a large number of ethnic groups. In Georgia there are Abkhazians (related to Circassians) and Adzhars (Muslim Georgians) as well as Ossetians and Kurds, among others. As a result of overlapping ethnic areas, Armenia separates an Azerbaijani enclave, Nakhichevan, from the rest of the country, and Nagorno-Karabakh is the disputed mountainous region in western Azerbaijan, inhabited largely by Armenians, that claims independence. It was the object of a war between the two countries in the early 1990s.

Because the Caucasus region covers a large area, there is a wide variety of climates and vegetation and, consequently a highly diversified and rich fauna and flora. While the northern slopes are inhabited by red deer, wild goat, and boar, there are also a number of game birds such as quail, partridge, mountain turkey, black grouse, and heath cock. Livestock, mainly sheep but also cattle, graze on heavily forested slopes; and seas, lakes, and streams yield a plentiful supply of seafood, ranging from carp and trout to a local specialty called *kramuli*, white-fleshed and delicately flavored fish.

Fortunately, the productive regions of the Caucasus have long been blessed by nature with an abundance of basic ingredients such as fruits, vegetables, nuts, and grains. While wheat and barley are grown on the northern Kuban plain and Armenian plateau, rice is cultivated in Azerbaijan where it remains a treasured delicacy. Ironically, in Western Georgia a favorite staple is corn, enjoyed roasted, as popcorn, and used to make breads. In the warmer southern regions one finds high-quality olives, dates, tea, citrus fruits (especially lemons), and wine grapes, important for the wine and brandy industries. Throughout the Caucasus there is a profusion of marvelous vegetables, prepared in many inviting dishes.

Because of its geographical and ethnic diversity, the colorful and vibrant cookery of the Caucasus, interwoven with the history of invasion and conquest, the influence of religious affiliation, and the effects of political and social orientation or allegiance, represents a mixture of tastes. We find distinct culinary influences from the Greeks, Romans, Persians, Arabs, Turks, and Central Asians as they passed through or occupied the area, and there are also some

Cuisines of the Caucasus Mountains

Slavic or Russian contributions. Today, the region's cuisine is perhaps best described as a joyful melange of Persian, Turkish, Greek, or Mediterranean dishes with many innovations and improvements. While there are subtle culinary differences among the area's three countries, one finds a lot of similarity.

Caucasians are noted for their creative dishes, many of them intricate, which cooks evolved over the years by the clever use of fragrant herbs and spices and tart flavorings from foods like lemons or sour plums. They also favor such foods as pomegranates, saffron, rose water, honey, olive oil, yogurt, onions, garlic, fresh and dried fruits, and a great variety of nuts, principally walnuts.

Outstanding among the dishes are a wealth of hearty soups with names as imaginative as the ingredients, succulent skewered grilled lamb, innumerable varieties of ground meat specialties, spitted chicken creations; aromatic stuffed vegetables and fruits; and all kinds of flavorful vegetable preparations featuring tomatoes, peppers, squash, and, especially, eggplants. Particularly prized are rich nut and honey sweets and flaky pastries as well as fruit puddings and compotes, similar to those of the Near East.

While there are some similarities in the cookery and a number of dishes are common to the three countries as well as neighboring regions, it is interesting to review the distinctive and individual specialties. For whatever the regional or cultural differences, all of the people share a fondness for fine food. It is a tribute to them that, despite the rigors of a checkered history and the effects of political grouping and regrouping, the cookery of the various locales retains national, and in some cases, regional, characteristics that make them praiseworthy. This is particularly true for Armenia, Georgia, and Azerbaijan. Brief reviews of factors contributing to the culinary heritage of each of them are intended to enhance the understanding of the cookery.

Some of the traditional ingredients in the Caucasus dishes are unfamiliar and difficult to obtain in American stores. Substitutions are possible and often an item may simply be left out, to no great detriment to the dish. A few suggestions for replacements are given with the recipes.

ARMENIA

The Republic of Armenia, which became an independent state on September 23, 1991, is located in a majestic landlocked area in the south-central section of Transcaucasia, south of the Greater Caucasus Mountains. Bordered by Georgia to the north, Azerbaijan to the east, Turkey to the west, and Iran to the south, almost all the country is extremely mountainous, dominated by the Lesser Caucasus range, consisting of a series of high plateaus. Surrounded by mountain crests with its highest mountains in the northwestern part of the nation, the plateau is broken up by short ridges, deep gorges, and narrow valleys with many small rivers and streams carving its surface. As mentioned above, the highest mountain is Mt. Aragats.

One of the world's most ancient countries, Armenia has endured a rich and turbulent history. Tradition has it that the country was founded by a descendant of Noah in the vicinity of Lake Van in what is now Turkey and where Noah's ark is said to have landed after the deluge. According to history, Armenia is the original seat of the one of the oldest civilized peoples who migrated to the area in the sixth century B.C., conquering an earlier, high civilization. Armenians speak an Indo-European language and call themselves *Hai*, from the name of *Hayk*, a legendary hero, and their country Haiastan. The term *Armenian* is said to have derived from the Armen tribe. Because of its strategic location, the nation was a buffer zone between empires and traders who left their imprints on the peoples and land.

Once a powerful great kingdom, stretching from the Black Sea to the Caspian Sea, it encompassed most of Transcaucasia and, reaching south into Iran, taking in the whole of Syria and a large area that included Turkish Armenia. It was briefly the strongest state in the Roman East. After contacts with centers of early Christianity, Armenia accepted it as an official religion in A.D. 301 and, ever since, it has flourished. More than 90 percent of the people belong to the Armenian Apostolic Orthodox faith.

Over the centuries Armenians, for various reasons, have emigrated to neighboring lands and faraway countries, including the United States, where they carried with them their religion, culture, and traditions, including the cookery, to which they remain loyal and have been important in maintaining a sense of national unity. Many of these have enriched the societies into which the Armenians settled.

Because of its unusually large variety of landscapes, Armenia has interesting crop variations. While fruits like figs, grapes, pomegranates, apricots, peaches, and melons are produced on the Ararat plain, potatoes and grains grow at higher altitudes. In the plateau and mountain valleys are grown cereals, vegetables, and orchard produce, namely cherries, apples, pears, almonds, hazelnuts, and grapes from which notable wines, brandies, and champagnes are made. Extensive mountain pastures support an important dairy industry and there are substantial numbers of sheep and pigs providing meat.

Traditional Armenian cookery has deep roots and a worldwide culinary reputation that has been promoted by enterprising Armenians who started and developed all kinds of commercial food businesses, from shops to restaurants. The cuisine also has derived notoriety from Armenian church societies who hold lively food festivals, bazaars, and holiday celebrations featuring traditional fare. Thus, of all the Caucasian cookery, the best known outside the area is that of Armenia.

Armenians have created some of the world's best and most interesting soups, ranging from simple kinds based on yogurt to hearty soup-stews featuring flavorful lamb-vegetable combinations. Fruits, especially apricots, are added to some of them. Like other peoples of the Caucasus, Armenians are fond of lamb, flat breads (including the well-known *lavash*), and have a wealth of nutritious salads, and dishes made with vegetables, from pickles to stews. Bulgur is the most common grain, and cheese, usually made of sheep or goat's milk, is eaten as snacks and at all meals, including breakfast.

Armenians are renowned for their imaginative use of spices and herbs that flavor such well-known dishes as rice or meat-filled grape leaves, cold white bean appetizers, chickpea pastes, lamb patties, kebabs, fruit-stuffed trout, and savory pies and pastries, among others.

For dessert, Armenians favor fruit and/or cheese but do eat more pastries, puddings, and cakes than other Caucasians, relishing luscious many-layered honey and nut-filled sweets and those flavored with rose or orange flower waters as well as pine nuts and pistachios, two favorite foods.

Contemporary travelers to Armenia can enjoy its warm climate, splendid mountains, and lush forests as well as archaeological sites, churches, monasteries, and historical monuments. The country has a number of health spas and resorts centered on medicinal springs offering possible health cures as well as field trips for bird watchers and botanists. There also are facilities for water sports, winter skiing, mountaineering, caving, hiking, horseback riding, and fishing. Above all great hospitality is offered in modern hotels and atmospheric dining places.

Yerevan, or Erevan, the capital and largest city dating back to 782 B.C., situated on the left bank of the Zanga River at an elevation of 3,00 feet, forms the center of the fertile Yerevan basin, which opens onto the Aras valley, a principal agricultural area. Once an important crossroads of many trade routes, the city has notable natural features. Overlooked by mountains in the north, it also has glorious views of Ararat, the country's holy mountain, to the south.

In *Eastward to Tartary*, Robert D. Kaplan gives a vivid description of the city and the mountain. "The Armenian capital of Yerevan sits under the spell of Mount Ararat, soaring 16,874 feet over the surrounding plain; a giant smoky-blue pyramid capped by a craggy head of silvery-white snow. On many days, the summit emerges from a platform of clouds halfway up the sky, like a new universe in formation. The name Ararat is from the Armenian root for 'life' and 'creation.' Mount Ararat is Armenia's national symbol, appearing on maps and banners and in paintings."

The architecture of modern Yerevan is distinguished by its contrast of colorful stone buildings in several styles. Republic Square is the center of the city. Among its numerous attractions are several outstanding museums and art galleries, the Matenadaran (a famous ancient manuscript library), National Opera House, Genocide Memorial, Government Palace, and a large Central Market, "Shuga," where one finds row and row of fresh fruits and vegetables, dried fruits, breads, and cheeses.

For dining there is the Old Erivan Tavern, offering traditional Armenian cuisine as well as a display of carpets and musical instruments; atmospheric Dolmama's with local specialties; and the Ararat Restaurant featuring a floor show; as well as cafés for snacks, pastries, and drinks.

Some other interesting places are mentioned elsewhere in the book.

GEORGIA

The Republic of Georgia, which became an independent state on April 9, 1991, is located in the western portion of Transcaucasia on the eastern shore of the Black Sea. It is bordered on the north by the Russian republics of Chechnya, Ingushetia, and North Ossetia. Neighbors to the southwest are Turkey, and to the southeast, Armenia and Azerbaijan. Divided by the Surami range into two distinct sections, western Georgia and eastern Georgia, in the north it is bounded by the Greater Caucasus and in the south by the Lesser Caucasus system. A country of extremely varied and attractive topography, it has forbidding mountains, snow-covered peaks, thick green forests, and multicolored alpine meadows with fertile valleys and deep ravines where rapid rivers flow. On the Black Sea coast there also are sandy beaches.

Despite its formidable mountains, Georgia's location at a major commercial crossroads and its a wealth of natural resources attracted invaders and travelers from neighboring and faraway lands dating back to the fifth millennium B.C. Over the centuries, the territory of Georgia varied considerably in size. Known to the ancient Greeks and Romans as Colchis (western Georgia) and Iberia (eastern Georgia), the country, in the form of a kingdom, accepted Christianity in the fourth century. Its "Golden Age" as an independent state, from the tenth to the thirteenth centuries, is remembered nostalgically for its greatness, particularly rich artistic and literary achievements, ranging from folk music and dances to poems that are still a part of the culture. The twelfth-century masterpiece, *The Knight in the Panther's Skin*, by Shota Rustaveli, has survived as the country's national epic. In the next generation a noteworthy poet was Ilia Chavchavadze, born in Kvareli in eastern Georgia at the foot of the greater Caucasus.

Although Saint George is the country's patron saint, the name Georgia derives from the Arabic and Persian words, *Kurj* and *Gurj*. Georgians, however, call themselves *Kartveli* and their land *Sakartvelo*. The people speak a distinct Caucasian language, written in a unique alphabet, and the great majority of Georgians belong to the Georgian Orthodox Church. Through the centuries, Georgians have been acclaimed for their independence, longevity, hospitality, and friendship, outstanding national characteristics of the high-spirited people.

Eighty-five percent of Georgia is mountainous, with the exception of a small area in the west bordering on the Black Sea known as the Kolkhida Lowland. This is the site of ancient Colchis, known for its immense wealth, which was colonized by ancient Greeks and is the setting for the legend of the Golden Fleece. Once mostly swampland, it now is a major producer of subtropical crops and winter vegetables.

Behind Kolkhida the land rises to reach two saddle ridges that connect the mountains of the Greater and Lesser Caucasus. Beyond that is a high plateau, known as the Kartilian Plain where fruit trees abound, including apples, pears, and various kinds of nuts. Dairying is practiced on the lower slopes of the mountains and vineyards are also widely cultivated.

Within the republic's territory are two autonomous republics, Abkhazia and Adzharia; and one autonomous region, South Ossetia, largely populated by a separate ethnic group speaking a language based on Persian. Its capital is Tskhinvali, formerly Rtskhinvali, meaning "hornbeam tree," which was once a market town. Today it is a commercial center for the area.

Abkhazia, a golden triangle of rugged land bordering the Black Sea in the northwest region bordering on Russia, is known for its picturesque coastline, health resorts, tropical fruits and gardens, vineyards, and for the miraculous longevity of its people. For centuries the Abkhazians, a distinct Caucasian ethnic group who once had their own kingdom and whom were primarily herdsmen, have been notorious because so many of them live to be 100 years or even older. Whatever the reasons, some say it's because of their enjoyment of lengthy good meals and fondness for "Bouquet of Abkhazia" wines.

Sukhumi, a small port, resort center, and the capital lying on Sukhumi Bay, is surrounded by mountains with striking views. Visitors can enjoy the Botanical Gardens, antiquities, palm-tree-lined promenades, and atmospheric seaside restaurants featuring highly seasoned Abkhazian dishes.

Adzharia, or Achara, a tiny subtropical region in southwest Georgia, is noted for its seaside resorts, alpine mountains, tea plantations, and unique culinary specialties such as *khachapuri*, a rich cheese bread, and chicken *satsivi*, roasted and topped with a ground walnut sauce. The capital Batumi, a port, popular resort, and the southernmost city on the Georgian Black Sea coast near the Turkish frontier, is known for its lush vegetation, museums, aquarium, evening promenade, and lively central market. It also has an inviting assortment of restaurants, cafés, and bars serving Acharian snacks and meals.

The traditional cookery of Georgia has won an international reputation for its unique dishes and innovative use of distinctive ingredients. Julianne Margvelashvili, author of *The Classic Cuisine of Georgia*, explains that "Georgians have a particular flair for adding the unexpected to produce the exotic." Her recipes prove this point.

While Georgians are devotees of healthful foods like olive oil, grains, fruits, nuts, cheese, yogurt, greens, and vegetables, especially a wide variety of beans, they favor meat and some fish dishes flavored with hot sauces and spices. Dining with a Georgian family is a pleasure as they spend hours at the table eating, drinking wine, and talking. You learn from them that their traditions, including cookery, date back to early times when the country was an independent kingdom, and that their style of living is quite different from that of their neighbors. Their culinary masterpieces are an important part of the culture that links the generations.

Generally speaking, the cookery of Georgia is divided into two main regions: the west, where Turkish and Greek influences prevail; and the east where there are Persian similarities. Western Georgian cooking is quite hot, employing a variety of spices as well as lots of peppers, walnuts, pomegranates, and herbs such as coriander. There are also cornmeal and corn specialties. Eastern specialties include wheat bread as the staple, and the cooking is subtle, relying on a lot of vegetables, grains, fruits, and dairy products. Yet, because the country comprises several small regions, each one has its own cuisine.

As previously mentioned in the preface, traveling and dining in Georgia is truly an exhilarating experience. Tbilisi, the cosmopolitan capital of Georgia and principal city of the Caucasus, has numerous attractions, historic as well as culinary, that range from art galleries and museums to a flourishing central market and Georgian restaurants with traditional dishes. At the popular Mukhrantubani, Caucasian specialties are served in an attractive courtyard as well as indoor dining areas, one of which is an old wine cellar.

A highlight of any trip to Georgia is a visit to the magnificent mountains regions of Tusheti, Khevsureti, Pshavi, and Svaneti where there are great opportunities for climbing, trekking, bird watching, enjoying the flora and fauna, and exploring the local culture and cookery. Most of the people live by farming and village communities offer a panorama of life as it was in the past. One finds old churches, lively folk festivals, small museums depicting regional crafts, as well as guest houses and lodges with hospitable hosts offering kebabs, spicy meat dumplings called *khinkali*, and marvelous breads.

Other places of interest in Georgia are mentioned elsewhere in the book.

AZERBAIJAN

Azerbaijan, the largest of the three Transcaucasus republics that became an independent state on October 18, 1991, is a partially mountainous land located in the eastern section of the Caucasus isthmus on the Caspian Sea.

It includes the southeastern spurs of the Greater Caucasus, which terminates in the Apsheron Peninsula, the easternmost section of the Lesser Caucasus. In ancient times it was the center of overland trade routes connecting Central Asia and the Middle East on the famed Silk Route, and was long known for its handsome carpets. Early Assyrian chronicles of more than 5,000 years ago mention the abundant riches of Azerbaijan.

Bordered by Iran to the south, Armenia and Georgia to the west, and Dagestan in the Russian Federation to the north, the country's area also includes the disputed enclave of Nagorno-Karabakh, mainly occupied by Armenians, and the geographically detached region of Nakhichevan. Its capital and largest city is Baku.

Although characterized by a variety of landscapes, three physical features dominate Aberbaijan. Foremost is the Caspian Sea, whose shoreline forms a natural boundary to the east; the above-mentioned Caucasus mountain range to the north; and the extensive flatland drained by the Kura River and its chief affluent, the Aras in the country's center. The highest elevations occur in the Greater Caucasus where Mount Bazar-dyuzi rises 13,500 feet about sea level.

As a crossroads of tribal migration and military campaigns during most of its history, the territory of the present country was under Persian influence. But as the Persian Empire declined, Russia began a 200-year dominance. A culturally and linguistically Turkic people, the Azeris or Azerbaijani have retained a rich cultural heritage despite long periods of foreign domination. Most of them are Shi'i Muslims. As stated above, the official language is Azeri, a Turkic language.

A legend explains that the name Azerbaijan is thought to have the meaning of "a land of flames," or "the land of fire," a reference either to the oil-fueled fires in the temples of the once-dominant Zoroastrian religion or the natural burning of surface oil deposits. Marco Polo, the first European to pinpoint a source of petroleum in the area, wrote that near the Caspian Sea was "a fountain which sends up oil in great abundance." He noted that the oil was good to burn, but also "to anoint the camels for the itch."

Because oil was important for lighting, heating, and cooking as well as medicine and warfare the oil wells of Apsheron were jealously guarded by the medieval fortresses of the local feudal lords.

The Azeris have sought to protect their cultural identity from long-standing outside influences by fostering indigenous forms of artistic and intellectual expression. They proudly point to a number of scientists, philosophers, and literary figures. The architecture of the Middle Ages survives in the bridges, mosques, mausoleums, and fortresses found throughout the country.

More than one third of the republic lies in the alluvial Kura River valley where wheat and vegetables are cultivated. Citrus fruits, tea, and rice are grown in the subtropical Lenkoran lowlands, and the slopes of the Caucasus are covered with vineyards and orchards. Besides being a major producer of grapes, the agricultural crops include rice, tea, olives, saffron, pomegranates, nuts, vegetables, figs, citrus fruits, and the sesame plant for seeds and oil. Vineyards are the basis for a wine making and distilling industry. The fishing industry plays an important role in the economy with the catch consisting mainly of herring, carp, and sturgeon, which is processed into caviar. Livestock and dairy products are also important to the economy.

Azerbaijanis are proud of their culinary heritage and, while having a little in common with the cooking of Armenia and Georgia, it is more closely related to that of Central Asia and Iran. Notably the cuisine has a character of its own and is delightfully varied, each region having its prized specialties. Many of the dishes are exquisitely refined and take time and skill to prepare. There are over a hundred varieties of rice dishes called *plovs*, made with a wide range of ingredients and served traditionally almost as a rite with each person helping himself according to taste.

On the other hand, the Azerbaijani appetizer spread is not as elaborate as that of Armenia and Georgia, relying primarily on simple combinations like dried fruits and nuts, fresh vegetables and herbs, salads, with breads, and perhaps yogurt and cheese. Soups play an important role in the meals and range from simple ones based on yogurt, flavored with aromatic herbs, to substantial kinds containing meatballs and stuffed pastries. A great number of the main dishes feature ground or cubed meat, usually lamb, and are served often with fruit or spice-flavored sauces and condiments. Among the most commonly used seasonings are dried and fresh fruits, flower waters, almonds, pistachios, and walnuts, as well as barberries and saffron, the national flavoring. Typical Azeri desserts are honey-nut sweets, cakes, and pastries laden with syrups, raisins, and nuts, but the common finale to a meal is a plate of luscious fresh fruit in season. Black tea, served in small glasses, starts off and ends an everyday repast, as wine, if served, is reserved for special occasions.

Because Azerbaijan possesses considerable oil reserves, rich industrial resources, and fertile agricultural lands, and is an important center of international trade, many contemporary visitors go there for business reasons or while traveling to Central Asia. But the country does have tourist attractions and one usually begins sightseeing in Baku, the capital and port of the world's first oil town on the landlocked Caspian Sea, long famed for its sturgeon and caviar. Situated attractively on a hillside around the horseshoe-shaped Il'ich Bay on the south side of the semiarid Apsheron Peninsula, Baku has a rich and complex ethnic background, a place whose economic fortunes rose and fell with oil, and which has long been viewed as a prize by neighboring countries.

Described by an early historian as a town of stone with "healthy airs," often plagued by devastating winds, the name Baku comes from the Persian for "windy place." The present-day city, however, is a complex of oil wells and refineries, industrial plants, and suburbs with little left of what was once the "inner town", at its center, down near the water. The present Old Town, a maze of alleys and mixture of medieval monuments, now is some distance from the shore and can be explored easily by foot.

At the old city's highest point stands the fifteenth-century palace of the Shirvanshahs, built on a series of walls that consists of several buildings, including a museum and harem, as wall as courtyards. Within sight of it are a Muslim watchtower, dating from the twelfth century; Madras Mosque, built in 1301; and the Synyk Kala Minaret, more than 900 years old. Baku's most famous landmark and symbol is the twelfth-century Maiden's Tower, rising to a height of 90 feet in alternating courses of indented, honey-colored stonework and comprising nine cylindrical stories supported by a spur-like buttress. The source of many legends, nobody knows for certain the tower's real name, age, or purpose. Nor can anyone verify if a young woman leapt to her death from its ramparts rather than accept an unwelcome arranged marriage with a medieval ruler.

Not far from the tower is the National Carpet Museum with a very large collection of rugs and detailed data about the textile arts. Baku's other treasures include art museums, a theater, opera house, and literary collections of two writers who compete for the title of national poet, Nizami and Fuzuli, remembered throughout the country with statues, streets, and buildings named for them. Among the numerous atmospheric dining places serving Azeri specialties is the Karvansaray Restaurant in the Old Town, housed in an actual fourteenth century caravansary that once served travelers on the Silk Route and now features traditional dishes. Another is the Mugam Club, located in another caravansary near the Maiden's Tower and featuring music and dancing.

Other places of interest in Azerbaijan are mentioned elsewhere in the book.

THE CAUCASUS IN LITERATURE

My interest in the Caucasus began when I was a student in Russian studies and journalism at Syracuse University's prominent Maxwell School of Citizenship, studying the difficult language as well as the economics, culture, geography, and literature of the vast Soviet Union as Russia was then called.

Ever since my geography professor, Dr. George B. Cressey, who wrote and spoke about his Russian journeys, described the Caucasus Mountains and lands in vivid terms the region held a certain mystique for me. Beyond its remote location and curious customs was the intrigue connected with its spirited people and their history. Adding further fascination were the textbook pictures of isolated settlements, the inner courtyard of a caravansary, a tea house, the Georgian Military Highway, and rich meadows providing summer pastures on the slopes of the northern Caucasus.

It was another professor, a vivacious lady from Leningrad, who introduced me to a casual style of dining she called a *zakuska* party. To improve our language skills I, along with our small group of seven students, gathered at her small apartment around a table covered with a bright cotton cloth and attractive dishes of hot and cold appetizers. We chatted amicably in Russian, listened to fascinating tales about her homeland, and savored the strange but tasty food she had prepared. I can still recall my first taste of red caviar, piquant pickled herring, and delectable small yeast-risen pancakes, spread with butter and sour cream, that were called *bliny*. I wanted to learn more about the cuisine.

Later, when I began reading Russian literature, my interest in the remote romantic Caucasian lands reached new heights. Ever since the first half of the nineteenth century some of Russia's young authors derived a great deal of inspiration from travels in the Caucasus and thus introduced the region and its peoples to the rest of the country and world. For at that time this was thought to be a wild, lawless, spectacular land, like the American "Wild

West," fabled in song and story. Its mountains, precipices, rushing torrents, beautiful Circassian women, and fierce, untamed tribesmen captured the imagination of aristocratic poets and novelists from St. Petersburg and Moscow and Russia and gave rise to their exotic tales and poems. Ironically, the Caucasus became also a favorite place of exile, the "Southern Siberia," for political prisoners, among them writers.

The renowned Alexander S. Pushkin, a romanticist who became Russia's greatest poet, was, as a young man, banished to South Russia in 1820 for writing too freely in his revolutionary poems against the government. That same year marked his first trip, for health, to the Caucasus where he became enamored of the people, culture, and food, and enjoyed experiences which he used in several poems, notably *The Prisoner of the Caucasus*, a story about the love of a native girl for a Russian. In 1825, after a brief stay at home, because of more inflammatory literature, he was exiled again, this time to the Caucasus. Here he continued to write about his travels, drinking, and adventures, including a colorful visit to the fabled Tiflis baths, described in *A Journey to Arzrum* (1835). Unfortunately, during a duel in 1837 the talented poet received a serious pistol wound from which he died.

It was, however, Mikhail Yurievich Lermontov, Russia's greatest literary figure after Pushkin, whose life and works are particularly associated with the Caucasus. He was the first writer to describe the grandeur of the scenery and places, and to record the hitherto unwritten folk tales and ballads of the colorful people.

Born the son of an army officer descended from a Scottish adventurer, George Learmont, who came to Russia in the early seventeenth century, claimed descent from Scotland's legendary Thomas the Rhymer. As a boy, Lermontov read widely and was taken on family excursions to the Caucasus, by then the focus of a Russian colonial war. It was a region that left him with strong, affectionate impressions and inspired literary efforts. His earliest poems were about the traditions and wonders of the enchanting place.

Later, as political punishment for writing *On the Death of a Poet* (1837), a eulogy implying court complicity in the death of his friend Pushkin, Lermontov was arrested and exiled for a year to military duty in the Caucasus. Here in the dramatic landscape of the mountains he wrote poetry about truth, freedom, and honesty, and completed narrative poems. Then, after a brief return to St. Petersburg where he continued to write critically about the imperial court, Lermontov was exiled again to the Caucasus, assigned to the front ranks and in danger for his life. There he completed his narrative poetic masterpiece, *The Demon* (1839), and his single completed prose work, *A Hero of our Time* (1840), the first Russian psychological novel and Lermontov's best known work.

Based on the exploits of an antihero, Grigory Pechorin, bored with his life and unable to respond to human affection, the book consists of five stories with the setting in the Caucasus. The action takes place during the Caucasian War of 1817-64, waged by tsarist Russia against the Caucasian mountain tribes. The Ossetians, Circassians, Kabardians, Chechens, and other nationalists who offer stubborn resistance to the Russian forces are frequently mentioned in the text, as are the names of Caucasian towns, rivers, and mountains.

Much of the author's writing centers around a resort region located on the northern spur of the central Caucasus, in the foothills of the Greater Caucasus, made up of four atmospheric spa towns: Pyatigorsk, Kislovodsk, Yessentuki, and Zheleznovodsk, all with a marvelous climate, lush vegetation, alluring mountain scenery, and fine dining facilities. Here one can take a variety of excursions to local scenic and historic attractions. The area is also known for its abundance of fruits and vegetables, fresh fish, dry and sweet wines, and mineral waters.

The region's oldest and best-known resort, frequently mentioned in Lermontov's novel, is Pyatigorsk (Five Peaks), located in the midst of the five Pyatigorsk mountains: Iron (2,795 feet), Snake (3,261 feet), Besh Tau or Mount Besh (4,590 feet), Mashuk (3,248 feet), and Bold (2,427 feet).

Lermontov writes dramatically about his mountain surroundings while staying in Pyatigorsk, at the foot of Mount Mashuk. "I have a marvelous view on three sides. Five-peaked Beshtau looms blue in the west like 'the last cloud of the storm blown over;' in the north rises Mashuk like a shaggy Persian cap concealing this part of the horizon.... Farther in the distance the massive amphitheater of mountains grows even bluer and mistier, while on the fringe of the horizon stretches the silvery chain of snow-capped peaks beginning with Kazbek and ending with twin-peaked Elbrus.... It is a joy to live in a place like this! A feeling of elation flows in all my veins. The air is pure and fresh like the kiss of a child, the sun is bright and the sky blue—what more could one desire?"

Unfortunately, it was just outside Pyatigorsk that in 1841 Lermontov provoked a duel with a fellow cadet and on July 15 was shot dead. In the town there are several places, a Lermontov Street, Square, Statue, and Gallery and Museum, situated in the central park, associated with the famous writer who loved and wrote so wonderfully about the Caucasus.

Beginning in 1851, Leo Tolstoy, Russia's acclaimed versatile author, spent two and a half years in the northern Caucasus where he saw action against the mountaineers, and the native setting and people of Chechnya had a profound effect upon him. He also visited Tiflis, the neighboring town of Kizlyar, took a trip to the Caspian shore, as well as a journey to Pyatigorsk during a momentous period in his life, vividly described in *Caucasian Reminiscences*. Whereas his remarkable novel, *The Cossacks* (1863), which is philosophical in tone, gives vivid descriptions of the Caucasian way of life against a magnificent scenic background.

Another novel, *Hadji Murad*, published in 1911 after Tolstoy's death, is also centered in the northern Caucasus. It's the enthralling tale of a mountaineer chieftain, *Hadji*, who out of vengeance and personal ambition deserts his leader, *Shamil*, and goes over to the Russians. An irresistible desire to see his son, held as a hostage by *Shamil*, leads him to escape into the mountains where he is run down and killed. *Hadji* is characterized as a shrewd, brave fighter, endowed with all the vices and virtues of his half-willed people. In essence it's a simple story about the tragic irony of dissension between men of different orders of civilization, a struggle that continues there today.

A more recent author, Fitzroy Maclean, a British diplomat and inveterate traveler, has written one of the best and most detailed books about the Caucasus, an area he knew intimately. To him it was "one of the most exciting places on earth" and "a region of high romance." In *To Caucasus: The End of all the Earth*, the author writes that be believes most people are fascinated by frontiers, and "...if there ever was a frontier, it is the Caucasus—the great mountain barrier stretching from the Black Sea to the Caspian, dividing Europe from Asia, West from East, Christendom from Islam."

In his book Maclean writes enthusiastically about the area by tracing its amazing history, gives marvelous descriptions of the splendid buildings, magnificent scenery, and portrays the people as "glamorous and dashing, with the true Highlander's non-chalant approach to life,"—all skillfully illustrated with his own evocative photographs. He also has marvelous accounts of the local cuisine, exotic food and drink. In North Ossetia Maclean dines on mushrooms cooked with sour cream and grated cheese, and, in Tibilisi, enjoys *shashlik*, a 'savory stew full of strange herbs,' and the local bread, *lavash*. In Kakhetia where "hospitality is spontaneous and lavish," he joins a group of villagers for a convivial outdoor feast under a tree. Whereas in Imeretia he favors the 'flowery white wines' and highly spiced dishes, and is given a surprise farewell luncheon that begins at eleven in the morning and lasts until five in the afternoon, "punctuated by toasts in honour of everybody and everything."

To Maclean the Caucasus is indeed a magic land, filled with fable, mystery, and inviting dining. Hopefully, the readers of the book will believe so also and that recipes and background data will enhance understanding of the cookery and the cultures.

APPETIZERS

"The sanctity of hospitality among Caucasians is such an article of faith that modesty in performing it is no virtue, and failing to deliver it would be considered eccentric, almost uncivilized."

Highlanders

One of the most delightful aspects of dining in the Caucasus is the pleasure of savoring tidbits of food or a spread of elaborate fare with wine, or other drinks, before a luncheon or dinner. Leisurely sampling of appetizers at an outdoor café, atmospheric restaurant, or in the home, prior to the main meal is a traditional way of life in these lands. Everyone loves to sit and while away the time by drinking, eating, chatting, or simply taking in the scene.

In the various regions of the Caucasus there are different traditions of appetizers, covering a delightful range of foods and dishes, both hot and cold, that have similarities but are distinctive. In the northern Caucasus a very typical and pleasurable Russian dining custom, which takes place before the main meal, is the enjoyment of a rich repertoire of stimulating dishes, *zakuski*, accompanied by vodka.

Believed to have been adapted from the Scandinavian smorgasbord when Rurik became the first czar of Russia, *zakuski* became particularly lavish during the nineteenth century, when the nobility gathered daily in handsome homes to partake of regal repasts. *Zakuska*, the singular of *zakuski*, means literally "bite down," and the tradition is to drink a glass of vodka neat and then to "bite it down" with one or more appetizers.

The simplest and most common *zakuska* is herring in one form or another. Generally, however, the herring is accompanied by other foods such as different kinds of fish, pickles, sausage, cheese, vegetable salads, breads, and butter. Traditionally the *zakuski* and vodka are set up in the living or reception room on a cloth-covered table with small plates, implements, and glasses. Each person, customarily standing, helps himself to the food and drinks during this pre-meal social hour or two.

From humble beginnings, the *zakuski* array expanded considerably to become one of the world's most appealing appetizer assortments, distinguished by artful seasonings, colorful garnishes, and inviting culinary contrasts. Imperial Russian tables groaned with sumptuous displays of as many as sixty or seventy creative dishes, which were eaten with a wide selection of vodkas downed in considerable quantity.

Today the Russians do not concentrate on the opulent settings of the bygone czarist days, but they do continue the treasured dining tradition with a more frugal presentation of the *zakuski* that includes traditional fare. In addition to the specialties mentioned above, the repertoire for a special occasion might be expanded to include cold meats and poultry, preserved fish, stuffed and pickled vegetables, pâtés, fish in aspic, filled pastries, savory soufflés, salads of cooked vegetables and fish or meat, and a particular favorite, buckwheat pancakes.

While Russian-style *zakuski* are not served traditionally in Armenia, Azerbaijan, and Georgia, the people in these countries do have national traditions and appetizer specialties called *meze*, *mezza*, or *mezze*, a word derived from the Persian *maza* meaning "taste" or "relish." Deeply rooted in the culture of each country it is the custom of hospitality to welcome guests with a presentation of hot and cold dishes. Usually placed along the center of the table, they are enjoyed with glasses of wine, or other drinks, and convivial conversation before the main meal of the day.

While traveling in Transcaucasia one soon discovers that many of the appetizer specialties are similar to those enjoyed in neighboring Near Eastern lands and, indeed, were introduced by the Persians, Greeks, and especially the Turks. All of them adhere to the belief that one does not partake of before-the-meal libations without something to eat, and it's long been the custom to serve a profusion of tasty dishes, or "miniature foods," before dining.

Like Near Easterners, the Caucasians have always been great nibblers and share a fondness for nuts in profusion, a fascinating variety of olives, raw and cooked vegetables, chickpeas, cubes of white and yellow cheese, slices of preserved meats, relishes, and all kinds of salads. Traditional fare also includes tangy mixtures we call dips or spreads, based on such nourishing and appealing fare as sesame seed paste, yogurt, ground chickpeas, fish roe, and broiled eggplant, prepared as in yesteryear.

Also in these lands we find deep-fried filled savory pastries, pickled and stuffed vegetables, and skewered tidbits of meat and seafood. Interesting variations of tiny well-seasoned meatballs, deep-fried fritters and croquettes, smoked fish, and vegetable dishes of many kinds, all created in the Caucasian kitchens.

The appetizer repertoire of each country was developed over the years by cooks relying on native resources and individual imagination and include a wealth of appealing specialties. While the choice of drinks is usually a matter of local taste, wine is the most popular. Russians, however, favor vodka; Moslems fruit juice; and in some areas of Transcaucasia the people imbibe a potent anise-flavored aperitif called *raki* or *arak*.

Included in this chapter are recipes for some of the best Caucasian appetizers.

A CENTERPIECE OF FRESH HERBS

In the Caucasus, fresh herbs, grown in home gardens or purchased at local markets, are highly prized foods, used imaginatively in many dishes and valued as a garnish. It's a beloved ancient tradition to adorn the dining table with a bowl or plate, filled or piled high with aromatic, colorful fresh herbs, with or without accompaniments. Not only do the "delicious grasses," as they are sometimes called, provide a decorative centerpiece, but they also are nibbled from in between courses, and, perhaps eaten with some bread at the end of a meal.

Typical herb choices are sprigs or leaves of fresh coriander, tarragon, mint, dill, opal or green basil, thyme, peppery cress, marjoram, summer savory, and, in Georgia, marigolds, among others. In addition to the fresh herbs, there also might be as assortment of raw vegetables such as the tender leaves of lettuce and spinach, scallions, and radishes with their tops, as well as tomato and cucumber wedges or slices, all arranged attractively on a plate or platter.

In many homes it has become traditional to enjoy the herbs and vegetables with bread and cheese. For a simple herb-cheese appetizer, cut 14 ounces of fresh white goat cheese like feta into small cubes and place them in the center of a large plate. Arrange washed and chilled fresh herbs around the cheese. On separate plates serve whole radishes, tomato wedges, cucumber slices, thin scallions, and slices of thin, crisp bread such as *lavash* (Armenian) or *lavashi* (Georgian), or pita. Spread bread slices with cheese; garnish with herbs. Eat with vegetable accompaniments.

SALTED ALMONDS

Makes 1 cup.

The delicate, nutritious sweet almond is a beloved food in Caucasian lands where it has been enjoyed for thousands of years. Marvelously flavorful, almonds are a basic source of nourishment and traditionally used in cookery to make a wide range of appealing dishes that are ever present as an appetizer. They are eaten plain, toasted, and fried in olive oil. Almonds blanched in the home will have a fresher flavor than if purchased already blanched. Here's the traditional method of preparing the nuts.

> *1 cup shelled whole almonds*
> *1 to 2 teaspoons extra-virgin olive oil*
> *Sea or coarse salt*

Preheat oven to 300 degrees.

Place almonds in a bowl; cover with boiling water. Let stand 2 to 3 minutes; drain. Plunge into cold water; drain. With the tip of a small sharp knife or the fingers, rub the skins off. Dry thoroughly.

Spread blanched whole almonds in a single layer in an ungreased pie plate or shallow baking dish. Put in oven. Toast, turning once, 5 minutes. Remove from oven. Sprinkle with olive oil. Return to oven and toast, turning once or twice, about 8 minutes, until just golden. Do not overcook or let nuts become charred. Remove from the oven. Sprinkle with salt to taste at once. Serve within a few hours after toasting.

Note: The almonds may also be fried in olive oil and seasoned with salt.

CASPIAN SEA CAVIAR

In the Caucasus, the choicest appetizer is caviar, the salted roe, or eggs, of any of several varieties of sturgeon or related fish. Treasured as an international luxury, the magical delicacy has an age-old romantic association with Russia where it was highly prized by royalty, and, particularly the Caspian Sea, the world's largest lake, home to the most popular members of the European and Asiatic sturgeons. Until recently, the Caspian was the source of over 90 percent of the world's sturgeon and black caviar harvest.

Although the term caviar may designate the salted processed roe from many species of fish, purists consider only sturgeon roe, often called "black pearls," worthy of the name caviar. Called *ikra* in Russia, the name outside of Russia is caviar, a word that derives from the Turkish word *khavyah*.

While sturgeons come in twenty-six species, the prized three are the Caspian's *beluga*, *ossetra* (or *asetra*), and *sevruga*. The biggest sturgeon, the beluga, produces the largest of choice firm fresh eggs, which are named for it. They have delicate membranes full of mild and creamy flavor and vary in color from silver, or steel, to gray or darker. The medium-sized *ossetra* roe have a distinctive fruity, nut-like flavor and vary in color from a golden yellow to dark brown. *Sevruga*, the smallest sturgeon, yields the smallest eggs ranging in color from light to dark gray. The most common and least expensive, they are praised for their lively and full flavor with a subtle aftertaste. Only the three top qualities of caviar are labeled "*malossol*," meaning lightly salted.

In recent years it has been more difficult and costly to purchase top quality caviar, a shortage that experts blame on over fishing, pollution, and a flourishing black market along the banks and in the towns of the Caspian.

Expensive fresh caviar should be accorded very special treatment. Remove from the refrigerator and let stand at room temperature 10 to 15 minutes. Open just before serving. Serve in its ice-packed container or a bowl set directly on ice. Caviar devotees spoon and eat the "black gold" directly from the container with a horn or ivory spoon. Some persons, however, prefer to serve caviar on points of unbuttered white-bread toast or unsalted crackers. Caviar does not require any embellishments or accompaniments such as lemon juice, capers, chopped hard-cooked eggs, or onions.

Pressed, damaged, or less choice eggs have a glossy black color and intense, yet good flavor. The red or pink eggs of fresh and saltwater salmon, also called caviar, are enjoyed as appetizers in various forms. Simply serve on buttered pumpernickel with a dab of sour cream as a garnish.

RED CAVIAR SPREAD

6 servings.

A popular creamy, pale pink spread called *taramosalata*, made with salted carp or other fish roe, and a few other ingredients, has a number of variations including this one made with red caviar. Caucasians serve it as a tangy dip with thin bread or fresh lettuce leaves, or sometimes as a salad dressing. While best made in a mortar with a pestle, it can also be mixed in a blender.

> *5 slices white bread, crusts removed*
> *1 jar (4 ounces) red caviar*
> *Juice of 1 large lemon*
> *1 small white onion, minced*
> *½ cup extra-virgin olive oil*
> *Garnishes: Chopped fresh coriander or parsley, tomato*
>   *wedges, and black olives*

Place bread slices in a shallow dish; cover with hot water. Press with the hands to remove any liquid; break into tiny pieces. In a wooden mortar or bowl, mash the bread pieces with a pestle or fork until smooth. Add the caviar, 1 teaspoon at a time, mashing and stirring constantly. Beat in the lemon juice, onion, and oil, adding 1 tablespoon at a time, until all the oil is absorbed. Refrigerate, covered, until ready to serve, Spoon into a mound on a plate or in a bowl. Garnish with the coriander or parsley, tomato wedges, and olives.

A GARNISHED HERRING PLATTER

4 servings.

Although caviar is the royal appetizer, the most popular and important food on the *zakuska* table is the humble salt herring, considered a national treasure and enjoyed in any number of dishes. Russians almost always eat this fish with vodka as it stimulates drinking.

While a grand *zakuska* spread may include several cold and hot herring specialties, an everyday appetizer will usually consist of a morsel or two of herring accompanied by pickles, a slice of cheese or sausage, cucumbers with sour cream, and pieces of dark bread with butter. Here's one way of serving the fish.

½ cup olive oil
3 tablespoons red wine vinegar
1 tablespoon sharp mustard
Freshly ground pepper
4 hard-cooked eggs, shelled
8 pickled herring fillets, rinsed, skinned, and boned
1 large yellow onion, chopped
1 cup diced cooked beets
2 tablespoons capers, drained

In a small bowl whisk the oil, vinegar, mustard, and pepper. Separate the egg yolks from the whites. Finely chop the whites; sieve the yolks.

To serve, cut the herring fillets into strips. Arrange on a platter. Surround with small mounds of chopped egg whites, onions, beets, and capers. Spoon the oil-vinegar mixture over the herring. Garnish with sieved egg yolks. Serve at once with pieces of black bread.

MTSKHETA
EGGPLANT CAVIAR

Makes about 3 cups.
6 to 8 servings.

The Caucasians use the word "caviar" to describe piquant fine mixtures or spreads based on a vegetable, usually mushrooms, beets, or eggplants. This version, sometimes called "poor man's" caviar, is made with the handsome shiny deep purple eggplant. Some people think that the seeds look like caviar grains. This is one of several variations.

Mtskheta, the ancient capital of Eastern Georgia and the country's leading religious center, situated at the convergence of the Mtkvari and Aragvi rivers northwest of Tbilisi, is now an important archaeological center. Here are the impressive ruins of ancient fortress walls, palaces, tombs, the magnificent Sveti Tskhoveli Cathedral, one of Georgia's great architectural treasures, and the castle of Bebris Tsikhe. For many years the town, on a major trade route linking the Mediterranean, Asia, and the Caucasus, was known for its caravansaries. Today, visitors can dine on local Georgian specialties, including eggplant dishes, at atmospheric restaurants located in pleasant settings near the cathedral and along the waterfront.

> *1 large eggplant (about 2 pounds), not pared*
> *¼ cup extra-virgin olive oil*
> *3 tablespoons freshly squeezed lemon juice*
> *2 garlic cloves, peeled and crushed*
> *1 cup thinly sliced scallions, with some green tops*
> *1 cup finely chopped green bell peppers*
> *2 tablespoons minced fresh coriander or parsley leaves*
> *Salt, freshly ground pepper*
> *Garnishes: A tomato "rose" and red and*
>   *green bell pepper strips*

Preheat oven to 400 degrees.

Remove and discard the eggplant stem and blossom end. With a fork prick the skin in several places. Put on a baking sheet. Bake, turning once or twice, until soft and skin is charred and blistered, about 50 minutes. While still hot, peel off the skin. Put the pulp in a medium bowl; mash finely with a fork. Add the oil, lemon juice, and garlic; mix well. Stir in scallions, bell peppers, and coriander or parsley leaves. Season with salt and pepper. Mix well. Refrigerate, covered, 6 to 8 hours. Serve at room temperature in a mound on a plate or in a shallow serving dish. For garnishes, place a tomato "rose" in the center and/or decorate the top with bell pepper strips. Serve with pieces of dark bread or romaine leaves.

GEORGIAN LOBIO FROM GORI

4 servings.

In Georgia, beans are called *lobio* and they are one of the most abundant and favorite vegetables in the country. Beans of every description, color, and kind, both fresh and dried, are not only relished as basic fare but are used to make delectable dishes. Georgians boast that they are great bean eaters and never tire of them. A characteristic appetizer or accompaniment called *lobio* is well seasoned with pounded walnuts, garlic, hot peppers, and coriander, a favorite herb. Another version calls for pomegranate juice and seeds.

Gori, an ancient city on the banks of the Kura River southwest of Tbilisi, is famous as the birthplace of Iosif Visarionovich Jugashvili, better known as Joseph Stalin. The house where he was born, the Stalin Museum, and other sites pertaining to the former USSR ruler can be visited. The name Gori derives from the word for hill, *gora*, and the original fortification or castle, Goris-Tsikhe, stands on a hill overlooking the valley below. Located in Kartli, the central region of Georgia, the town is a good place to sit at a café and enjoy Georgian dishes including those made with beans.

½ cup shelled walnut pieces
1 garlic clove, crushed
¼ cup red wine vinegar
½ to 1 teaspoon cayenne pepper
3 scallions, sliced, with some green tops
3 tablespoons minced fresh coriander or parsley
1 tablespoon chopped fresh mint
Salt, freshly ground pepper
3 cups cooked or canned red kidney beans, drained and
rinsed under cold water

In a mortar with a pestle or in a nut grinder, pound or grind the walnuts and garlic. In a medium bowl, combine the nut mixture with the wine vinegar; mix well. Stir in the cayenne pepper, scallions, coriander or parsley, and mint. Season with salt and pepper. Add beans. Toss to mix well. Refrigerate, covered, 4 to 6 hours. Serve accompanied by *lavash* or pita triangles or as a salad.

SESAME-ALMOND APPETIZER

4 to 6 servings.

Sesame, a herbaceous plant, has been grown in Caucasian lands since time immemorial. Its tiny grayish-white or black seeds have a sweet nutty flavor and yield a valuable light, milk and healthfully unsaturated oil. It is good for salads as well as cooking. The seeds, often toasted and eaten like nuts, are also sprinkled on breads and pastries, and are good combined with other foods, especially butter and cheese.

Tahini, a rich and creamy paste made of crushed sesame seeds, is noted for its pleasant nutlike flavor and versatility. The healthful oily cream is used in soups, sauces, salad dressings, sandwich spreads, and to make dips: mixed with nuts, herbs, yogurt or mashed chickpeas. Here is a recipe for a flavorful dip.

> *1 garlic clove*
> *½ teaspoon salt*
> *⅓ cup fresh lemon juice*
> *1 cup well-mixed* tahini *(sesame seed paste)*
> *¼ teaspoon dried mint*
> *½ cup ground blanched almonds*
> *Garnishes: Whole blanched almonds, chopped fresh mint*

In a medium bowl crush the garlic with salt. Gradually add the lemon juice and *tahini*, beating as adding. Add a little cold water, if needed, to make a thick smooth cream. Stir in the mint and ground almonds. Mix well. Refrigerate, covered, 1 to 2 hours, up to 12, to blend flavors. Serve in a bowl, garnished with the whole almonds and fresh mint.

ANCHOVY PURÉE

Makes about ½ cup.

Russians are very fond of anchovies, or *kilky*, small herring-like fish, which are appreciated for their salty, tangy taste. They enjoy them with a piece of buttered dark bread or wrapped around a red or black radish as well as in a number of inviting dishes.

Here are recipes for two easy-to-prepare anchovy appetizers.

1 can (2 ounces) anchovy fillets, drained and
*   rinsed in cold water*
3 garlic cloves, crushed
2 tablespoons olive oil
2 teaspoons wine vinegar
Freshly ground pepper

In a shallow dish, mash anchovies with a fork. Add the garlic, oil, and vinegar. Season with pepper. Beat until smooth. Refrigerate, covered, 24 hours, up to 2 days. Serve on rounds of dark bread sprinkled with finely chopped scallions or fresh herbs, if desired.

ANCHOVY-PEPPER RELISH FROM SHEKKI

Makes about 4 cups.

This zesty relish featuring green peppers and anchovies is from Shekki in the northwest corner of Azerbaijan, reached by car from Baku on a winding road that rises and traces the southern brow of the high Caucasus. In the valleys are grown pomegranates, custard apples, bananas, and the cornel cherry, whose white variety is unique to the district. Shekki is also a popular destination for Leo Tolstoy aficionados. It was here that Hadji Murad, a colorful nineteenth-century Tartar fighter, died in defiance of the forces of Czar Nicholas I, and his last days were chronicled in Tolstoy's masterpiece, *Hadji Murad*.

While traditionally made in a mortar with a pestle, the appetizer can also be prepared in a blender.

1 can (2 ounces) flat anchovy fillets
2 garlic cloves, crushed
12 scallions, sliced, with some green tops
2 cups finely chopped green bell pepper
1 cup finely chopped celery
½ cup chopped fresh parsley
¼ cup ground almonds
1 tablespoon olive oil
2 tablespoons red wine vinegar
1 tablespoon fresh lemon juice
Freshly ground pepper

Drain anchovies, reserving the oil. Finely chop anchovies; turn into a medium bowl. Add the scallions, bell peppers, celery, parsley, and almonds; mix well. In a small dish combine the reserved oil, olive oil, vinegar, and lemon juice. Add to the pepper mixture. Mix well. Season with pepper. Refrigerate, covered, stirring occasionally, for 1 day before serving.

EGGPLANT WITH WALNUT SAUCE

Makes about 3 cups.

A native of Persia, or Iran, the walnut has long been a treasured food in the Caucasus, particularly in Georgia where the nuts are plentiful and used to make important pastes, sauces, confections, and to flavor several vegetable and poultry dishes. This is a typical dish made in several variations that can be served as a spread with crusty white bread.

> *1 long narrow eggplant, about 1½ pounds, washed*
> *½ cup shelled walnuts*
> *2 garlic cloves, crushed*
> *1 medium yellow onion, cut into quarters*
> *3 tablespoons extra-virgin olive oil*
> *2 tablespoons freshly squeezed lemon juice*
> *2 tablespoons pomegranate juice*
> *2 tablespoons minced fresh coriander leaves*
> *⅛ teaspoon paprika*
> *Salt, freshly ground pepper*
> *Garnish: Pomegranate seeds, optional*

Preheat oven to 400 degrees.

Remove and discard stem and blossom end from eggplant. With a fork pierce the skin in several places. Put on a baking sheet. Bake, turning once or twice, until soft and a knife goes into it with no resistance, about 50 minutes. When cool enough to handle, peel off and discard skin. Scoop out the pulp onto a large plate. Press with a spoon or squeeze with the hands to remove all moisture. With a fork mash finely. Spoon into a medium bowl.

In a blender or nut grinder, finely grind the walnuts. Add garlic and onion; process again. Add the olive oil, lemon juice, pomegranate juice, coriander leaves, and paprika; purée. Stir into eggplant purée. Season to taste with salt and pepper. Mix well. Refrigerate, covered, 24 hours, up to 3 days, before serving. Serve at room temperature, spooned into a mound on a plate or in a shallow dish. Garnish the top with pomegranate seeds, if desired.

ARMENIAN BULGUR-VEGETABLE DIP

6 servings.

This traditional Near Eastern appetizer dip, or salad, called *tabbouleh*, is made with nutty-flavored cracked wheat (bulgur), a favorite grain in Armenia, and a variety of chopped vegetables and herbs, chosen according to local tastes. This version includes fresh mint, an aromatic, sweet refreshing herb that is commonly used in Caucasian dishes, as well as red and green peppers, and pine nuts, two other favorite foods.

> *1 cup fine bulgur*
> *1 cup sliced scallions, with some green tops*
> *½ cup chopped fresh parsley*
> *1 cup chopped fresh mint*
> *1 cup chopped green bell peppers*
> *1 cup chopped red bell peppers*
> *1 cup peeled and chopped tomatoes*
> *¼ cup chopped pine nuts or blanched almonds*
> *½ cup extra-virgin olive oil*
> *⅓ cup freshly squeezed lemon juice*
> *Dash of cayenne pepper*
> *Salt, freshly ground pepper*
> *Fresh romaine lettuce leaves or pita*

In a medium bowl cover the bulgur with cold water. Let stand about 15 minutes. Drain and, with the hands, squeeze out any excess moisture. Turn into a large bowl. Add the scallions, parsley, mint, green and red bell peppers, tomatoes, and pine nuts or almonds. Mix well. Sprinkle with the oil and lemon juice. Season with cayenne, salt, and pepper. Mix well. Refrigerate, covered, 4 to 6 hours. Serve chilled or at room temperature, with romaine leaves or pita to be used as "scoops."

EUGENIA'S COLD WHITE BEANS

6 to 8 servings.

While living in Istanbul, Turkey, I learned to prepare a number of Caucasian appetizers from Eugenia, our enthusiastic Armenian cook who loved to talk about the culinary specialties of her homeland. One of her favorites was a bowl of cold cooked white beans, seasoned with a lot of garlic, spices, and olive oil, and decorated with colorful garnishes, served as an appetizer or salad. "My beans are different from and better than the Turkish cold beans," she boasted with nationalistic pride. I agree.

> *2 cups dried white beans, washed and picked over*
> *3 to 4 garlic cloves, crushed*
> *2 medium yellow onions, finely chopped*
> *2 medium carrots, scraped and chopped*
> *¾ to 1 cup extra-virgin olive oil*
> *Salt, freshly ground pepper*
> *3 tablespoons fresh lemon juice or wine vinegar*
> *2 teaspoons sugar*
> *4 scallions, sliced, with some green tops*
> *4 tablespoons chopped fresh herbs (parsley, mint, dill, and/or coriander)*
> *Garnishes: Tomato wedges, black olives, radish "roses"*

In a large saucepan, cover beans with water; bring to a boil; boil 2 minutes. Let stand, covered, for 1 hour. Place the pan over medium-high heat; bring to a boil. Reduce heat to medium-low. Cook slowly, covered, until partially cooked, about 45 minutes. Add a little more water while cooking, if needed. Add garlic, onions, carrots, and olive oil. Season with salt and pepper. Continue to cook slowly, covered, until beans are just tender, about 30 minutes. Stir in lemon juice or vinegar, sugar, and scallions. Cook another 5 minutes. Remove from the heat and cool. Serve cold garnished with the fresh herbs, tomato wedges, olives, and radish "roses."

A PINK CABBAGE "ROSE"

Makes 1 cabbage "rose."

This attractive appetizer is prepared with a head of green cabbage that is colored pink in a beet-vinegar marinade. The leaves are folded back so the cabbage resembles a large rose. It is a marvelous centerpiece for an appetizer or buffet table. Guests will enjoy picking off the petals and eating them with their fingers.

1 firm white head cabbage, about 1½ pounds
2 medium beets, cooked, peeled, and cubed
1 large stalk celery, chopped
¼ cup chopped fresh parsley
1 teaspoon paprika
Salt, freshly ground pepper
½ cup red wine vinegar
1½ cups boiling water

Remove and discard outer leaves from the cabbage. Put the cabbage in a kettle. Cover with cold water. Bring to a boil over high heat. Reduce the heat to medium-low and cook slowly, covered, until soft, 12 to 15 minutes. Drain. Put in a large bowl. Add the beets, celery, parsley, and paprika. Season with salt and pepper.

In a medium saucepan combine the vinegar and boiling water. Bring to a boil. Remove from the heat; pour over the cabbage. Leave at room temperature for 1 day. Refrigerate, covered, turning the cabbage occasionally, until it turns pink, 4 to 5 days. To serve, remove cabbage from the bowl; drain thoroughly. Place in the center of a large plate or platter. Pull back leaves so the cabbage resembles a large rose. Garnish with small whole beets or radish "roses," if desired.

JERMUK CUCUMBER-YOGURT APPETIZER

4 to 6 servings.

Throughout Transcaucasia a popular appetizer is made from cucumbers, one of the oldest cultivated vegetables, and yogurt, a treasured staple food, with the addition of other ingredients according to local tastes. Most often the inviting cool combination is flavored with herbs, lemon juice or vinegar, and garlic, or, perhaps, yellow or golden raisins, and chopped nuts. Called *jakik* in Armenia, this version is from Jermuk, a small resort town on the Arpa River in the picturesque northern mountainous region of Vayots Dzor, "gorge of woes." Famous for its hot mineral springs, one of the attractions is the Gallery of Waters where the various waters are said to have different properties, each good for a particular illness. Visitors also enjoy the resort for its lush alpine vegetation, forests, and the Tsolk waterfall that surround the hill upon which the town is located. Local cafés and hotel restaurants serve typical Armenian fare, including this appetizer.

> *2 medium cucumbers, peeled, seeded, and finely chopped*
> *Salt*
> *2 cups plain yogurt*
> *1 to 2 garlic cloves, crushed or minced*
> *2 tablespoons wine vinegar or fresh lemon juice*
> *2 teaspoons chopped fresh dill*
> *Freshly ground white or black pepper*
> *2 tablespoons extra-virgin olive oil*
> *1 tablespoon chopped fresh mint*

Put cucumbers in a strainer over a bowl; sprinkle with salt. Leave about 20 minutes. Drain off all liquid. In a medium bowl combine the yogurt, garlic, vinegar or lemon juice, and dill. Season with pepper. Refrigerate, covered, 4 hours, up to 6. Serve sprinkled with the oil and mint in small bowls as individual appetizers or as a dip with pita triangles.

RICE-STUFFED GRAPE LEAVES

Makes about 55.

In the Caucasus a favorite appetizer is made from fresh vine or grape leaves that are stuffed with various fillings ranging from lentils and/or bulgur to ground meat mixtures. In Armenia there is a Blessing of the Grapes on the Sunday nearest the Feast of Assumption. Great trays of the fruit are brought into the churches, and after they are blessed, members of the congregation carry them home. This flavorful rice stuffing is from Azerbaijan. If fresh grapevine leaves are not available, the appetizers may be made with preserved leaves sold in jars or cans in specialty food stores.

1 jar (12 ounces) grape or vine leaves, drained
½ cup olive oil
1 cup finely chopped yellow onions
¼ cup chopped pine nuts
1 cup uncooked long-grain rice
1 large ripe tomato, peeled and chopped
2 cups chicken broth
2 tablespoons dried currants
½ teaspoon ground cinnamon
Salt, freshly ground pepper
3 tablespoons chopped fresh parsley

Drain the grape leaves. Separate and rinse in cold water. Set aside. In a large skillet heat the oil over medium-low heat. Add onions. Sauté 4 minutes. Add pine nuts and rice; continue to sauté, stirring continuously, until rice is transparent and well coated with oil, about 7 minutes. Add tomato, chicken broth, currants, and cinnamon. Season with salt and pepper. Mix well. Reduce heat to low. Cook, uncovered, until liquid has evaporated, about 10 minutes. Stir in parsley. Remove from heat. Cool.

On a flat surface arrange each grape leaf, glossy side down. Cut off any stem end from each leaf. Mix cooled rice mixture well. Place a spoonful of the mixture in center of each grape leaf. The exact amount will differ according to the size of the leaf. Roll up, beginning at bottom, and fold in sides. Be sure that the stuffing is well enclosed. Place, one on top of the other, in a large saucepan. Heat 2 cups water in the skillet in which the stuffing was cooked. Slowly pour over the grape leaf packets. Cook slowly, covered, over medium-low heat 40 minutes. With a slotted spoon, remove from the pan. Cool. Serve cold with lemon wedges or yogurt.

SPINACH-YOGURT APPETIZER FROM LAHIC

4 servings.

The picturesque mountain village of Lahic, reached with difficulty up a winding road along the narrow Girdimanchai river gorge from the sunny vineyards of Shemakha, is a remote arts and crafts center in northeastern Azerbaijan. Said to have been founded by a Persian "Shah of the Shirvans" who took refuge there with his treasures and wealth, today's artisans claim descent from the craftsmen who accompanied the ruler to his mountain retreat. The quality of the village crafts was known as early as the tenth century and they have been sought after by merchants ever since. Today's visitors can purchase highly prized carpets, copper ware, and leather goods at the marketplace known as Gapandibe, "Under the Scales," and shop along the cobbled street called Aghale for samovars, braziers, covered pilaf dishes, and sets of nested bowls used for making richly garnished rice-and-meat dishes. There are also a History Museum, housed in a former mosque, where visitors can learn about the village's designs, and a New Life Restaurant serving tea, kebabs, and *dolmas*, stuffed vegetables.

Many of the local dishes, including this appetizer, called *borani*, came to the village from Persia. Although it is traditionally made with fresh spinach, frozen spinach is a good substitute. It may also be served as a salad.

1 package (10 ounces) frozen chopped spinach
2 tablespoons peanut or vegetable oil
½ cup finely chopped yellow onions
1 garlic clove, crushed
¾ cup plain yogurt
½ teaspoon ground nutmeg or cinnamon
Salt, freshly ground pepper
2 tablespoons chopped fresh mint or coriander

Cook spinach according to package directions until tender; drain; press out all liquid. Spoon into a bowl. Meanwhile, in a medium skillet heat the oil over medium-high heat. Add the onions and garlic; sauté 4 minutes. Add, with the yogurt and nutmeg or cinnamon, to the spinach. Season with salt and pepper. Refrigerate, covered, 1 to 2 hours before serving. Serve cold sprinkled with the mint or coriander.

PICKLES AND RELISHES

Caucasians usually have dishes of homemade pickles and relishes on the appetizer table. They are fond of preserved fruits, vegetables, and mushrooms that provide basic nutrients and add color and flavor to the appetizer display. Here are recipes for two of them.

CUCUMBER PICKLES

Makes about 3 cups.

These pickled cucumber slices, combined with scallions and peppers in a vinegar-sugar marinade, are served with a dill garnish.

> *2 medium-large cucumbers, peeled and sliced thinly*
> *1 teaspoon salt*
> *6 scallions, thinly sliced, including some green tops*
> *3/4 cup chopped green bell peppers*
> *1/3 cup vinegar*
> *1 tablespoon sugar*
> *Freshly ground white pepper*
> *1 tablespoon snipped fresh dill*

Place cucumber slices in a colander over a bowl. Sprinkle with salt. Let stand at room temperature about 30 minutes. Drain. Rinse in cold water. Return to bowl. Add scallions and bell peppers; mix well. In a small dish combine the vinegar, sugar, and pepper. Pour over cucumber mixture. Refrigerate, covered, 6 hours, up to 2 days. At serving time, drain; sprinkle with salt. Serve garnished with dill.

PICKLED MUSHROOMS

4 to 6 servings.

Russians and Caucasians are extremely fond of mushrooms, a staple food eaten in great quantity and variety. In the autumn families gather many kinds of wild mushrooms, which they dry or preserve for use throughout the year. For this treasured *zakuska* specialty the pickled mushrooms are made with cultivated kinds.

> *1 pound fresh small white mushrooms*
> *⅔ cup distilled white vinegar*
> *1 large garlic clove, minced*
> *1 small bay leaf*
> *6 whole peppercorns*
> *2 whole cloves*
> *2 teaspoons salt*
> *2 tablespoons vegetable oil*

Clean mushrooms by removing any dirt with wet paper towels or by rinsing quickly under running water. Remove stems and save for use in some other dish. In a medium saucepan cover the mushrooms with lightly salted water over medium-high heat. Bring to a boil. Reduce the heat to medium-low. Cook slowly, covered, 5 minutes. Drain and cool. Spoon mushrooms into a jar.

Meanwhile, in a small saucepan combine the vinegar, garlic, bay leaf, peppercorns, cloves, and salt over medium-high heat. Bring to a boil. Pour over mushroom caps. Top with the oil. Cover jar tightly. Leave for at least 3 days before serving. Remove from marinade before serving.

SOUPS

While traveling about the Caucasus one will always find a tempting variety of imaginative soups, made with a wide range of ingredients. These dishes have been important mainstays of the everyday diet, ranking just after breads and grains, and are generally superb. Creative cooks not only relied on them for nourishment but were discerning enough to make them appealing to the palate. Each cuisine has a noteworthy number of praiseworthy national favorites, prepared and flavored according to local traditions.

Whether a clear vegetable, fish, or meat broth, seasoned with fresh herbs, and commonly taken as a tonic, or a hearty meat and vegetable combination, each dish is a pleasure to prepare, serve, and to eat. Indeed, there is nothing more enjoyable at mealtime, or in between, than a superb soup that plays a significant role in Caucasian dining.

Soup-making has long been an essential accomplishment and laudable art in the Caucasus home. Soups are among the earliest and most traditional culinary creations, providing basic sustenance, the mainstay at many tables through good and bad times. In these ancient lands, where many of our soups originated, the earliest varieties were made simply with meats, greens, vegetables, grains, and especially legumes, wisely flavored with garlic, onions, herbs, spices, yogurt, olive oil, lemon juice or vinegar, to enhance the appeal of the bland lentils, beans, and chickpeas.

Of all the superb soups, those made with vegetables are particularly noteworthy for their rich and interesting variety. The practice of placing one or more vegetables and the necessary liquid, with or without other foods, into some sort of pot dates back to prehistoric times. Some of the soups are still made simply with greens and herbs. Particularly desirable are those enhanced with noodles, dumplings, or grains.

Many of the thick and substantial soups, age-old creations made with a medley of the native bounty of land and sea, are often served as one-dish meals. Quite naturally hearty varieties of meat soups utilized bits and chunks of meat or game or split animal bones with clinging particles of meat, simmered in water. Later, legumes, vegetables, and seasonings, and sometimes even fruit and nuts were added to the basic dishes. Not only were they nutritious but could be prepared with readily available foods.

In the North Caucasus traditional Russian soups, made especially with cabbage, root vegetables, and grains, and flavored with sour cream, are staple dishes. Many soups of Transcaucasia, similar to those of Central Asia and the Near East, are hearty well-seasoned dishes featuring lamb or mutton. One typical substantial specialty, called *bozbash*, made in several varieties, generally includes fatty breast of lamb, vegetables, fresh herbs and spices, and perhaps fruits and pasta. Azerbaijan is known for its thick lamb soups called *piti*, made with chickpeas and vegetables, cooked and served in individual earthenware casseroles.

Traditionally all parts of the animal, including the head, innards, and feet, go into the flavorful soups often enriched with greens. Some of them are still prepared for religious festivals and family celebrations and taken as "cures" for various ailments. In Georgia a flavorful nourishing beef bouillon, called *khash* or *khashi*, made with tripe, knuckles, and perhaps calves' hooves, is served with cold *chacha* (vodka) in the morning as a remedy for hangovers. Another concoction, said to have therapeutic value for digestive problems, includes milk, grated garlic, and bread that are mixed and stirred into the soup just before serving.

Although many of the soups are similar, there are distinctive regional favorites. One Armenian specialty includes *tarhana*, a grain product made with a basis of crushed wheat and yogurt, allowed to rest and sour, then formed into sheets or pellets which are dried in the sun and crumbled. Used commonly in soups, it is also eaten as a sort of cereal. Another special ingredient is hulled wheat or *dzedzadz*. One of the most commonly used foods for the flavorful soups is yogurt, a treasured staple.

Of all the diverse variety of Caucasian soups, hot or cold, clear or creamy, simple or hearty, each holds a place of honor on the table. All are culinary delights. The recipes in this chapter comprise only a few of the vast repertoire but are representative of those that can be made easily in our homes.

BORSHCH

8 to 10 servings.

This famous soup prepared in numerous variations throughout Russia, is an ancient dish that probably originated in the Ukraine, where it is still a favorite. The name *borshch*, or derivations of it, comes from an old Slavic word for beet. This one ingredient appears in all versions and provides the soup's characteristic red color. While *borshch* can be made simply with beets and broth, it also may include additional vegetables, meats, poultry, or game. Served hot or cold, it is often garnished with sour cream. This hearty version is an excellent one-dish meal that can be prepared beforehand and reheated. Serve with pumpernickel or rye bread.

8 medium beets, washed
Salt
½ cup cider vinegar
2 pounds soup beef or chuck
3 cracked soup bones
½ pound lean fresh pork
1 bay leaf
8 peppercorns
2 sprigs parsley
1 clove garlic, halved
3 medium carrots, scraped and thinly sliced
2 medium yellow onions, chopped
2 medium leeks, white parts only, sliced
½ small head green cabbage, coarsely chopped
3 medium tomatoes, peeled and chopped
4 medium potatoes, peeled and cubed (optional)
1 to 2 teaspoons sugar
1 cup sour cream, at room temperature

In a large saucepan put 7 of the beets, whole and unpeeled, in salted water to cover with ¼ cup vinegar over medium-high heat. Bring to a boil. Lower heat to medium-low and cook, covered, about 30 minutes, until just tender. Drain beets; peel; cut into thin strips.

In a large pot combine the beef, bones, pork, and 10 cups cold water over medium-high heat. Bring to a boil. Skim. Add bay leaf, peppercorns, parsley, garlic, carrots, onions, and leeks. Reduce heat to medium-low. Cook slowly, covered, 1½ hours, until meat is tender. Add cabbage, tomatoes, cooked strips of beets, and potatoes, if desired. Continue to cook slowly another 20 minutes, or until ingredients are tender. Remove meat and cut up, discarding any bones and gristle. Take out and discard bones, bay leaf, peppercorns, parsley, and garlic, Return cut-up meat to pot. Season with salt. Peel and grate the remaining beet. In a small saucepan combine 1 cup hot soup, the remaining ¼ cup vinegar, and sugar over medium-high heat. Bring to a boil. Stir into hot soup. Ladle soup into bowls and garnish with a spoonful of sour cream.

COLD BEET SOUP
WITH SOUR CREAM

6 servings.

This is a refreshing and easy-to-prepare version of *borshch* that is prepared by a Russian friend who lives in Washington, D.C. She serves it as a first course for a summer dinner.

> *2 cups or 1-pound can beets, drained and*
>   *cut into julienne strips*
> *4 cups beef bouillon*
> *1 bay leaf*
> *3 tablespoons cider vinegar*
> *1 teaspoon sugar*
> *Salt, freshly ground pepper*
> *½ cup sour cream*
> *2 tablespoons chopped fresh dill or parsley*

In a large saucepan combine the beets, bouillon, bay leaf, vinegar, and sugar over medium-high heat. Season with salt and pepper. Bring to a boil. Reduce the heat to medium-low. Cook slowly, covered, 10 minutes. Remove from the stove and cool. Refrigerate, covered, 4 hours, up to 8. Serve cold, garnished with a spoonful of sour cream and some dill or parsley.

GEORGIAN LEMONY CHICKEN SOUP

6 servings.

This characteristic Georgian soup called *chikhirtma* is made with chicken or lamb broth and has a pleasing tart flavor achieved with lemon juice or vinegar. In some versions spices and dried herbs, including marigold petals, are used as flavorings. This easy-to-prepare variation has a combination of fresh herbs.

2 tablespoons unsalted butter
1 cup finely chopped yellow onions
2 garlic cloves, crushed
1 tablespoon cornstarch or flour
6 cups hot chicken broth, well seasoned,
  preferably homemade
Salt, freshly ground pepper
3 egg yolks
3 tablespoons fresh lemon juice
½ teaspoon powdered saffron, dissolved in a little
  hot water (optional)
2 cups slivered cooked white chicken
½ cup chopped mixed fresh herbs (coriander, basil, mint,
  parsley)

In a large saucepan melt the butter over medium-high heat. Add the onions and garlic; sauté about 4 minutes. Sprinkle in the cornstarch or flour. Cook, stirring, 1 minute. Gradually add the hot broth. Bring to a boil. Reduce the heat to medium-low. Season with salt and pepper.

Meanwhile, in a medium bowl whisk the eggs yolks and lemon juice to blend well. Gradually add 1 cup of hot broth, whisking until smooth. Stir into the hot soup. Cook slowly, stirring, until the soup thickens, about 5 minutes. Stir in the saffron and chicken. Leave over low heat 5 minutes. Serve garnished with the herbs.

EGG AND LEMON SOUP FROM GYUMRI

4 to 6 servings.

In the Caucasus typical soups are made with a simple chicken broth flavored and thickened with eggs and lemon juice. While an Armenian version called *havabour* includes fine egg noodles, this one is made with rice. Serve as a first course for a luncheon or dinner.

Gyumri, the second largest city of Armenia, is situated on the banks of the Akhurian River in the northwestern Shirak region near the Turkish border. Located in the Lesser Caucasus range at an elevation of 4,600 feet in an area where destructive earthquakes have created great havoc, it was heavily damaged by a massive one in 1988. It was known previously as Leninakan, and as Alexandropol, named for the wife of Czar Nicholas I, before that. Once the home of famous Armenian poets, writers, composers, and minstrels, travelers may visit its national museum, located in a typical Armenian house, as well as attractive nineteenth century houses and churches. An important trading center since ancient times, the city is now in the center of a main farming area on the Armenian plateau. One of its good dining places is the Restaurant Gyumri, located in an in an old, atmospheric cellar, that offers a variety of Armenian dishes, including soups.

> 6 cups chicken broth
> ⅓ cup long-grain rice
> Salt, freshly ground pepper
> 3 egg yolks
> Juice of 2 lemons
> 2 tablespoons finely chopped coriander or parsley

In a large saucepan bring the chicken broth to a boil over medium-high heat. Stir in the rice. Reduce heat to medium-low and cook slowly, covered, about 15 minutes, until rice is tender. Season with salt and pepper. Meanwhile, in a small bowl whisk egg yolks until light and creamy. Add a few spoonfuls of the hot broth and the lemon juice. Whisk to mix well. Slowly stir into the soup and leave on low heat only a few minutes, long enough for the soup to thicken. Do not boil or the mixture will curdle. Serve at once, garnished with the coriander or parsley. Do not reheat.

COLD
MEAT-VEGETABLE SOUP

6 servings.

A refreshing slightly tart cold meat or fish and vegetable ancient soup called *okroshka* is a popular Russian warm-weather dish that includes a variety of unusual colorful ingredients that blend surprisingly to make a pleasing medley. Essential to the soup is a flavoring called *kvass*, a lightly fermented and sour-sweet liquid having a low alcoholic content that is rich in vitamins. Made generally from bread or grain but also fruit, *kvass* somewhat resembles beer in flavor. Often consumed as a relatively healthful common drink, it has long been used in soups. While there is no real substitute for the fermented beverage, some suggestions are given in this recipe.

1 cup diced cold cooked beef, ham, or veal
1 medium cucumber, peeled, seeded, and diced
½ cup sliced scallions, with some green tops
2 hard-cooked eggs, chopped
About ½ cup sour cream
4 cups cider, beer, or a mixture of 3 cups bouillon and
    1 cup dry white wine
2 teaspoons sharp prepared mustard
1 teaspoon sugar
Salt
3 tablespoons chopped dill or parsley

In a large bowl combine the meat, cucumber, scallions, and eggs. In a medium bowl mix together the sour cream, cider or other liquid, mustard, and sugar. Season with salt. Beat well. Add to the meat mixture. Refrigerate, covered, 2 hours, up to 6. Serve cold garnished with dill or parsley.

GEORGIAN MEAT-RICE SOUP

8 servings.

An aromatic and slightly spicy hearty soup called *kharcho* is one of Georgia's best known dishes that can be made with beef, lamb, poultry, or game and seasoned variously. Characteristic flavorings are garlic, red peppers, fenugreek, sour plum juice, and several fresh herbs. As the dish became more popular in areas outside the Caucasus the list of ingredients has changed considerably and now the soup is made in many variations. This one is a favorite of a Georgian friend whom I knew in Turkey.

> 1½ pounds boneless stew meat,
>   cut into 1-inch cubes
> 1 medium carrot, scraped and chopped
> 2 parsley sprigs
> Salt
> ½ cup long-grain rice
> 1 large yellow onion, finely chopped
> ½ teaspoon dried thyme
> ¼ teaspoon dried basil
> ¼ teaspoon freshly ground pepper
> ½ cup finely chopped walnuts (optional)
> 3 tablespoons tomato paste
> ½ teaspoon paprika
> 2 to 3 cloves garlic, crushed
> 3 tablespoons fresh lemon juice
> ¼ cup finely chopped fresh coriander
> ¼ cup finely chopped fresh parsley,
>   basil, or dill

In a large pot combine the meat cubes, carrot, parsley, 1 teaspoon salt, and 8 cups cold water over medium-high heat. Bring to a boil. Lower the heat to medium-low. Cook slowly, covered, 1 hour, occasionally skimming off any foam as it rises to the top. Remove and discard the carrot and parsley.

Stir in the rice, onion, thyme, basil, and pepper. Continue to cook slowly, covered, 15 minutes. Meanwhile, in a small bowl combine the walnuts, tomato paste, paprika, and garlic. Stir into the soup. Continue cooking an additional 15 to 20 minutes, until the rice is tender. Stir in the lemon juice. Simmer 1 minute. Serve sprinkled with the fresh coriander and other herbs.

KISLOVODSK YOGURT-CHICKEN SOUP

6 to 8 servings.

Kislovodsk, one of the four famous health spa resorts of the northern Caucasus in an area on the northern spur of the central Caucasus, is located in a valley, at an elevation of 2,695 feet on the banks of the Olkhovka and Beryozovka rivers, which have several small waterfalls. Founded in the early 1800s, the town is renowned for its Narzan "drink of the gods" mineral water, used in medicinal baths. A number of the scenic outdoor cafés and restaurants serve nutritious fare such as this yogurt-flavored soup.

Some of the best and most interesting Caucasian soups are made with yogurt, which imparts an attractive flavor and nutrient richness both to the light and hearty varieties. Since ancient times yogurt has been prepared as soup with such flavorings as garlic, onions, and herbs that were mixed with it. During the summer it is eaten cold and in winter months enjoyed hot. There are excellent clear soups made with broth and yogurt, and more substantial kinds laced with yogurt. Fortunately, it mixes well with spicy seasonings so popular in some of the soups, and imparts an appealing addition to those that include noodles, dried beans, rice, and such vegetables as onions, tomatoes, and cabbage. Included below are recipes for some of them.

6 cups chicken broth
Salt, freshly ground pepper
2 cups plain yogurt
1 tablespoon flour
2 egg yolks, well beaten
2 tablespoons unsalted butter
2 tablespoons chopped fresh mint, dill, or parsley

In a large saucepan bring the broth to a boil over medium-high heat. Season with salt and pepper. Reduce the heat to medium-low. In a small bowl combine the yogurt, flour, and beaten egg yolks. Stir in some of the hot broth; mix well. Gradually stir into the broth. Cook slowly, stirring, 1 or 2 minutes. Add the butter and mint, dill, or parsley. Serve at once. Do not reheat.

ARMENIAN BARLEY-YOGURT SOUP

6 servings.

One of the favorite soups of Armenia called *tanabour* is made simply with barley and yogurt and flavored with mint. It is surprisingly tasty as well as nourishing.

> 2 tablespoons unsalted butter
> 1 medium yellow onion, finely chopped
> ⅓ cup pearl barley
> 4½ cups chicken broth
> 1 egg, lightly beaten
> 1 tablespoon all-purpose flour
> 2 cups plain yogurt
> 1 tablespoon chopped fresh mint
> 1 tablespoon chopped fresh coriander or parsley
> Salt, freshly ground pepper
> 2 to 3 tablespoons minced scallions, with some green tops

In a large pot melt the butter over medium-high heat. Add the onion; sauté 3 minutes. Add the barley; sauté, tossing to coat with the onion mixture. Add chicken broth; heat to boiling. Reduce heat to medium-low. Cook slowly, covered, about 50 minutes, until barley is tender. In a medium bowl combine the egg, flour, yogurt, mint, and coriander or parsley. Slowly stir into the soup. Warm through but do not boil. Season with salt and pepper. Serve garnished with minced scallions.

YOGURT-MEATBALL SOUP

8 servings.

This characteristic Caucasian soup illustrates what an appealing flavor yogurt can impart to two other regional favorites, meatballs and rice.

> *1 pound ground beef*
> *½ pound ground lamb*
> *1 medium yellow onion, minced*
> *3 eggs*
> *2 cloves garlic, crushed*
> *2 tablespoons chopped fresh coriander or parsley*
> *Salt, freshly ground pepper*
> *1½ cups beef bouillon*
> *⅔ cup long-grain rice*
> *2 cups plain yogurt*
> *Juice of 1 large lemon*
> *¼ cup chopped fresh parsley*

In a large bowl combine the ground beef and lamb, onion, 1 egg, garlic, and coriander or parsley. Season with salt and pepper. With a spoon or the hands, work to thoroughly combine the ingredients. Shape into small balls about 1 inch in diameter. Set aside. In a large saucepan bring the bouillon to a boil over medium-high heat. Drop in the meatballs. Add the rice. Stir well. Reduce the heat to medium-low. Cook slowly, covered, about 30 minutes, or until the meatballs and rice are tender. Gradually add the yogurt. Meanwhile, in a medium dish combine the remaining 2 eggs and lemon juice. Stir in 1 cup hot broth; mix well. Stir into the soup, beating constantly while adding. Leave over low heat, stirring, until thickened. Stir in the parsley. Serve at once.

Note: If the soup is partially prepared beforehand, do not add the yogurt or the mixture of eggs and lemon juice and parsley until just before serving.

COLD YOGURT SOUPS

Throughout Transcaucasia light and refreshing cold yogurt soups are made with cucumbers and seasonings that may vary from herbs and onions to fruits and nuts. They are also eaten as appetizers and salads. Here are recipes for two superb soups.

ZAQATALA WALNUT-YOGURT SOUP

4 to 6 servings.

In Azerbaijan's scenic northwest region one of the historic towns is Zaqatala, a popular tourist destination for outdoor enthusiasts in the thickly forested area of the Caucasus Mountains. It is a lovely green town planted with ancient plane trees and has an attractive park with a tea house as well as marvelous views of the distant snow-capped mountains. The town is also the center of a nut-producing area and has nut-processing factories.

> *2 medium cucumbers, peeled, seeded, and diced*
> *Salt*
> *4 cups plain yogurt*
> *½ cup finely chopped walnuts*
> *2 or 3 garlic cloves, crushed*
> *1 tablespoon fresh lemon juice*
> *2 tablespoons extra-virgin olive oil*
> *Freshly ground white pepper*
> *2 tablespoons minced fresh dill*

Put diced cucumbers in a colander over a bowl. Sprinkle with salt. Leave to drain for 30 minutes. Turn cucumbers into a large bowl. Add yogurt, walnuts, garlic, lemon juice, and olive oil. Season with salt and pepper. Refrigerate, covered, 2 hours, up to 8. Serve in chilled soup bowls garnished with the dill

GARNISHED COLD YOGURT SOUP

4 servings.

This is a colorful and flavorful soup to serve for a company meal.

> *1 medium cucumber, peeled, seeded and diced*
> *Salt*
> *3 cups plain yogurt*
> *⅓ cup raisins*
> *⅓ cup chopped scallions, with some green tops*
> *2 hard-cooked eggs, chopped*
> *3 tablespoons chopped fresh parsley*
> *2 tablespoons chopped fresh mint or dill*
> *Freshly ground pepper*

Put diced cucumber in a colander over a bowl. Sprinkle with salt. Leave to drain for 30 minutes. Turn cucumbers into a large bowl. Add yogurt, raisins, scallions, eggs, parsley, and mint or dill. Season with salt and pepper. Refrigerate, covered, 2 hours, up to 8.

LENTIL-SPINACH SOUP

6 servings.

Since ancient times lentils have been staple fare in the Caucasus countries. They are highly prized for their nutritional value and are used interestingly in soups, each flavored well with seasonings according to local preference. One of the traditional dishes includes spinach and lemon juice.

1 cup dried lentils, washed and picked over
Salt, freshly ground pepper
⅓ cup olive oil
1 medium yellow onion, minced
1 clove garlic, crushed
Juice of 1 lemon
1 pound spinach, chopped

In a large pot combine the lentils and 8 cups water over medium-high heat. Season with salt and pepper. Bring to a boil. Reduce the heat to medium-low. Cook slowly, covered, about 20 minutes, until lentils are just tender. Meanwhile, heat the oil in a small skillet over medium-high heat. Add the onion and garlic; sauté 4 minutes. When lentils are cooked, stir in the onion mixture, lemon juice, and spinach. Cook about 10 minutes longer, until spinach is tender.

LAMB-LENTIL POT

6 to 8 servings.

This hearty soup includes such favorite Caucasian foods as lamb, garlic, onions, and tomatoes. It's a good supper dish to serve with crusty dark bread.

4 lamb shanks, about 3½ pounds total
Salt, freshly ground pepper
About 2 tablespoons unsalted butter
1 large yellow onion, chopped
1 garlic clove, crushed
1 can (1 pound, 12 ounces) tomatoes, undrained
½ teaspoon dried thyme
1 medium bay leaf
3 sprigs parsley
1 cup dried lentils, washed and drained
2 tablespoons fresh lemon juice
⅓ cup chopped fresh parsley

Trim the shanks of any excess fat. Discard the fat. Rub the shanks with salt and pepper. In a large pot melt 2 tablespoons butter over medium-high heat. Add the shanks and brown on all sides. Remove to a plate. Add the onion and garlic to the drippings, adding more butter, if needed. Sauté 2 minutes. Add the tomatoes, thyme, bay leaf, and parsley. Season with salt and pepper. Cook 2 minutes, breaking the tomatoes with a spoon while cooking. Return the shanks to the pot. Reduce the heat to medium-low. Cook slowly, covered, for 1 hour. Add the lentils and 8 cups water. Continue to cook slowly, covered, about 30 minutes, until the ingredients are tender. Stir in the lemon juice and parsley. Remove from the heat. Take out the shanks. Cut all the lamb from them. Return the lamb to the soup. Remove and discard the bay leaf and parsley. Reheat if necessary.

DERBENT FISH SOUP

6 servings

A traditional hearty soup or stew called *solianka* or *selianka*, made with either fish or meat, reflects the Russian fondness for a tart flavor. In this dish, tartness is achieved with the addition of salted cucumber, capers, and olives. It is traditionally made with sturgeon, but any firm white-fleshed fish will do.

Derbent, a southern port city on the Caspian Sea and one of the world's oldest cities, has notable architectural monuments. Among its culinary specialties are flavorful fish soups.

> *2½ pounds whole white-fleshed fish*
> *3 medium yellow onions, chopped*
> *1 bay leaf*
> *3 sprigs parsley*
> *2 whole cloves*
> *6 peppercorns*
> *Salt*
> *2 tablespoons unsalted butter*
> *2 large tomatoes, peeled and chopped*
> *1 medium cucumber, peeled, chopped, and*
>   *sprinkled with salt*
> *3 tablespoons capers, drained*
> *12 pitted olives*
> *1 lemon, thinly sliced*
> *2 tablespoons chopped fresh dill or parsley*

Have fish dealer dress and fillet fish. Take home trimmings, heads, and bones, as well as fillets. Cut fillets into bite-size pieces. To cook, in a large pot combine the trimmings, heads, and bones with 1 chopped onion, bay leaf, parsley, cloves, peppercorns, and salt with 10 cups water over medium-high heat. Bring to a boil. Reduce heat to medium-low. Cook slowly, covered, 30 minutes. Strain broth and discard solid ingredients.

Meanwhile, in a medium saucepan melt the butter over medium-high heat. Add remaining 2 onions; sauté 3 to 4 minutes. Add tomatoes. Cook, stirring, 2 minutes. In a large pot combine this mixture with the cucumber, capers, olives, fish pieces, and strained broth. Cook slowly, covered, about 10 minutes, until the fish is tender. Remove and discard the bay leaf, cloves, and peppercorns. Correct the seasoning. Serve in bowls garnished with lemon slices and dill or parsley.

NAZRAN BARLEY-
MUSHROOM SOUP

8 to 10 servings.

North Caucasians are partial to dried mushrooms that figure prominently in many of their nourishing soups such as this one named after Nazran, capital of Ingush or Ingushetia, Russia's smallest autonomous republic. It is a lazy, overgrown village on a plateau that was transformed into a capital only in 1992. The soup is a substantial one dish meal.

3 ounces dried mushrooms
3 tablespoons unsalted butter
½ cup chopped yellow onions
1 medium leek, white part only, chopped
1 cup diced carrots
⅓ cup pearl barley
4 peppercorns
Salt
2 cups peeled diced potatoes
2 medium bay leaves
1 cup sour cream
Chopped fresh dill

In a small dish soak the mushrooms in lukewarm water to cover for 20 minutes. Drain, pressing to extract water. Slice the mushrooms. In a large saucepan melt the butter over medium-high heat. Add the onions and leek; sauté 5 minutes. Add the carrots, barley, peppercorns, and 8 cups water. Season with salt. Bring to a boil. Reduce the heat to medium-low. Cook, covered, for 1 hour. Add the potatoes, bay leaves, and sliced mushrooms. Continue to simmer until the vegetables are tender, about 45 minutes. Just before serving, mix in the sour cream. Garnish with chopped dill.

MUSHROOM-HERB SOUP FROM TUSHETI

4 servings.

This tasty healthful soup is named for Tusheti, an isolated mountain area of northeastern Georgia bordering Dagestan that is rich with flora and fauna as well as mushrooms. Tushetians maintain individual ancient religious rituals dating back to pagan times and celebrate with lively festivals. They also put out the welcome mat for nature lovers and hikers. Serve this soup for a first course at an informal meal or as an in-between snack.

> *⅓ cup unsalted butter*
> *1 cup finely chopped yellow onions*
> *2 tablespoons fresh lemon juice*
> *2 cups sliced fresh mushrooms*
> *4 cups vegetable or chicken bouillon*
> *½ cup chopped mixed fresh herbs (basil, mint,*
> *   parsley, or coriander)*
> *Salt, freshly ground pepper*

In a large saucepan melt the butter over medium-high heat. Add the onions; sauté 3 minutes. Add the lemon juice and mushrooms; sauté 4 minutes. Pour in the bouillon. Bring to a boil. Stir in the herbs. Season with salt and pepper. Reduce the heat to medium-low. Cook slowly, covered, 15 minutes.

LAK WINTER VEGETABLE SOUP

6 to 8 servings.

The Laks, an indigenous mountain people of the Greater Caucasus area of Dagestan, once had their own nation where a long line of khans, or "warrior-dukes," reigned. Ghazi-Ghumug, the capital of the former Lak state and now a quiet town, is surrounded by hillsides of fields of cabbages, the mainstay of the economy and a favorite food. From the site of the former khan's citadel one has a magnificent panoramic view of the surrounding mountains.

3 tablespoons unsalted butter
1 large yellow onion, sliced
1 leek, white part only, sliced
2 medium carrots, scraped and cut into
  ¼-inch-thick slices
1 large stalk celery, chopped
½ turnip, peeled and cubed
8 cups beef bouillon
1 small head green cabbage, about 1½ pounds,
  cored and shredded
1 can (6 ounces) tomato paste
3 tablespoons chopped fresh dill or parsley

In a large saucepan melt the butter over medium-high heat. Add the onion, leek, carrots, celery, and turnip. Sauté 5 minutes. Add the bouillon; bring to a boil. Stir in the cabbage and tomato paste. Reduce the heat to medium-low. Cook slowly, covered, about 1 hour, until vegetables are cooked. Serve sprinkled with dill or parsley.

RUSSIAN CABBAGE SOUP

6 to 8 servings.

This hearty, nutritious specialty called *shchi* or *s'chee*, is one of the most famous Russian soups, made with a variety of ingredients and served as a treasured staple in all family homes. In Leo Tolstoy's famous novel, *Anna Karenina*, Oblonsky invites Levin to dine at a fashionable Moscow restaurant. Oblonsky orders an elaborate French meal with wines but Levin indicates he would prefer a simple meal of *shchi*, or cabbage soup, and *kasha*, porridge. This is one of many recipes for the soup.

3 tablespoons vegetable oil or unsalted butter
1 large yellow onion, sliced
1 leek, white part only, sliced
2 medium carrots, scraped and cut into
  ¼-inch-thick slices
1 medium stalk celery, sliced
½ white turnip, peeled and cubed (optional)
8 cups beef bouillon or water
1 head green cabbage, about 1½ pounds, cored and
  shredded
1 can (6 ounces) tomato paste
3 tablespoons chopped fresh dill or parsley

In a large pot heat the oil or melt the butter over medium-high heat. Add the onion, leek, carrots, celery, and turnip. Sauté 5 minutes. Add the bouillon or water; bring to a boil. Stir in the cabbage and tomato paste. Reduce the heat to medium-low. Cook slowly, covered, about 1 hour, until vegetables are cooked. Stir in the dill or parsley. Serve hot.

DAIRY DISHES

From the Caucasus a wealth of imaginative dairy dishes has emerged utilizing some of man's earliest and most versatile foods—eggs, milk, cream, butter, yogurt, and cheese. Either by themselves, together, or combined with other ingredients, they are superb for all meals and in between. Fortunately, they give us an interesting repertoire of innovative and nourishing fare.

Over the centuries these basic nutritious and important foods have not been treated as ordinary fare and are accorded great respect by Caucasian cooks. One of nature's almost perfect foods, the egg, highly valued for the amount and high quality of protein it contains, has long been an important part of the everyday dining, used in every type of dish. Even combined with humble ingredients, egg dishes become artistic achievements. Consider the flavoring of a simple hard-cooked egg by rolling it in spices. Omelets in various forms and with ingenious flavorings belong to each cuisine. Several national dishes combine colorful vegetables with scrambled eggs. The repertoire of such dishes is indeed fascinating.

Since ancient times the egg has been not only important as a food but also as a meaningful religious symbol, particularly to signify new life. In pagan days it was customary to offer and receive brightly colored eggs at the annual spring festival. Later on, people in these lands attached other meanings to eggs and considered them important to Christian celebrations and holiday repasts.

Even before the domestication of animals and the beginnings of agriculture, early man relied on milk from his goats, sheep, or camels as the mainstay of his diet. Soured or fermented milk, rather than fresh, was soon recognized to be far more valuable as it would last longer and had an appealing flavor. Throughout the Caucasus there is a wide range of milks and creams that have been developed over the years by various processes. *Kaymak* is a rich clotted cream served as a pastry or dessert topping. Sour cream, or *smetana*, one of the most important ingredients in the Russian cuisine, is a rich sweet versatile food that can be an important flavoring and topping for hot dishes, and is widely used to enhance any number of cold specialties. While it is often made in the home by adding a little lemon juice to fresh cream or mixing buttermilk with heavy cream, commercial products are readily available and good.

Yogurt, a tangy, semisolid cultured milk, is highly esteemed as a delicacy as well as an everyday food that is marvelously versatile and adaptable. In itself, the "milk of eternal life" is an enjoyable and nutritious treat that also imparts flavor and richness to all elements of the culinary repertoire. Low in fat and calories, high in nutritional value, very easily digested, and effective in maintaining a healthy intestinal system, yogurt has often been called a perfect food.

According to legend, yogurt was an accidental discovery. Desert nomads, traveling over the vast expanses of southwestern Asia, carried their milk supplies in bags made of sheep's stomachs slung over the backs of their animals. Because of the joggling and hot sun the milk not only fermented but changed into a semisolid or concentrated consistency. Unknown to the nomads, the transformation had been caused by bacteria from the sheep's stomach. These would be identified later as specific kinds of *lactobacilli* (milk bacteria), which differentiates yogurt from clabber or fermented milk.

Once the tribesmen had acquired their first batches of yogurt they were able to make more of it by inoculating fresh milk with a small amount of yogurt already prepared. As they settled in villages and towns in the Near East, Central Asia, and other lands, these ancient peoples undertook the preparation of yogurt as a necessary daily household chore. In the Caucasus yogurt is still prepared as it was centuries ago, primarily in the homes or in small factories, and is very rich and creamy. Because it is made with whole milk, generally from sheep and/or goats, the butterfat content is quite high and the flavor is definitely tart or piquant. The word yogurt comes from the Turkish *yogurt*. It is called *madzoon* or *matsun* in Armenia; *matsoni* in Georgia and Azerbaijan; and *laban* in Arabic.

Cheese is one of the world's oldest man-made foods. Its creation, however, was probably accidental. One legend credits an ancient traveler in the desert with the discovery. When stopping to eat, he poured milk from a pouch made of a sheep's stomach and found that the liquid had separated into curds and whey. The rennet of the stomach had done the trick. The unknown wanderer presumably found the curds, or cheese, both tasty and refreshing and told others about it.

Cuisines of the Caucasus Mountains

Caucasians are especially fond of cheese that they eat throughout the day as a snack and at meals, from appetizers to desserts. It is also widely used in cookery to make an extensive array of dishes. Over the years the people have developed a fine selection of interesting and unique varieties. Commonly used throughout the area are bland fresh white cheeses made of sheep or goat milks such as *panir* or *peynir*, the Persian and Turkish words for cheese. When left to ripen in brine, the white cheese known as feta is mildly salty with a tangy flavor. A similar one called *brindza* or *bryndza* has a soft texture and is mildly pungent.

In Georgia two favorites are fresh moist *Emeretian* and *sulugundi*, with a texture similar to fresh mozzarella. There are also semi-hard and hard yellow cheeses including the semi-sharp *tushuri*, from the region of Tusheti, a mountainous region in the northeastern corner of Georgia where sheep and cattle farming is the major occupation.

Armenians have numerous types of white cheeses including a twisted thin string cheese called *peynir*, served with bread and sliced fresh vegetables or pickles as a favorite snack or appetizer. One particular favorite is a "green" or blue cheese similar to Roquefort that has a pleasant sharp taste.

The following culinary creations cover a range of good and creative dairy dishes that demonstrate the rich inventiveness of Caucasian cooks.

SPICED EGGS FROM TARKI

Makes 8.

This age-old way of preparing eggs is as good today as it was in yesteryear. According to legend it was a favorite snack in Tarki, an ancient town over-looking Makhachkala, the capital of Dagestan, and the vast Caspian Sea beyond it. Once the capital of the Kumyk nation, which for centuries was the leading power of the northern Caspian lands, it was visited by Peter the Great in 1722. Contemporary visitors to what was once a flourishing town can see the ruins of a royal palace and enjoy a beautiful view from the hilltop.

> *8 hard-cooked eggs, shelled*
> *¼ cup olive oil*
> *1 teaspoon ground cinnamon*
> *½ teaspoon ground cumin*
> *½ teaspoon ground coriander*
> *Salt*

With the tines of a fork, prick the eggs all over. In a medium skillet, heat the oil over medium-high heat. Add the eggs and sauté, turning with a spoon so the oil penetrates on all sides, until hot and golden. Sprinkle all over, turning once or twice, with the spices and salt, mixed together. Remove from the skillet. Serve whole or cut into halves, hot or cold.

GARNISHED EGGS

One of the most appealing ways of serving eggs is to fill or cover the hard-cooked white shells with colorful mixtures and garnishes. While they are standard fare on the appetizer table, the attractive eggs are also good for buffets and luncheons.

EGGS À LA RUSSE

Makes 12.

It's an ancient Russian custom to serve caviar as a filling for hard-cooked eggs or as ingredient in a "sauce" spooned over them. Here's one suggestion.

> *6 hard-cooked eggs, shelled, halved lengthwise*
> *1 cup sour cream*
> *½ cup red caviar*
> *1 tablespoon fresh lemon juice*
> *3 tablespoons chopped chives*
> *Freshly ground white pepper*

Place egg halves, yolk-sides down, on a plate or in a shallow serving dish. In a small bowl combine the sour cream, caviar, lemon juice, and chives, and season with pepper. Spoon over the eggs, Refrigerate, covered with plastic wrap, up to 6 hours.

SOUR CREAM-STUFFED EGGS

8 servings.

Stuffed eggs, filled with all kinds of foods, from caviar to herring, complement the appetizer tables of the Caucasus. This one is always a winner.

> *8 hard-cooked eggs, shelled*
> *¼ cup sour cream*
> *2 tablespoons minced scallions*
> *2 tablespoons minced fresh dill or parsley*
> *Salt, freshly ground pepper*
> *Paprika*

Cut eggs into halves lengthwise. Remove egg yolks to a small bowl. Add sour cream, scallions, dill or parsley. Season with salt and pepper. Mix well. Spoon mixture into the egg halves. Sprinkle with paprika. Refrigerate, covered with plastic wrap, up to 6 hours.

GREEN BEANS AND EGGS

4 servings.

This favorite Caucasus dish is made by combining vegetables and eggs with seasonings to make a main dish for a light meal.

> *2 tablespoons unsalted butter or vegetable oil*
> *1 medium yellow onion, minced*
> *1 tablespoon all-purpose flour*
> *⅛ teaspoon cayenne pepper*
> *Salt, freshly ground pepper*
> *1 cup chopped, cooked green beans*
> *4 eggs, slightly beaten*
> *½ cup plain yogurt or sour cream,*
> *   at room temperature*
> *2 teaspoons chopped fresh dill*

In a medium skillet melt the butter or heat the oil over medium-high heat. Add the onion; sauté until tender, about 4 minutes. Stir in the flour and cayenne. Season with salt and pepper. Cook 1 minute. Reduce the heat to medium-low. Add the green beans; mix well. Stir in the eggs, yogurt or sour cream, and dill. Cook slowly, stirring occasionally, until the eggs are cooked and still a little moist. Serve at once.

POACHED EGGS IN YOGURT

2 servings.

This is a characteristic luncheon or supper dish in the Caucasus.

1 garlic clove, halved
2 cups plain yogurt
1 or 2 tablespoons wine vinegar
Salt
4 eggs
2 tablespoons unsalted butter, melted
1 teaspoon paprika

Rub a shallow serving dish with garlic. Add the yogurt and vinegar. Season with salt; mix well. Leave at room temperature up to 1 hour. Meanwhile, poach the eggs in lightly salted water. With a slotted spoon, remove from the water. Place in the yogurt mixture. Sprinkle the top with melted butter and paprika. Serve at once.

SCRAMBLED EGGS WITH WHITE CHEESE

4 servings.

Cubes of salty white cheese and raisins add allure to eggs in this dish.

> 8 eggs
> ½ cup crumbled white cheese (feta or farmer)
> ⅓ cup golden raisins
> ⅓ cup milk
> Salt, freshly ground pepper
> 3 tablespoons unsalted butter

Break eggs into a medium bowl; mix well. Add crumbled cheese, raisins, and milk. Season with salt and pepper. In a medium skillet melt the butter over medium-high heat. Pour in egg mixture. Cook, stirring occasionally, until eggs are thickened but still moist. Serve on toasted crusty dark bread, if desired.

POACHED EGGS IN SPINACH

4 servings.

Typical colorful dishes for light meals include eggs poached in fresh vegetables such as spinach, tomatoes, or green beans. Frozen spinach is a good substitute.

> *2 packages (10 ounces each) frozen chopped spinach,*
>   *cooked and drained*
> *8 eggs*
> *2 garlic cloves, crushed*
> *1½ cups plain yogurt*
> *½ cup grated yellow cheese*
> *3 tablespoons chopped fresh dill*

Preheat oven broiler.

Spoon the cooked, drained spinach into a buttered shallow baking dish. With the back of a large spoon make 8 depressions in the spinach. Break 1 egg into each depression. In a small dish combine the garlic, yogurt, and grated cheese. Spoon over eggs, spreading evenly. Sprinkle with dill. Put under broiler about 5 minutes, long enough to become hot and bubbly.

Cuisines of the Caucasus Mountains

BATUMI FISHERMEN'S OMELET

4 to 6 servings.

Batumi, the capital, a port and seaside resort on the eastern shores of the Black Sea in the Adzharia region of western Georgia, was once a fortified Turkish city. Situated in an attractive subtropical coastal area where a variety of flora and citrus fruits are grown, Batumi has several inviting cafés serving Turkish-inspired sweets, as well as restaurants specializing in local specialties and dishes including those made with fish, such as this omelet.

> 3 tablespoons olive oil
> 1 medium yellow onion, chopped
> 1 garlic clove, crushed
> 2 large tomatoes, peeled and chopped
> ½ teaspoon dried oregano
> Salt, freshly ground pepper
> 2 cups diced cooked white fish
> 2 tablespoons fresh lemon juice
> 6 eggs, beaten
> 3 tablespoons chopped fresh herbs (parsley, oregano, basil)

In a large skillet heat the oil over medium-high heat. Add the onion and garlic. Sauté 4 minutes. Add the tomatoes and oregano. Season with salt and pepper. Cook 5 minutes.

In a large bowl combine the fish, lemon juice, eggs, and herbs. Season with salt and pepper. Mix gently and pour over the tomato mixture. Stir to mix the ingredients. Reduce the heat to medium-low and cook until the omelet is set and top is dry, occasionally lifting the edges of the mixture to let the liquid run underneath. Remove from the heat. To serve, cut into wedges.

Dishes called pancakes, made with vegetables and eggs, and fried or baked, are served hot or cold for breakfast or other meals in the Caucasus. This is one of the best.

> *4 large potatoes, peeled*
> *Salt*
> *3 tablespoons minced scallions, with some green tops*
> *4 tablespoons sour cream*
> *1 egg, beaten*
> *3 tablespoons grated yellow cheese*
> *⅛ teaspoon paprika*
> *Freshly ground pepper*
> *Unsalted butter or vegetable oil for frying*

In a medium saucepan cook the potatoes in salted water to cover over medium-high heat for about 25 minutes, until just tender. Drain; turn into a large bowl. While still warm, mash until smooth. Mix in the scallions, sour cream, egg, cheese, and paprika. Season with salt and pepper. Refrigerate, covered, 30 minutes.

In a large skillet heat or melt enough butter or fat to cover the surface over medium-high heat. Drop in 2 heaping tablespoons of potato-egg mixture; shape with a spoon to form a pancake. Fry until golden and crisp on both sides. Repeat until all the mixture is used. Serve warm.

Thick omelet cakes, made with eggs and meat, poultry, or vegetables that are baked or fried, cut into wedges and served hot or cold, are typical Caucasian fare for breakfast, snacks, or light meals.

> *6 thin slices bacon, diced*
> *2 medium yellow onions, peeled and diced*
> *2 cloves garlic, crushed*
> *1 cup diced cooked carrots*
> *1 cup cooked green peas*
> *1½ cups diced cooked peeled potatoes*
> *8 eggs, beaten*
> *3 tablespoons chopped fresh parsley*
> *Dash cayenne pepper*
> *Salt, freshly ground pepper*

In a large skillet fry the bacon over medium-high heat until crisp; remove; drain on paper towels; set aside. Pour off all but 3 tablespoons fat. Add onions and garlic to the fat. Sauté 4 minutes. Add the carrots, peas, and potatoes. Meanwhile, in a medium bowl combine the beaten eggs and parsley. Season with the cayenne, salt, and pepper. Add to vegetable mixture. Reduce the heat to medium-low. Cook until eggs are set and the surface is dry, about 10 minutes. While cooking, slip a knife around edges and tilt pan to let wet mixture run underneath. Sprinkle top with bacon pieces. Cut into wedges.

AZERBAIJAN BAKED EGGS WITH VEGETABLES

4 servings.

This favorite Azerbaijani specialty is a good luncheon dish.

> *1 medium eggplant, about 1 pound, washed and dried*
> *About 1 cup olive oil*
> *2 garlic cloves, crushed*
> *Salt, freshly ground pepper*
> *1 large yellow onion, chopped*
> *6 medium tomatoes, peeled and chopped*
> *8 eggs*
> *½ cup chopped fresh herbs (dill, parsley, coriander, basil)*

Preheat oven to 350 degrees.

Cut stem end from eggplant. Do not peel. Cut into small cubes. In a large skillet heat ½ cup of oil over medium-high heat. Add the eggplant cubes and garlic. Season with salt and pepper. Fry about 8 minutes, until fork tender, adding more oil if needed. With a slotted spoon remove to a plate and set aside. Add the onion to the drippings. Sauté 4 minutes. Add tomatoes. Season with salt and pepper. Cook 10 minutes. Spoon eggplant mixture into a large shallow baking dish. Surround with the onion-tomato mixture. With the back of a large spoon make 8 depressions in the vegetables. Break an egg into each depression. Sprinkle with herbs. Bake about 15 minutes, until the eggs are just set. Serve at once.

A cake-like specialty made with vegetables and eggs that is baked in a round dish and unmolded, then cut into wedges, is a favorite Caucasus creation.

> *1 pound fresh green beans, stemmed and shredded*
> *Salt*
> *2 tablespoons unsalted butter*
> *2 tablespoons chopped fresh dill or dillweed*
> *¼ cup chopped fresh parsley*
> *Few grains nutmeg*
> *Freshly ground pepper*
> *4 eggs, lightly beaten*

Preheat oven to 400 degrees.

In a medium saucepan cook the green beans in lightly salted water to cover over medium-high heat until tender, about 12 minutes. Drain. Turn into in a buttered shallow baking dish. Add the butter, dill or dillweed, parsley, and nutmeg. Season with salt and pepper. Toss and spread evenly. Pour eggs over green bean mixture, tipping dish to spread evenly. Bake until eggs are set, about 20 minutes. Run a spatula around edges of dish and invert onto a warm plate or platter. Cut into wedges.

KOBUSTAN ZUCCHINI CAKE

4 servings.

A baked vegetable, chicken or meat, and egg dish similar to the Persian *kuku* is a popular dish in Azerbaijan and can be served cold as well as warm. It is often enjoyed as picnic fare.

One of the main attractions in Azerbaijan is the world's finest prehistoric petroglyphs in Kobustan, "ravine land," located southwest of Baku where the spurs of the Greater Caucasus descend to the sea and the soft clay soil led to the formation of numerous ravines. First discovered in 1939, the rock carvings date back to the Stone Age and show stick-figures of men and women engaged in rituals and dancing, including the "food dance," presumably a magic rite done before hunting. The area is a unique source of knowledge on the period from 10,000 B.C. to the Middle Ages covering the fields of history, culture, art, and archaeology. There is also a small museum.

Zucchini is an attractive green-and-yellow striped variety of summer squash that is popular in Azerbaijan and other areas of the Caucasus. It should not be peeled before cooking. Just wash it and cut off the ends.

> *3 small zucchini (about 1 pound)*
> *Salt*
> *3 tablespoons olive oil*
> *1 medium yellow onion, minced*
> *2 tablespoons fresh lemon juice*
> *⅛ teaspoon ground nutmeg*
> *Freshly ground pepper*
> *6 eggs, beaten*
> *¼ cup chopped fresh parsley*
> *½ cup chopped walnuts*
> *1 cup plain yogurt*
> *⅓ cup chopped fresh mint*

Preheat oven to 350 degrees.

Remove stem ends from zucchini; cut into small julienne-style shreds. Put into a colander; sprinkle with salt; let stand 15 minutes. Wrap zucchini in a clean towel or paper towels; wring out all moisture. Pat dry. In a medium skillet heat the oil over medium-high heat. Add the zucchini and onion. Sauté about 5 minutes, until zucchini is tender but still crisp. Remove from heat. Add lemon juice, and nutmeg. Season with salt and pepper.

In a medium bowl, combine the eggs with parsley and walnuts. Add to zucchini mixture. Spoon into a greased round shallow dish. Bake about 25 minutes, until set. Remove from the oven and let stand several minutes. Cut into wedges to serve. Top with yogurt combined with mint.

FRIED CHEESE WITH OLIVES

4 servings.

This is a typical appetizer or snack that is easy to prepare. Cut 8 ounces firm white "pickled" cheese such as feta into ½-inch cubes. In a small skillet heat 1 to 2 tablespoons olive oil over medium-high heat. Add cheese cubes. Sauté gently until golden and crisp. Serve with black olives and wedges of flat bread.

GEORGIAN FRIED CHEESE

4 servings.

Usually made with a cheese called *sulugundi*, mozzarella is a good substitute.

> *½ pound fresh mozzarella*
> *2 tablespoons unsalted butter*
> *1 egg, beaten*
> *All-purpose flour*

With a sharp knife cut the mozzarella into ¼-inch-thick slices. In a medium skillet melt the butter over medium-high heat. Dip each cheese slice in beaten egg and dust lightly with flour. Fry, turning once, until golden on both sides. Serve warm with fresh herbs and cornbread. Or serve with a spicy tomato sauce.

CHEESE PANCAKES

Makes about 12 patties.

A traditional Russian specialty called *sirniki* or *syrniki*, these are simple, flavorful cheese pancakes that may be served for a morning meal or evening supper. The name derives from the Russian word for cheese, *syr*.

> *1 pound pot, cottage cheese, or farmer cheese*
> *2 eggs*
> *½ cup all-purpose flour*
> *Salt*
> *2 to 3 tablespoons unsalted butter*
> *Sour cream*

Put cheese through a sieve into a medium bowl to remove any liquid and make smooth. Add the eggs and flour. Season with salt. Mix well. Turn out on a lightly floured board. Pat the mixture into about 2-inch rounds, turning to flour on both sides. In a medium skillet melt butter over medium-high heat. Add the patties, a few at a time, and fry until golden and crisp on both sides, about 8 minutes. Transfer to a heated platter. Serve warm with sour cream.

WALNUT-CHEESE SPREAD

Makes about 3½ cups.

8 ounces feta cheese
4 ounces farmer cheese
½ cup grated mild yellow cheese
1 cup sour cream
2 tablespoons chopped fresh dill, mint, or coriander
½ cup minced walnuts

In a food processor or in a bowl blend the feta, farmer, and yellow cheeses. Add the sour cream; dill, mint, or coriander; and walnuts. Mix well. Serve as a spread with flat bread triangles.

CHEESE-GARLIC SPREAD

Makes 1½ cups.

> 2 tablespoons olive oil
> 3 tablespoons sliced scallions
> 2 cloves garlic, crushed
> ½ pound (8 ounces) feta cheese
> 3 tablespoons plain yogurt
> 1 tablespoon chopped fresh mint or ½ teaspoon dried

In a small skillet heat the oil over medium-high heat. Add scallions; sauté 1 minute. Stir in garlic; remove from the heat. Let cool about 3 minutes. In a medium bowl mash the cheese or process in a food processor until smooth. Add scallion-oil mixture, yogurt, and mint. Blend well. Turn into a small crock or bowl. Refrigerate, covered with plastic wrap, 2 hours, up to 2 days. Twenty minutes before serving remove from refrigerator. Serve with pita triangles or toast rounds.

YOGURT RAW VEGETABLE DIP

Makes about 2¼ cups.

Serve as a dip with such vegetables as cucumber fingers, carrot sticks, cauliflower flowerets, radishes, cherry tomatoes, celery, and green or red pepper strips.

> *2 cups plain yogurt*
> *1 or 2 garlic cloves, crushed*
> *2 tablespoons prepared mustard*
> *⅓ cup chopped scallions, with some green tops*
> *2 tablespoons chopped drained capers*
> *¼ cup minced fresh dill or parsley*
> *Salt, freshly ground pepper*

In a large bowl combine the yogurt, garlic, mustard, scallions, capers, and dill or parsley. Season with salt and pepper. Refrigerate, covered, 2 hours, up to 6.

YOGURT
CHEESE

A tasty white cheese can be easily made with yogurt and served in a number of interesting ways. To make, stir a 1-quart container of plain yogurt and pour off any liquid. Put in a bag, made with two or three layers of cheesecloth or muslin, and knot the top. Put in a colander or strainer in the sink and leave to drain three or four hours, or until most of the liquid or whey has drained off and the yogurt has thickened. Leave overnight to drain further. Remove the yogurt cheese from the bag. Season with salt. It should have a fairly thick consistency, similar to cream cheese. Because yogurt becomes tarter as it ages, the flavor of the cheese will be more piquant if the yogurt is several days old.

In the Caucasus the cheese is served garnished with olive oil and eaten with flat bread and olives. It is also mixed with a combination of local spices, herbs, and olive oil and served as a spread on bread. Or, combine the cheese with olive oil and dried mint. Other suggestions include flavoring the cheese with minced scallions, fresh herbs, or seeds, such as sesame or mustard. The cheese may be also offered as a topping for or with fruit as the piquant flavor is a good contrast to that of fresh pears, apples, or others.

YOGURT
CHEESE BALLS

In the Caucasus yogurt cheese is shaped into small balls, stored in olive oil and kept for several weeks. To make the balls, drain 1 quart of yogurt and make it into cheese according to the above directions. When the cheese is firm season with salt and mix well. Shape into smooth balls, about 1 inch in diameter. Leave overnight on a large plate in the refrigerator. Place in a large glass jar; cover with olive oil. Cover the jar. The balls will keep at room temperature for several days. Remove as needed. They may be eaten by themselves or mixed with a little oil, spices, or herbs, and used as a spread for bread.

FRESH MINT YOGURT DRESSING

Makes about 1¼ cups.

This is a good dressing to serve with cooked lamb, grilled chicken, or fresh fruits.

> *½ cup chopped fresh mint*
> *2 teaspoons sugar*
> *1 tablespoon fresh lemon juice*
> *Salt, freshly ground pepper*
> *1 cup plain yogurt*

In a medium bowl crush the mint leaves. Add the sugar and lemon juice. Season with salt and pepper. Fold in the yogurt. Refrigerate, covered, 2 hours, up to 6.

COTTAGE CHEESE-YOGURT DRESSING

Makes about 2¼ cups.

Serve with salad greens.

> *1 cup cottage cheese, drained*
> *1 tablespoon chopped onion*
> *1 tablespoon fresh lemon juice*
> *¼ cup chopped fresh herbs (dill, parsley, basil, oregano)*
> *1 cup plain yogurt*
> *Salt, freshly ground pepper*

In a medium bowl combine the cottage cheese, onion, lemon juice, and herbs. Mix well. Add the yogurt. Season with salt and pepper.

FISH

From the lakes and cool mountain streams of the Caucasus Mountains to the waters of the Black Sea, the Caspian Sea, and Lake Sevan come delectable fish that are prepared in imaginative ways. Fishing has always been important throughout the Caucasus and creative cooks utilized the daily catch to make nourishing dishes for themselves and to serve as special occasion fare. Nothing can compare with the fresh flavor of each fish whether served in the home or in an atmospheric seaside restaurant.

The roster of inviting specialties prepared with fish is impressive. Ancients passed on the art of skewering firm-fleshed fish, grilling tender fillets, baking fish in paper, frying seafood in oil, stuffing large fish with flavorful mixtures, baking whole ones on a bed of vegetables, and slowly cooking several kinds to make soups and stews.

Some of the fruits of the sea are not only native to the waters of the Caucasus but exist solely in certain locales. Trout taken from Armenian lakes and Georgian mountain brooks are highly prized for their delicate and sweet flesh. A tiny small brook trout called *tsotskhali*, or "I'm alive," is a treasured specialty in Georgia where it is kept alive until ready to be cooked. The most cherished fish, however, are various kinds of sturgeon, enjoyed fresh or smoked and prized for its luxurious roe known as caviar.

Despite pollution, the Caspian Sea, a great salt lake that is the largest inland body of water in the world, lying between Europe and Asia east of the Caucasus Mountains, yields valuable fish. From it is taken whitefish varieties; herring; grey mullet, noted for its firm white flesh; and almost of the annual Russian supply of sturgeon, which Caucasians prepare with an interesting variety of ingredients including coriander, tarragon, walnuts, and fresh and dried fruit.

Sea of the Ancients, or Black Sea, was once connected with the Mediterranean, then isolated, and later reconnected with the larger sea through the Bosporus. A deep kidney-shaped pool, the Greater Caucasus rise majestically along the sea's eastern shore in the north, and, further south, the mountains of the Lesser Caucasus appear at the sea's edges. Once called the "hospitable sea" because of its abundance of fish, its fisheries yield bonito, herring, mackerel, pike, perch, bream, and *hamsi*, the Black Sea anchovy.

Always superb, the Caucasian fish dishes are noted for their many flavorings ranging from herbs and spices to fruit juices and yogurt. Cooking and serving these creations will reward the diner with unusual and delicious fare.

MAKHACHKALA HERRING SALAD

6 servings.

The Russian cuisine makes extensive use of the herring and has a number of interesting dishes featuring the humble fish. This colorful combination salad includes vegetables, fruit, piquant flavorings, as well as herring.

The salad is named for Makhachkala, the capital of Dagestan, largest city in the North Caucasus, and an important commercial port of the Caspian Sea. It is noted for its rich folk art and fish specialties served in restaurants along the shore.

> *1½ cups cold diced cooked potatoes*
> *1 cup cold diced cooked beets*
> *1 cup cold diced cooked carrots*
> *1 large tart apple, peeled, cored, and diced*
> *1 medium yellow onion, finely chopped*
> *2 medium dill pickles, diced*
> *2 hard-cooked eggs, chopped*
> *1 jar (8 ounces) pickled herring, skinned, boned, and diced*
> *1 cup (about) sour cream*
> *3 tablespoons wine vinegar*
> *2 tablespoons sharp mustard*
> *1 to 2 teaspoons sugar*
> *Salt, freshly ground pepper*
> *Garnishes: Cooked beet slices, hard-cooked egg wedges*

In a large bowl combine the potatoes, beets, carrots, apple, onion, pickles, chopped eggs, and herring. In another bowl mix together the sour cream, vinegar, mustard, and sugar. Season with salt and pepper. Add to the vegetable-herring mixture, adding more sour cream if necessary to bind the ingredients. Mix well. Serve in a mound on a plate or in a bowl. Garnish with beet slices and egg wedges.

STURGEON BAKED IN SOUR CREAM

4 servings.

Of the many species of fish enjoyed in Russia, the greatest favorite is sturgeon, which is prepared in many creative dishes. The most characteristic way of cooking sturgeon, as well as other fish, is with piquant sauces sharpened with mustard, capers, pickles, horseradish, or sour cream. In America, this dish can be made with any firm white-fleshed fish as a substitute for fresh sturgeon.

> *2 pounds white-fleshed fish fillets*
>   *(haddock, mackerel, or cod)*
> *All-purpose flour*
> *Salt, freshly ground pepper*
> *2 hard-cooked eggs, sliced*
> *2 tablespoons unsalted butter*
> *1 tablespoon fresh lemon juice*
> *½ pound fresh mushrooms, sliced*
> *1 cup sour cream, at room temperature*
> *3 tablespoons chopped fresh dill or parsley*

Preheat oven to 350 degrees.

Cut fish into serving portions and wipe dry. Dust with flour. Sprinkle with salt and pepper. Arrange in a greased shallow baking dish. Top with the egg slices. Meanwhile, melt the butter in a small skillet over medium-high heat. Add the lemon juice and mushrooms. Sauté for 3 minutes. Spoon over the fish and eggs. Top with sour cream, Sprinkle with dill or parsley. Bake about 20 minutes, until the fish is tender.

FISH WITH APPLE-HORSERADISH SAUCE

4 servings.

This is another Russian fish dish that features a piquant flavored sauce.

> *2 pounds white-fleshed fish (halibut, cod, or haddock)*
> *1 cup wine vinegar*
> *1 leek, white part only, sliced*
> *2 medium yellow onions, sliced*
> *2 small bay leaves*
> *¼ teaspoon dried thyme*
> *2 sprigs parsley*
> *6 peppercorns*
> *Salt*
> *¼ cup freshly grated or prepared horseradish,*
>   *well drained*
> *1 cup puréed apples*
> *1 tablespoon sugar*
> *Lemon wedges*

Cut fish into serving portions. In a large saucepan combine the fish and vinegar over medium-high heat. Bring to a boil. Remove from the stove. Set aside. In a medium saucepan combine the leek, onions, bay leaves, thyme, parsley, peppercorns, and salt, with water to cover, over medium-high heat. Bring to a boil. Reduce the heat to medium-low. Cook, covered, for 5 minutes. Remove fish from the vinegar. Add to the vegetable mixture. Cook, covered, about 5 minutes, or until the fish is fork-tender. Remove fish to a warm platter; keep warm. Meanwhile, in a small dish combine the horseradish, apples and sugar. Thin with a little vinegar, if desired. Serve the sauce and lemon wedges with the fish.

KOBULETI BREAM STUFFED WITH KASHA

6 servings.

A small freshwater fish called bream, which in appearance resembles the carp, is eaten in the Black Sea regions where it is filled with *kasha*. A good place to enjoy fish specialties is Kobuleti, a popular seaside resort on the Black Sea, north of Batumi in the western region of Adzharia.

> *6 tablespoons unsalted butter*
> *2 medium yellow onions, chopped*
> *2 cups cooked* kasha
> *2 hard-cooked eggs, chopped*
> *2 tablespoons chopped fresh parsley*
> *2 tablespoons chopped fresh dill*
> *Salt, freshly ground pepper*
> *6 small white-fleshed fish (porgies, crappies, sunfish),*
> *each fish about 1 pound*
> *Fine dry bread crumbs*
> *1 cup sour cream, at room temperature*

Preheat oven to 400 degrees.

In a medium skillet melt 3 tablespoons butter over medium-high heat. Add onions; sauté 4 minutes. Add the cooked *kasha*, eggs, parsley, and dill. Season with salt and pepper. Mix well. Wash fish and wipe dry. Sprinkle cavities with salt. Fill with the stuffing. Arrange fish in a greased shallow baking dish. Meanwhile, in a small skillet melt remaining 3 tablespoons butter over medium-high heat. Sprinkle over the fish. Then sprinkle with bread crumbs. Bake until fish is tender, about 10 minutes. Spoon the sour cream over the fish. Cook another 5 minutes.

Note: If there is any stuffing left over, serve it with the fish.

ARMENIAN FISH PLAKI

4 servings.

A characteristic manner of preparing fish in Armenia is by baking it on a bed of vegetables, generally those in season, flavored with olive oil and lemon juice.

> ½ cup olive oil
> 2 medium yellow onions, sliced
> 1 or 2 garlic cloves, crushed
> 3 medium tomatoes, peeled and chopped
> 2 medium carrots, scraped and thinly sliced
> 2 stalks celery, sliced
> Salt, freshly ground pepper
> 2 pounds white-fleshed fish fillets (halibut, cod, mackerel, haddock)
> 2 large lemons, sliced
> 3 tablespoons chopped fresh dill or parsley

Preheat oven to 350 degrees.

In a medium skillet heat the oil over medium-high heat. Add the onions and garlic; sauté 4 minutes. Add the tomatoes, carrots, and celery; cook 5 minutes. Season with salt and pepper. Arrange fish fillets in a buttered shallow baking dish; cover with vegetable mixture. Arrange lemon slices over them. Sprinkle with dill or parsley. Bake about 20 minutes, or until fish is fork-tender. Serve hot or cold.

LAKE SEVAN TROUT

4 servings.

Lake Sevan, one of the largest and highest mountain lakes in the world, fed by some thirty rivers and streams, is 6,000 feet up the slopes of the Caucasus Mountains in northeastern Armenia. Known for its unusual bright blue-green waters, its name comes from an ancient word meaning "country of lakes." It has only one outlet, the Razdan River. An ideal summer and winter vacation area, the region of Sevan has many attractions for outdoor enthusiasts. Along the lake's rocky beaches are also remains of age-old settlements. From the lake comes a delicate pink salmon trout with silvery scales and reddish flesh that Armenians call *ishkhan*, meaning "prince." Known for its fine flavor and succulence, the fish is cooked and prepared in several ways such as this one.

4 fresh trout, cleaned
Salt
½ cup ground walnuts
1 small yellow onion, finely chopped
¼ cup fresh lemon juice or vinegar
1 teaspoon sugar
Pinch of cayenne pepper
Freshly ground pepper
3 tablespoons chopped fresh coriander or parsley

Wash and dry trout thoroughly. Sprinkle inside and out with salt. In a large skillet cover the trout with water over medium-low heat. Simmer, covered, about 15 minutes, until fish are tender. Carefully remove to a platter. Meanwhile, in a small saucepan combine the walnuts, onion, lemon juice or vinegar, sugar, and cayenne over medium-low heat. Season with salt and pepper. Cook, uncovered, 5 minutes. Stir in the coriander or parsley. Pour over the fish. Serve hot or cold.

Cuisines of the Caucasus Mountains

These trout are best cooked on an outdoor grill, preferably in a mountain setting. Otherwise, cook under an oven grill.

> *4 trout, cleaned*
> *Salt, freshly ground pepper*
> *8 thin slices lemon*
> *4 tablespoons minced scallions, with some green tops*
> *½ cup chopped fresh coriander*
> *Olive oil*
> *Garnishes: Scallion slivers, tomato and cucumber slices*

Wash and dry trout thoroughly. Sprinkle inside and out with salt and pepper. In the cavities place the lemon slices, scallions, and coriander. Brush the skin of each trout with oil. Cook on a lightly oiled grill over a prepared charcoal fire until the flesh is fork tender, about 5 minutes on each side. Or broil under a preheated oven broiler. Serve with garnishes.

BLACK SEA OLIVE-STUFFED CARP

4 to 6 servings.

Carp, an esteemed fish that comes from the Black Sea and nearby rivers, is made into flavorful soups and stews or baked with other ingredients such as vegetables and seasonings. Given below are two characteristic dishes made with the fish.

1 (3 to 4 pound) fish (carp, hake, cod)
Salt, freshly ground pepper
1 cup chopped green olives
1 garlic clove, crushed
2 tablespoons fresh lemon juice
5 tablespoons olive oil
¼ cup chopped fresh parsley
2 large yellow onions, sliced
1 lemon, sliced
About ½ cup fine bread crumbs

Preheat oven to 400 degrees.

Wash fish and wipe dry. Sprinkle inside and out with salt and pepper. In a small dish combine the olives, garlic, lemon juice, 1 tablespoon olive oil, and parsley; spoon into fish cavity. In a buttered shallow baking dish arrange the onions and lemon slices evenly. Place the fish over them. Sprinkle with salt, pepper, and bread crumbs. Add remaining 4 tablespoons olive oil and ¼ cup hot water. Bake, allowing 10 minutes per pound, until fish is fork tender.

STEPANAKERT BAKED FISH

4 to 6 servings.

In the Caucasus cooks have an interesting way of flavoring fish and vegetable dishes with fresh and dried fruits as well as herbs. This specialty is named for Stepanakert, the capital and largest city of Nagorno-Karabakh that means "Mountainous Black Garden." A disputed region between Armenia and Azerbaijan in the center of the Lesser Caucasus that has endured a long and turbulent history, it has an abundance of home-grown vegetables and fruits, including pomegranates, olives, grapes, and raisins. Near Stepanakert is the town of Shusi known for its curative springs and sanitarium as well as two Christian churches.

> *2 pounds white-fleshed fish fillets*
>   *(carp, cod, pike, perch, flounder)*
> *½ cup olive oil*
> *2 medium yellow onions, sliced*
> *2 garlic cloves, crushed*
> *2 leeks, white parts only, sliced*
> *½ cup diced scraped carrots*
> *½ cup sliced green beans*
> *3 medium tomatoes, peeled and chopped*
> *3 tablespoons chopped fresh dill*
> *⅓ cup chopped fresh parsley*
> *¼ cup raisins*
> *½ cup chopped apricots*
> *2 tablespoons fresh lemon juice*
> *Salt, freshly ground pepper*

Preheat oven to 350 degrees.

Wash and dry fish fillets. Place in a greased baking dish. In a medium skillet heat the oil over medium-high heat. Add the onions, garlic, and leeks. Sauté 5 minutes. Add carrots, green beans, and tomatoes. Sauté 5 minutes. Stir in dill, parsley, raisins, apricots, and lemon juice. Season with salt and pepper. Mix well. Spoon the vegetable-fruit mixture over the fish fillets, spreading evenly. Bake, covered, about 25 minutes, until fish is tender.

FISH COOKED IN PAPER

An excellent Caucasus method of cooking fish is in parchment paper. The finished dish is truly delightful as the juices and flavorings of the fish and accompaniments are retained within the paper. Aluminum foil is an excellent substitute for the paper. It can be prepared beforehand and cooked either on an outdoor grill or in the kitchen stove.

For each serving, buy any kind of dressed small white fish weighing about 1 pound each. Cut heart-shapes or squares of foil large enough to enfold each fish. Place the fish on the foil; brush with olive oil on both sides. Sprinkle or top with one or more of the following: bits of unsalted butter, lemon juice, white wine, minced garlic, onion slices, bay leaves, herbs, salt, and freshly ground pepper.

Fold over the other half of the foil. Pinch edges to close securely. Arrange in a baking dish or on a baking sheet. Bake in preheated hot oven (400 degrees) about 20 minutes, until fish flesh is fork tender. Or cook over hot coals on an outdoor grill, turning once, about 8 minutes. Remove from heat. Serve on a plate or platter for each person to open at the table.

MOUNT ARAGATS SKEWERED FISH KEBABS

6 servings.

In the Caucasus a favorite way of cooking fish is on skewers over open fires in the mountains or countryside, along beaches, or in the home. This typical preparation can also be broiled indoors.

Snow-covered Mt. Aragats in the northwest region of Armenia, filled with high mountains and steep valleys, has four challenging summits that attract climbers during the summer months. The nearest place to stay is the village of Aghtsk, northwest of Yerevan.

> *2 pounds firm fleshed fish (halibut, salmon, swordfish)*
> *½ cup olive oil*
> *Juice of 1 large lemon*
> *¾ teaspoon crumbled dried oregano*
> *Salt, freshly ground pepper*
> *1 large onion, cut into large pieces*
> *4 large bay leaves, broken up*

Remove and discard any skin from the fish. Cut into 1-inch cubes. In a large bowl combine the fish cubes, olive oil, lemon juice, and oregano. Season with salt and pepper. Leave at room temperature to marinate about 2 hours, stirring occasionally. Thread fish cubes on skewers, alternating with onion and bay leaf pieces. Brush well with marinade and broil over hot coals or under heated broiler about 10 minutes, until fish is tender, turning once or twice.

RICE-NUT STUFFED FISH

4 to 6 servings.

In the Caucasus a common method of preparing freshwater fish is to stuff it with a flavorful rice mixture and then cook by baking.

3 tablespoons olive oil
1 medium yellow onion, chopped
⅓ cup chopped pine nuts
½ cup long-grain rice
1 cup chicken broth
¼ cup dried currants
¼ teaspoon ground cinnamon
3 tablespoons chopped fresh coriander or parsley
Salt, freshly ground pepper
2 whole white-fleshed fish (3½ to 4 pounds each)
Garnishes: Chopped fresh parsley, lemon wedges

Preheat oven to 350 degrees.

In a medium saucepan heat the olive oil over medium-high heat. Add the onion; sauté 4 minutes. Add pine nuts and rice. Sauté, stirring, until grains are translucent, about 4 minutes. Add broth, currants, cinnamon, and parsley. Season with salt and pepper. Reduce the heat to medium-low. Cook, covered, about 20 minutes, or until liquid has been absorbed and grains are separate.

Meanwhile, wash the fish and wipe dry. Sprinkle inside and out with salt and pepper. Stuff the fish with the rice filling; close openings. Place in a greased baking dish. Bake, allowing about 10 minutes per pound, until tender. Serve garnished with parsley and lemon wedges, if desired.

FRIED FISH
WITH CAPER SAUCE

6 servings.

In the Caucasus frying fish is a common method of cooking. Often the fish is served with a flavorful sauce such as this one made with capers and lemon juice.

1 pound fish fillets (cod, halibut, haddock)
All-purpose flour
Salt, freshly ground pepper
Olive or vegetable oil for frying
¼ cup unsalted butter
2 tablespoons drained capers
2 tablespoons fresh lemon juice
Garnishes: Chopped fresh dill, coriander, or parsley;
*   lemon and cucumber slices*

In a large shallow dish sprinkle the fish fillets with flour, seasoned with salt and pepper. In a large skillet heat enough oil to cover the bottom of it over medium-high heat. Add fillets; pan fry 3 to 5 minutes on each side, turning carefully. Remove to a platter. Meanwhile, in a small saucepan melt the butter over medium-low heat. Add the capers and lemon juice. Heat 1 minute. Pour over the cooked fish. Serve at once garnished with dill, coriander, or parsley, and lemon and cucumber slices.

BASS WITH TOMATOES

4 to 6 servings.

Cooks in the Caucasus have created many nourishing and tasty dishes based on fish and vegetables, ranging from onions and potatoes to eggplants and tomatoes. This is always a winner.

> *8 bass fillets, washed and dried*
> *3 large tomatoes, peeled and chopped*
> *2 tablespoons lemon juice*
> *3 tablespoons olive oil*
> *3 bay leaves*
> *2 tablespoons chopped fresh coriander or parsley*
> *Salt, freshly ground pepper*

Heat oven to 350 degrees.

Arrange bass fillets in a greased shallow baking dish. Top with the tomatoes, lemon juice, olive oil, bay leaves, and coriander or parsley. Season with salt and pepper. Bake until fish is fork tender, about 20 minutes.

BAKED MACKEREL WITH YOGURT SAUCE

6 servings.

Yogurt imparts flavor and richness to fish dishes such as this one, a marvelous main course for a summer luncheon or dinner.

1 whole mackerel, 3½ to 4 pounds
Salt
⅓ cup olive oil
1 cup finely chopped yellow onions
¼ cup pine nuts
½ cup long-grain rice
1 cup chicken broth or water
⅛ teaspoon ground cinnamon
Freshly ground pepper
¼ cup currants
½ cup chopped fresh parsley
1 cup plain yogurt, at room temperature
1 lemon, thinly sliced

Preheat oven to 350 degrees.

Wash and dry the mackerel. Sprinkle inside and out with salt. Set aside. In a medium saucepan heat 2 tablespoons oil over medium-high heat. Add the onions; sauté 4 minutes. Add the pine nuts and rice. Sauté until rice is translucent. Add the chicken broth or water, and cinnamon. Season with salt and pepper. Bring to a boil. Reduce the heat to medium-low. Cook, uncovered, until rice grains are tender and liquid has been absorbed, about 20 minutes. Add the currants and ⅓ cup parsley. Mix well. Remove from the heat. Stuff the mackerel with the fish mixture. Close the opening with skewers. Place the fish in a greased shallow baking dish. Cover with the remaining oil, parsley, yogurt, and lemon slices. Bake about 1 hour, until fish flakes easily when tested with a fork. While baking, baste occasionally with the drippings.

FISH STEW

6 to 8 servings.

This stew is made with a typical inexpensive and hearty mixture of fish, vegetables, and seasonings that could be served for an outdoor meal.

⅓ cup olive oil
2 medium yellow onions, sliced
2 garlic cloves, crushed
1 can (29 ounces) tomatoes
1 bay leaf
½ teaspoon dried basil
3 parsley sprigs
1 cup dry white wine
3 pounds mixed fish, cut into serving pieces
3 anchovy fillets, drained and cut-up
Freshly ground pepper
3 tablespoons unsalted butter
1 tablespoon fresh lemon juice
1 pound whole fresh mushrooms
¼ cup chopped fresh parsley
Slices of crusty white bread

In a large saucepan heat the oil over medium-high heat. Add the onions and garlic; sauté 4 minutes. Add the tomatoes, bay leaf, basil, and parsley. Cook 5 minutes. Add the wine, fish, and anchovies. Season with pepper. Add enough water to cover the ingredients. Cook, covered, until fish is tender, about 12 minutes.

Meanwhile, in a medium skillet melt the butter over medium-high heat. Add the lemon juice and mushrooms. Sauté 5 minutes. Add, with the parsley, to the stew. Remove from the heat. Discard the bay leaf and parsley sprigs. To serve, spoon the fish, mushrooms, and broth over crusty bread slices in soup bowls.

ARMENIAN STUFFED MUSSELS

4 to 6 servings.

Midia Dolma, or stuffed mussels, a favorite Armenian dish that is said to have originated in Turkey, is prepared by stuffing the mollusks with an aromatic rice mixture.

> *20 to 24 large mussels*
> *½ cup olive oil*
> *1 large onion, finely chopped*
> *¾ cup long-grain rice*
> *¼ cup pine nuts*
> *1 large tomato, peeled and chopped*
> *2 tablespoons currants*
> *½ teaspoon ground cinnamon*
> *Salt, freshly ground pepper*
> *1 teaspoon sugar*
> *¼ cup chopped fresh parsley*
> *Lemon wedges*

Scrub mussels well and hold under running water to remove any sand. Open the shells without separating the two sides. Do not remove the mussels. Cut off the black part of the mussels and beards. Soak in cold water while making the stuffing.

In a large skillet heat the oil over medium-high heat. Add the onion; sauté 4 minutes. Add the rice and pine nuts. Sauté, stirring, for several minutes, until rice becomes translucent and is well coated with oil. Add the tomato, currants, cinnamon, and 1½ cups water. Season with salt and pepper. Reduce the heat to medium-low. Cook, covered, about 20 minutes, until rice grains are tender and liquid is absorbed. Stir in the sugar and parsley. Cool.

Place a large spoonful of the stuffing into each mussel. Close tightly. Tie with thread. Arrange in layers in a large kettle. Cover with water. Place a heavy plate over them to prevent moving while cooking. Over medium-low heat cook, tightly covered, for 20 minutes. Remove the mussels from the liquid. Take off the threads. Cool. Serve with lemon wedges.

MEAT, POULTRY, AND GAME

"Maksim Maksimych was well versed in the culinary arts and turned out a wonderful roast pheasant with an excellent pickled cucumber sauce. I must admit that without him I would have had to content myself with a cold snack. A bottle of Kakhetian wine helped us to overlook the modesty of the meal which consisted of only one course."

A Hero of Our Time

Diners in the Caucasus truly appreciate meat, poultry, and game, which appears frequently on their tables. They do not pick and choose among the selections but relish all of whatever is available, both domesticated and wild. Some are purchased in the markets but, very often, chickens might be raised at home and wild birds or small game acquired by hunters. While these foods are frequently roasted on spits over open fires, they may be also fried, grilled, baked, or used to make rich and aromatic pot-dishes or stews.

Particularly relished in the Caucasus are tiny birds that, since ancient times have been in plentiful supply. There is something special about serving tiny woodcock, delectable duck, or perhaps a partridge, quail, or a pheasant in the Caucasian locales, for it is usually a festive dish. Very often this fare is reserved for company and presented with tremendous pride. In the hinterlands a visitor might be welcomed with a dish prepared with a home-raised bird. Holiday tables are often graced with a fine catch from the field or forest.

Lamb, or mutton, has always been the staple Caucasian meat, and extraordinarily good things are done with it. Whole lamb or sheep roasted on a slow-turning spit is still a treasured treat for special celebrations. Because the flesh was tough it was generally cut into small pieces and sometimes treated with seasoned marinades. When strung on sticks and cooked over an open fire, shish kebab was introduced to the world. Skewered meats are popular fare in these lands and there is a wealth of choice kebab dishes.

All parts of the lamb, including the feet and head, have been traditionally relished. One of the choicest of dishes is roasted baby lamb, sometimes called spring lamb. This is a prize well worth ordering in restaurants. Perhaps it is best, however, when cooked on a spit in the backyard or, if on a picnic, in an open field—customary for many holiday meals. The peoples of the Caucasus love cooking and dining out-of-doors, particularly in rustic settings.

The earliest meat and game specialties were well-seasoned stews, fragrant with herbs and spices, and cooked slowly. The lengthy cooking process tenderized the tough flesh and the spices acted as important preservatives.

Ground meat dishes are other favorites in the Caucasus where cooks developed a number of meatball creations as well as many inexpensive and nourishing baked dishes or casseroles. Thousands of years ago cooks discovered that meat, when chopped, scraped, or minced, not only cooked more easily and used less fuel but was more tender and digestible. Combined with grains, spices, or other seasonings, the meat mixtures were found to be more flavorful, went further, and could be fried, cooked on skewers, baked, or simmered in sauces. They are also popular stuffing for vegetables and poultry.

While the diner in the Caucasus will not usually find a great many beef dishes, especially such cuts as roasts and steaks, there are some notable veal dishes. And, because the Caucasus is a mountainous region, there always has been an abundance of game such as wild boar, venison, and mountain sheep and goat to prepare in a number of ways.

This is a representative selection of the unusual dishes made with meat, poultry and small game that are known for their goodness and appealing variety.

BEEF KOTLETY

6 servings.

While lamb and mutton are the favorite Caucasian meats, Circassian beef was believed by Russians to be superior. We read in Ivan Turgenev's novel, *Fathers and Sons*, that for the preparation of special meals a servant is dispatched at dawn for Circassian beef.

In Russia, a variety of everyday dishes is made with ground meat mixtures. Notable among them are *bitky*, tiny meatballs with sauces, served as appetizers or entrées, and the so-called Russian hamburgers, *kotlety*, which are characteristic restaurant and family fare. *Kotlety* differ from American hamburgers in that they are golden and crisp on the outside and moist and tender on the inside. Typically they are served plain or with sour cream, mushroom or tomato sauce, and accompanied by *kasha*, macaroni, or potatoes.

3 slices thick, day-old crusty white bread
Milk
1 pound lean ground beef
2 eggs
1 medium yellow onion, minced
1 tablespoon chopped fresh dill or 1 teaspoon dried dill
Salt, freshly ground pepper
About ⅓ cup fine dry bread crumbs
Unsalted butter or vegetable oil for frying
3 tablespoons sour cream, at room temperature

In a shallow dish soak the bread in milk to cover for 20 minutes, or until bread is softened. Squeeze bread dry. In a large bowl combine the bread bits with the beef. Mix thoroughly. Add the eggs, one at a time, mixing after each addition. Add the onion and dill. Season with salt and pepper. Mix again. Shape into flattened oval patties; roll in bread crumbs. In a large skillet, heat about ¼ inch butter or oil over medium-high heat. Add the patties, a few at a time, and fry until golden and crisp on the outside, turning once. Remove to a warm plate and keep warm. When all are fried, scrape drippings in the pan; stir in sour cream. Leave over low heat 3 minutes. Spoon over the patties.

SHASHLYK

6 to 8 servings.

This classic Caucasian dish, grilled meat called *shashlyk*, has many variations. Generally made with lamb, it also can be prepared with beef, pork, innards, or a combination of these. The name is said to have come from *shashka*, meaning "sword," as once mountain tribesmen roasted meat on their swords over open fires. In Lesley Blanch's recipe for *shashlyk* she writes: "The Georgian tribesmen in the Caucasus sometimes grill meat on their sword; then throw a glass of brandy over it, and set fire to it, so that it is brought to the table flaming. And sometimes they dance, brandishing the lighted swords; their tall black sheepskin caps cocked over on the side of their heads, very exciting."

Marinades and seasonings for *shashlyk* differ according to regions and personal taste. Georgians prefer to marinate the meat in pomegranate juice, red wine, and/or lemon juice, and, when cooked, to sprinkle it with herbs. Others prefer an herb-flavored vinegar and olive oil marinade. Grated onions and spices are other common ingredients. Usually, the dish is prepared simply, using the marinade only with the specific purpose of enhancing the flavor of the meat and as a tenderizer for tough meats. *Shashlyk* is generally cooked outdoors over wood embers or hot coals. It is a festive company dish.

In Georgia a favorite barbecue specialty called *basturma* is made with cubes of beef that are marinated in a red wine and/or pomegranate juice mixture. Grilled on long skewers over an outdoor fire, preferably in a mountain setting, the meat is served on a large platter, attractively garnished with an assortment of colorful vegetables.

> *3 pounds boneless leg of lamb, trimmed of fat and cut*
>   *into 1½-inch cubes*
> *1 large yellow onion, minced*
> *3 tablespoons fresh lemon juice or wine vinegar*
> *Salt, freshly ground pepper*
> *2 medium onions, cut into chunks*
> *Garnishes: Fresh herbs, scallion strips, sliced tomatoes,*
>   *and lemon wedges*

In a large bowl combine the lamb cubes, minced onion, and lemon juice or wine vinegar. Season with salt and pepper; stir. Leave to marinate 2 hours, up to 4. When ready to cook, thread lamb cubes, interlarded with chunks of onion, on skewers. Broil over hot coals or under a heated broiler for 12 minutes or longer, turning once during the cooking, until desired degree of doneness. Serve on skewers on a platter with the garnishes.

The Balkars are a Turkic-speaking mountain people of the North Caucasus who share a political union with the Kabardins in the Republic of Kabardino-Balkaria. Celebrated for their longevity, they live in a harsh land making their livings primarily by raising sheep. The tradition of warm hospitality stipulates that guests be given a bountiful meal featuring a freshly slaughtered lamb, including the prized head, and many toasts of vodka.

This recipe is for a favorite lamb-rice specialty that has been prepared for centuries in Caucasian homes.

½ cup olive oil
2 medium yellow onions, chopped
2 pounds leg or shoulder of lamb, cut into 1-inch cubes
¼ cup tomato paste
1 cup tomato juice
½ teaspoon dried thyme or oregano
Salt, freshly ground pepper
1½ cups long-grain rice
About 2 cups chicken broth
¼ cup chopped fresh parsley

In a large saucepan or pot heat the oil over medium-high heat. Add the onions. Sauté 4 minutes. Push aside. Add lamb cubes; several at a time, to brown on all sides. Mix in the tomato paste, tomato juice, and thyme or oregano. Season with salt and pepper. Reduce the heat to medium-low. Cook, covered, for 1 hour, adding a little water during the cooking, if needed. Mix in the rice and chicken broth. Continue to cook about 30 minutes, or until the rice is tender and most of the liquid has been absorbed, adding a little more broth during the cooking, if necessary. Do not stir during the cooking. Mix in the parsley just before serving.

ARMENIAN LAMB STEW WITH SPINACH

4 servings.

Two favorite Armenian foods, lamb and spinach, are combined in this flavorful stew.

3 tablespoons olive or vegetable oil
2 pounds lamb shoulder, cut up and trimmed of excess fat
1 large yellow onion, sliced
2 pounds fresh spinach, stemmed and cut into large
  pieces
2 cups tomato juice
½ teaspoon dried oregano
Salt, freshly ground pepper
2 tablespoons chopped fresh coriander or parsley

In a large saucepan heat the oil over moderate-high heat. Add the lamb pieces and brown on all sides. Add onion; sauté 4 minutes. Add spinach, tomato juice, and oregano. Season with salt and pepper. Bring to a boil. Reduce heat to medium-low. Cook slowly, covered, about 45 minutes, until lamb is tender. Stir in coriander or parsley.

GHIVETCH

6 to 8 servings.

A baked meat and vegetable dish called *ghivetch*, or variations of the name, is common to the Caucasus regions where there are slight differences in the ingredients and preparation. It is best when prepared in the summer with as many as a dozen or more fresh vegetables. Given below is one recipe suggestion but other vegetables may be used as substitutes, if desired.

> *2 pounds boneless lamb shoulder,*
>   *cut into 1½-inch cubes*
> *Vegetable oil for frying*
> *2 medium yellow onions, chopped*
> *1 teaspoon paprika*
> *Salt, freshly ground pepper*
> *4 medium potatoes, peeled and*
>   *cut into 1½-inch cubes*
> *1 medium eggplant, unpeeled and*
>   *cut into 1½-inch cubes*
> *3 large green or red bell peppers, cut into strips*
> *1½ cups fresh green beans, cut up*
> *1 cup okra, cut-up*
> *4 large tomatoes, peeled and sliced*
> *3 eggs, beaten*
> *¼ cup chopped fresh parsley*

Wipe meat dry. Heat 3 tablespoons oil in a large saucepan over medium-high heat. Add lamb cubes; brown on all sides. Push aside; add onions and more oil, if needed. Sauté 4 minutes. Mix in paprika. Season with salt and pepper. Add water to cover. Reduce heat to medium-low. Cook, covered, for 1 hour.

Heat oven to 350 degrees. Spoon the meat and other ingredients from the saucepan or kettle into a large round casserole. Top with the potatoes, eggplant, bell peppers, green beans, and okra. Season with salt and pepper. Add water to just cover ingredients. Put in the oven. Cook, covered, for 1 hour, until ingredients are tender. Put tomato slices over the vegetables 10 minutes before the cooking is finished. In a small dish combine the eggs and parsley. Stir with a fork. Spoon over the ingredients. Return to the oven for several minutes, long enough for the egg mixture to set. Cool a little before serving.

AZERBAIJAN SPINACH-VEAL STEW

6 servings.

In Azerbaijan cooks have long filled stew pots with their highly seasoned favorite foods such as those found in this recipe.

2 pounds veal shoulder, cut into 1½-inch cubes
About 2 tablespoons olive or vegetable oil
1 large yellow onion, sliced
½ cup sliced scallions, with some green tops
1 garlic clove, crushed
⅓ cup tomato paste
½ teaspoon ground allspice
⅛ teaspoon cayenne pepper
2 pounds fresh spinach, cut up
Salt, freshly ground pepper
1 cup plain yogurt, at room temperature
1 tablespoon chopped fresh coriander or dill

Trim any excess fat from the meat; wipe dry. In a large saucepan or pot heat the oil over medium-high heat. Add the meat cubes; brown on all sides. Push aside and add the onions, scallions, garlic, and more oil, if needed. Sauté about 5 minutes. Stir in the tomato paste, allspice, cayenne, and spinach. Season with salt and pepper. Mix well. Add water to cover. Bring to a boil. Reduce the heat to medium-low. Cook, covered, about 1¼ hours, until meat is cooked, adding a little more water during the cooking, if needed. When cooked, stir in the yogurt and coriander or dill.

Cuisines of the Caucasus Mountains

LAMB-STUFFED VEGETABLES

About 8 servings.

Favorite main dishes in the Caucasus are vegetables stuffed with rice and meat (generally lamb but sometimes beef or pork). They are flavored according to regional tastes and may be eaten warm or cold, with or without a sauce. This is a general recipe that can be used for stuffing green bell peppers, tomatoes, eggplants, or zucchini. The necessary amount of stuffing will vary according to the size of the vegetables. Any leftover stuffing can be shaped into small meatballs and cooked with the vegetables.

> *1 medium yellow onion, minced*
> *1 pound ground lamb*
> *½ cup long-grain rice*
> *1 egg*
> *3 tablespoons tomato paste*
> *2 tablespoons finely chopped dill, mint, or parsley*
> *Salt, freshly ground pepper*
> *About 8 prepared green bell peppers,*
> *   tomatoes, eggplants, or zucchini*
> *1 cup chicken or vegetable broth*
> *¼ cup olive oil*

In a large bowl combine the onion, ground lamb, rice, egg, tomato paste, and dill, mint, or parsley. Season with salt and pepper. Mix to thoroughly combine the ingredients.

To prepare vegetables, scoop out the centers, rinse and drain. Spoon lamb mixture into prepared vegetables, stuffing lightly. Place in a kettle. Add broth, oil, and enough hot water to half cover the vegetables. Cook covered, over medium-low heat, about 40 minutes, until ingredients are thoroughly cooked. Serve hot or cold.

RICE-LAMB MUSAKA

4 servings.

This Turkish-inspired meat and vegetable casserole, also called *moussaka*, is prepared variously, with or without a sauce topping, in the Caucasus. This is a typical recipe.

> 2 tablespoons unsalted butter or vegetable oil
> 1 large yellow onion, minced
> 2 garlic cloves, crushed
> 1 pound lean ground lamb
> ½ cup minced green bell pepper
> 2 large tomatoes, peeled and chopped
> 1 teaspoon paprika
> Salt, freshly ground pepper
> ½ cup long-grain rice
> 1½ cups tomato juice
> 2 eggs, beaten
> 1 cup milk

Preheat oven to 350 degrees.

In a large saucepan melt the butter or heat the oil over medium-high heat. Add the onion and garlic. Sauté 4 minutes. Add the lamb. Cook, mixing with a fork, until any redness disappears. Stir in the green pepper, tomatoes, and paprika. Season with salt and pepper. Cook 1 minute. Add the rice and tomato juice. Mix well. Spoon into a greased shallow baking dish. In a medium bowl combine the eggs and milk. Pour over the lamb mixture. Bake 50 to 60 minutes, until topping is set.

AZERBAIJAN HERBED LAMB PATTIES

4 servings.

These patties are flavored with herbs and lemon juice. They are good for an informal outdoor meal.

> *1 pound lean ground lamb*
> *1 small yellow onion, minced*
> *1 to 2 garlic cloves, crushed*
> *1 tablespoon fresh lemon juice*
> *½ teaspoon cayenne pepper*
> *2 tablespoons chopped fresh herbs (coriander, dill,*
> *   parsley, and/or thyme)*
> *Salt, freshly ground pepper*
> *2 to 3 tablespoons olive or vegetable oil*
> *Garnishes: Scallion strips, cucumber and tomato slices*

In a large bowl combine the lamb, onion, garlic, lemon juice, cayenne, and herbs. Season with salt and pepper. Form into flat patties about 3 inches in diameter. In a large skillet heat the oil over medium-high heat. Add the patties a few at a time to brown on both sides, turning once, about 8 minutes. Serve with garnishes.

8 servings.

Armenians are partial to a dish called *küfte*, a mixture of ground meat, usually lamb, bulgur, and seasonings, which may be served uncooked or baked, fried, boiled, sauced, or stuffed. Here's a basic recipe for one preparation.

> *1 pound lean ground lamb or beef, ground twice*
> *½ cup finely chopped scallions, with some green tops*
> *½ cup minced green bell pepper*
> *¼ teaspoon cayenne pepper*
> *⅓ cup chopped fresh coriander or parsley*
> *Salt, freshly ground pepper*
> *1 cup fine bulgur*
> *Garnishes: Chopped scallions, fresh coriander or parsley,*
> *   and/or tomatoes*

In a large bowl combine the lamb or beef, scallions, bell pepper, cayenne, and coriander or parsley. Season with salt and pepper. Mix thoroughly. Refrigerate, covered, 1 to 2 hours.

Preheat oven to 350 degrees. Add 2 tablespoons cold water and bulgur to the meat mixture. Mix together by kneading with the hands to thoroughly combine the ingredients. Form the mixture into small patties, about 2½ inches in diameter and ½ inch thick. Cover and chill if made ahead. Place on a greased baking sheet. Brush with oil or melted butter, if desired. Bake 15 to 20 minutes, until cooked. Serve hot or cold with garnishes and flat bread.

MINT KÖFTAS

6 servings.

Round or oval meatballs or patties called *köftas* are favorite Caucasian dishes that are good for informal meals. Here's the recipe for one variation that is flavored with onions, lemon juice, and mint.

3 slices day-old white or whole wheat bread
1½ pounds ground lamb or beef
1 large yellow onion, minced
2 eggs, beaten
2 tablespoons fresh lemon juice
2 tablespoons chopped fresh mint or 2 teaspoons dried
  mint
Salt, freshly ground pepper
1 large white or yellow onion, cut into pieces or slices

In a shallow dish soak the bread slices in water to cover. Squeeze dry. Cut into tiny bits. In a large bowl combine the bread bits, lamb or beef, minced onion, eggs, lemon juice, and mint. Season with salt and pepper. Mix thoroughly. Form into meatballs, about 1½ inches in diameter. Thread on skewers interlarded with onion pieces. Grill over hot charcoal or under a broiler, turning to cook evenly, until cooked, about 10 minutes.

KEBABS

6 servings.

In the Caucasus there is a wide variety of meat dishes called kebabs or similar names. While the best known is shish kebab, meaning small chunks of meat grilled on a skewer, not all kebabs are skewered. Some kebab dishes are made of cubes of lamb and other ingredients that are stewed, baked, or broiled. Others are made with ground meat.

Particularly good and popular are the kebabs cooked outdoors. These are favorite street snacks sold on small skewers and eaten directly from them. Some are removed from the skewers and wrapped in unleavened bread. A great kebab for parties is the one called commonly *doner kebab* (ever turning). Large cuts of well-seasoned meat on a vertical spit slowly revolve in front of a charcoal fire and the exterior is sliced as it browns.

Given below is a basic kebab recipe that can be changed as desired. For seasonings Azerbaijanis favor allspice, cinnamon, cloves, or nutmeg. Armenians are partial to thyme or coriander. Georgians prefer coriander or mint. Garlic and onions can also be used. Some cooks like to interlard the meat cubes with slices or pieces of vegetables such as eggplant, onions, or green peppers. Because of their acidity tomatoes are not included with the meat but cooked separately.

Here is a basic recipe for shish kebab.

> *2 pounds loin or leg of lamb or boneless beef,*
>   *cut into 1½-inch cubes*
> *3 tablespoons olive oil*
> *3 tablespoons fresh lemon juice*
> *Salt, freshly ground pepper*
> *Fresh or dried herbs or spices*
> *Vegetable cubes, pieces or slices*

In a large bowl combine the lamb cubes with the olive oil and lemon juice. Season with salt and pepper. Add fresh or dried herbs or spices. Mix well. Leave at room temperature to marinate 1 to 2 hours. Remove meat cubes from marinade. Thread on skewers interlarded with vegetables. Grill over hot charcoal coals or under a broiler until desired degree of doneness, turning once, about 10 minutes. Serve on skewers.

Cuisines of the Caucasus Mountains

SHISH KEBAB WITH YOGURT SAUCE

6 servings.

An interesting way of serving shish kebab is to serve it over pieces of flat bread and covered with a yogurt sauce.

> *⅓ cup olive oil*
> *3 tablespoons freshly made onion juice*
> *1½ teaspoons dried thyme*
> *Salt, freshly ground pepper*
> *3 pounds lean lamb, cut into 1½ -inch cubes*
> *Vegetable slices (optional)*
> *6 large pieces pita*
> *1½ cups plain yogurt, at room temperature*
> *3 tablespoons butter, melted*
> *1 tablespoon cayenne pepper or paprika*

Preheat broiler.

In a large bowl combine the oil, onion juice, and thyme. Season with salt and pepper. Add the lamb cubes; mix well. Leave to marinate at room temperature for 1 to 2 hours. Thread lamb cubes on small skewers interlarded with vegetable slices, if desired. Place on a broiler rack. Broil, turning once or twice, about 10 minutes, depending on the desired degree of doneness. Meanwhile, arrange pita pieces on 6 plates. In a small saucepan, heat the yogurt over medium-low heat. Heat until just warm. When meat is cooked, with a fork remove the lamb cubes from the skewers onto the bread. Spoon yogurt over the meat. Combine the melted butter and cayenne or paprika. Sprinkle over the yogurt. Season with salt at the table.

ARMENIAN GROUND MEAT KEBABS

8 servings.

These ground meat kebabs, made with beef or lamb, seasoned with tomato sauce and spices, and formed into various shapes, are called *luleh* or *liulia*.

> *2 slices day-old bread, crumbled*
> *½ cup tomato sauce*
> *1 medium yellow onion, minced*
> *¼ teaspoon paprika*
> *½ teaspoon ground allspice*
> *¼ teaspoon ground cumin*
> *Salt, freshly ground pepper*
> *1½ pounds lean ground lamb or beef*
> *Garnishes: Chopped onions, fresh parsley, and tomatoes*

Preheat oven to 450 degrees.

In a large bowl combine the crumbled bread, tomato sauce, onion, paprika, allspice, and cumin. Season with salt and pepper. Mix well. Add the lamb or beef. Mix thoroughly. Shape into sausage-like cylinders, 3½ by 1½ inches. Place in a shallow pan or on a baking sheet. Cook, turning once, about 6 minutes on each side. Serve with garnishes.

MEATBALLS WITH EGG-LEMON SAUCE

6 servings.

These piquant meatballs include rice and herbs and are served with a smooth lemony sauce. Serve for a weekend supper.

1½ pounds ground lamb or beef
½ cup long-grain rice
½ cup minced onion
1 egg
2 tablespoons tomato sauce
¼ cup chopped fresh parsley
½ teaspoon dried oregano
Salt, freshly ground pepper
2 cups beef bouillon
2 tablespoons unsalted butter
3 egg yolks
¼ cup fresh lemon juice

In a large bowl combine the lamb or beef, rice, onion, egg, tomato sauce, parsley, and oregano. Season with salt and pepper. Mix well. Shape into 2-inch meatballs. In a large saucepan bring the bouillon to a boil over medium-high heat. Add meatballs and butter. Reduce the heat to medium-low. Cook, covered, until meatballs are tender, about 30 minutes. Test one to see if rice is tender. Meanwhile, in a small bowl beat the egg yolks. Stir in lemon juice. Add ½ cup hot liquid; mix well. Add to meatballs, stirring constantly while adding. Leave over low heat about 5 minutes, long enough to thicken a little. Serve at once. Do not reheat.

GEORGIAN SPITTED CHICKEN WITH PLUM SAUCE

4 servings.

In Transcaucasia, a favorite method of preparing poultry is to serve either spitted or broiled chicken with a sauce made with green gooseberries, pounded walnuts, sour cream, or fruits. One of the most typical sauces is *tkemali*, which is made with a base of wild or sour plums that grow in Georgia. While it is difficult to duplicate the recipe outside the region, a good substitute can be attempted. This is an excellent entrée for an outdoor meal.

> *2 broiler chickens, about 2½ pounds each*
> *Salt, freshly ground pepper*
> *Unsalted butter*
> *1½ cups puréed cooked plums*
> *1 garlic clove, crushed*
> *2 tablespoons chopped fresh coriander or parsley*
> *⅛ to ¼ teaspoon red pepper*
> *Garnishes: Slices of tomatoes and cucumbers*

Preheat oven broiler.

Wash chickens and wipe dry. Season with salt and pepper. Arrange, skin side down, on a grill or broiler rack. Brush well with butter. Put in preheated broiler and cook under medium heat about 50 minutes, or until tender, brushing occasionally with butter. Turn a few times during cooking. While chicken is cooking, in a medium saucepan combine the plums, garlic, coriander or parsley, and red pepper over medium-low heat. Season with salt and pepper. Cook just long enough to heat through. To serve, arrange cooked chicken on a platter. Garnish with tomatoes and cucumbers. Serve sauce separately to be poured over the chicken.

CIRCASSIAN CHICKEN

6 servings.

The Circassians, an indigenous mountain people of the western Caucasus that are also called Cherkess, have long been renowned for their bravery, love of independence, and beautiful women. Many of the lovely girls introduced their native dishes to the sultans' courts of fabled Constantinople, now Istanbul, from where they spread throughout the Near East. Legend has it that this chicken dish was named for a beautiful Circassian girl who lovingly ground nuts by hand in preparing the dish for her lover.

1 stewing chicken, 3½ to 4 pounds
1 small carrot, scraped and diced
2 medium yellow onions, chopped
¼ cup chopped fresh parsley
Salt, freshly ground pepper
2 cups shelled walnuts
3 slices day-old white bread
1 tablespoon paprika

In a large pot put the chicken, carrot, 1 chopped onion, parsley, and 5 cups water over medium-high heat. Season with salt and pepper. Bring to a boil. Reduce heat to medium-low. Cook, covered, about 2 hours, until chicken is tender. Remove chicken from kettle to a platter to cool. Strain broth and reserve. When chicken is cool enough to handle, cut meat from the bones, discarding bones and skin. Cut chicken meat into shreds.

Meanwhile, put the walnuts through a nut grinder or grind in a food processor, reserving the oil separately from the nuts. In a shallow dish, soak the bread in some of the strained chicken broth until soft. Squeeze dry and mix with the ground walnuts, 1 chopped onion, and pepper. Put mixture in a food processor or grinder to thoroughly blend the ingredients. Turn into a bowl. Gradually add about 1 cup of the strained chicken broth to make a paste or sort of mayonnaise-type sauce. Combine half of this paste or sauce with the chicken shreds. Mix well. Spread evenly on a platter. Cover with remaining paste or sauce. Garnish with the reserved walnut oil by sprinkling it, along with the paprika, over the sauce. Do not chill. Serve at room temperature.

RICE-NUT STUFFED CHICKEN

6 servings.

A good dish for a holiday meal.

> *1 roasting chicken, about 4 pounds*
> *Salt, freshly ground pepper*
> *1 cup chicken broth*
> *½ cup long-grain rice*
> *¼ cup currants or raisins*
> *⅓ cup chopped walnuts*
> *1 tablespoon sugar*
> *1 teaspoon ground cinnamon*

Preheat oven to 325 degrees.

Wash chicken and wipe dry. Season inside and out with salt and pepper. In a large saucepan bring the chicken broth to a boil over medium-high heat. Add the rice. Reduce the heat to medium-low. Cook about 15 minutes, until the rice is soft and the liquid has been absorbed. Add the currants or raisins, walnuts, sugar, and cinnamon. Season with salt and pepper. Remove from the stove. Stuff chicken with the rice mixture. Arrange in a roasting pan. Cook, uncovered, for 2½ to 3 hours, until tender. Remove from heat and cut up as desired.

CHICKEN CHAKHOKHBILI

4 to 6 servings.

This flavorful Georgian chicken and tomato specialty, fragrantly scented with several herbs and spices, is one of the country's best-known dishes and is served in restaurants as well as homes. It is best made in summer when fresh herbs are available. This is one of its many versions.

> *1 chicken, about 4 pounds,*
> *cut into serving pieces, washed and dried*
> *3 to 4 tablespoons unsalted butter*
> *Salt, freshly ground pepper*
> *2 medium yellow onions, minced*
> *1 to 2 garlic cloves, crushed*
> *6 medium tomatoes, peeled and chopped*
> *1 can (6 ounces) tomato paste*
> *⅓ cup dry white wine*
> *2 tablespoons fresh lemon juice*
> *¼ teaspoon cayenne pepper*
> *1 cup chicken broth*
> *2 tablespoons chopped fresh coriander*
> *2 tablespoons chopped fresh basil or thyme*
> *2 tablespoons chopped fresh parsley*

Trim any excess fat from chicken. Cut off wing tips and backbone pieces. In a large heavy skillet heat 3 tablespoons butter over medium-high heat. Add chicken pieces, seasoned inside and out with salt and pepper. Fry 10 minutes on each side. Remove to a deep, heavy pot or casserole.

Add onions and garlic to the skillet drippings, adding more butter, if desired. Sauté 4 minutes. Add the tomatoes, tomato paste, wine, lemon juice, and cayenne. Season with salt and pepper. Bring to a boil. Reduce heat to medium-low. Cook, covered, for 10 minutes. Add to chicken pieces in the pot or casserole over medium-high heat. Pour in the broth. Bring to a boil. Reduce heat to medium-low. Cook, covered, for 30 minutes, until chicken pieces are tender. Add 1 tablespoon each coriander, basil or thyme, and parsley. Cook another 5 minutes. Serve garnished with remaining herbs.

CHICKEN TABAKA

1 serving.

A classic Georgian dish called *tabaka* or *tapaka* is pressed, fried chicken that is made with a tiny chicken similar to the American rock Cornish hen. To prepare, the chicken has to be flattened and cooked with a weight over it. Traditionally it's served with spicy seasonings or sauces and eaten with the fingers. Serve one chicken per person.

> *Rock Cornish hen, 1 to 1½ pounds*
> *2 tablespoons unsalted butter*
> *Salt, freshly ground pepper*
> *2 garlic cloves, peeled and crushed*
> *Garnishes: Tomato wedges, fresh coriander*
> *and/or parsley springs*

Hold the hen firmly, the back downward, on a wooden board or surface. With a sharp knife, cut along the breast from neck to tip. From the center spread open until flat, breaking the rib cage. Remove and discard the breast bone, leaving the rest of the hen intact. Place on a flat surface and pound with a wooden mallet to flatten it. Rinse and dry. Meanwhile, melt the butter in a large heavy skillet over medium-high heat. Place the hen, inside down, in the skillet. Top with a weight (such as a skillet filled with cans of food) on top of the hen. Fry the hen for 15 minutes. Remove the weight. Turn the hen gently over and fry on the other side another 10 to 15 minutes. Pour off the melted butter and drippings. Fry an additional 5 minutes on each side until deep brown and crisp and hen is cooked through. Remove from skillet. Place, skin side up, on a plate. Season with salt and pepper. Sprinkle with crushed garlic. Serve hot or at room temperature with the garnishes or a bowl of a piquant tomato sauce.

APSHERON CHICKEN WITH OKRA

4 to 6 servings.

The Apsheron Peninsula, jutting forty miles out into the Caspian Sea south-east of Baku in Azerbaijan, at the easternmost section of the Lower Caucasus, is now a large industrial area but was once known for its vine-yards, orchards of almond and olive trees, and vegetable gardens. The name is said to derive from *ab* and *shoran*, water and salt, and there are many salt lakes on the peninsula. This is one of several dishes made with okra, a mucilaginous and aromatic vegetable commonly used in soups and stews.

> *2 frying chickens, about 2½ pounds each, cut up*
> *Salt, freshly ground pepper*
> *3 tablespoons unsalted butter*
> *2 large yellow onions, sliced*
> *⅛ teaspoon cayenne pepper*
> *2 cups sliced fresh okra*
> *1 cup chopped green bell peppers*
> *About 1 cup hot chicken broth*
> *3 tablespoons tomato paste*
> *3 tablespoons chopped fresh coriander or parsley*

Wash and wipe chicken pieces dry. Season with salt and pepper. In large skillet melt the butter over medium-high heat. Add the chicken pieces and fry, turning once, cooking about 6 minutes on each side. Remove to a large saucepan or heavy casserole. Add onions to the drippings. Mix in the cayenne pepper. Sauté 4 minutes. Spoon over the chicken. Top with okra and bell peppers. Meanwhile, in a small saucepan combine 1 cup chicken broth and tomato paste over medium-high heat. Bring to a boil. Pour over the chicken and vegetables. Reduce the heat to medium-low. Cook, cov-ered, about 35 minutes, until chicken is tender, adding a little more broth if needed. Stir in the coriander or parsley.

SALAD OLIVIER

6 servings.

This classic salad, often served as a *zakuska* specialty, is usually made with chicken but traditionally, cold cooked game, and vegetables. It was created by Olivier, Czar Nicholas II's French chef, and named by the czar in his honor. The ingredients vary considerably, but generally they are a rich medley combined with a flavorful sauce and garnished ornately. In the Caucasus the salad is a restaurant specialty and served for luncheon in some city homes.

1 cup diced cold cooked white meat of chicken or game
3 medium potatoes, boiled, peeled, and diced
2 medium carrots, scraped, cooked, and diced
1 cup cold cooked green peas
6 scallions, sliced, with some green tops
½ cup mayonnaise, preferably homemade
About ½ cup sour cream
2 tablespoons drained capers
1 tablespoon snipped fresh dill
Salt, freshly ground pepper
Garnishes: Pitted black olives, tomato wedges,
  hard-cooked egg wedges

In a medium bowl combine the chicken or game, potatoes, carrots, peas, and scallions. In a small bowl mix the mayonnaise, sour cream, capers, and dill. Add to chicken or game mixture. Season with salt and pepper. Mix well. Refrigerate, covered, 4 hours, up to 8. Serve shaped as a mound or pyramid on a plate or in a bowl, covered with the garnishes.

GEORGIAN PHEASANT

6 servings.

The pheasant, *Phasianus colchicus*, a highly prized and beautiful game bird, is indigenous to the Caucasus. The name *colchicus* refers to Colchis where Jason and the Argonauts went to find the Golden Fleece, and while there, according to legend, caught a few pheasant and brought them back to Greece. They are said to have traveled along the Rioni River that was known as the River Phasis, hence the name of the bird. Cooks in western Georgia have created many innovative pheasant dishes including one in which the bird is braised commonly with walnuts, pomegranate juice, or citrus fruits. A dish, called Pheasant, Georgian-Style, that became fashionable in Russian cities and France, is flavored with green, or underripe walnuts, green tea, wine, and the fresh juice of purple grapes. This is another specialty that can be served for a company dinner.

> *2 young pheasants, 2½ to 3 pounds each, dressed*
> *Salt, freshly ground pepper*
> *¼ cup (½ stick) unsalted butter*
> *1 cup finely chopped walnuts*
> *1 cup grape juice*
> *1 cup orange juice*
> *½ cup dry red wine*
> *½ teaspoon ground allspice*

Wash and wipe dry the pheasants. Sprinkle inside and out with salt and pepper. In a casserole or pot melt the butter over medium-high heat. Add pheasants and brown on all sides, about 10 minutes. Add the walnuts, grape and orange juices, wine, and allspice. Reduce heat to medium-low. Cook, covered, about 45 minutes, until pheasants are tender. Serve with the sauce.

BRAISED QUAIL WITH PILAF

4 servings.

Small game birds such as quail are served traditionally on a bed of flavorful pilaf in the Caucasian countries. This is a typical recipe for them.

> *¼ cup (½ stick) unsalted butter*
> *4 quail, cleaned*
> *Salt, freshly ground pepper*
> *3 tablespoons tomato paste*
> *1 medium tomato, peeled and chopped*
> *1 cup dry red wine*
> *⅛ teaspoon cayenne pepper*
> *4 rounds buttered white bread*

In a large skillet melt the butter over medium-high heat. Add the quail. Season with salt and pepper. Brown on all sides. Add the tomato paste, tomato, wine, and cayenne. Mix well. Reduce the heat to medium-low. Cook, covered, about 30 minutes, until the birds are just tender. Remove to a warm platter. Fry rounds of bread and soak in warm drippings. Serve each quail placed over a round of bread. Spoon the remaining sauce into a bowl and serve with the quail.

VEGETABLES
AND SALADS

Delightfully prepared vegetables available in exceptional variety and superb salads are Caucasian gastronomic delights. Each region has an enviable number of the delectable and interesting dishes. Fortunately, cooks have long been experts in making the gifts of the garden into inviting creations that enhance the pleasure of dining. The highlight of many meals is often an attractive, flavorful vegetable specialty, for in these lands the nutritious foods are accorded a place of honor on the table. No matter how humble, each one is deeply appreciated, cooked with respect, and savored as a delicacy.

A fascinating aspect of this cookery is the discovery of the wondrous ways that both familiar and unfamiliar vegetables can be prepared. Over the years a great deal of attention has been paid to their growth, method of cooking, seasoning, and presentation.

Throughout the Caucasus one finds colorful displays of fresh vegetables at sidewalk stalls, open-air markets, and groceries. Root and tuber, seed and pod, stem and flower, as well as leafy greens are delightful to behold. Although canned and frozen vegetables are available, cooks still prefer the fresh varieties and go to the market daily to purchase the household supply.

In most regions the vegetables are eaten in season, enjoyed while garden-fresh and tender. The desire for the freshest possible vegetables is so great that shoppers shrewdly pick and choose them with knowledge and care, for to seek and find the best is a pleasurable experience, as is the preparation and cooking. Long ago every aspect of how each kind could best be handled and seasoned was well understood and the art survived through the generations. The flavor, texture, and color are not only preserved but enhanced during the cooking procedure.

Rarely is a vegetable cooked simply by itself in water or another liquid. Instead, one or more vegetables will be combined with seasonings, sauces, or broth and, perhaps, such foods as poultry, meat, eggs, or grains. Caucasian cooks are renowned for their imaginative use of seasoning vegetables and rely on all the members of the onion family, tomatoes, and especially their native fresh herbs.

Vegetables cooked with olive oil are customarily served cold. Whereas vegetable stews, often differing only in name and flavorings, are characteristic Caucasian fare found in all locales.

Certainly among the most appealing and popular of the Caucasian dishes are the ingenious varieties of stuffed vegetables. Flavorful tomatoes, green peppers, squash, eggplants, and vine and cabbage leaves filled with aromatic combinations of grains or sometimes meat, and seasonings are standard fare. There are so many inviting ways of stuffing eggplant alone that a chapter could be written only on that subject.

Raw vegetables are nibbled as snacks, appetizers, and salads. A typical breakfast for many people might be a few raw scallions, tomato or green pepper slices, an olive or two, and perhaps cheese, with some bread. Garlic, highly regarded as a nutritious food, is eaten raw and is used lavishly in cookery.

The Caucasus vegetable repertoire is extensive. In the northern Caucasian regions where Russian and Slavic culinary influences are important, vegetables such as beets, cabbage, carrots, turnips, and potatoes are frequently used in the dishes. Early cooks became experts in the art of pickling, and today most meals include a pickled specialty. Another favorite is fermented green cabbage, or sauerkraut, that appears in a wide number of creations. Whereas the versatile herb dill is the favorite Russian flavoring, sour cream goes into many of the dishes or is served with them.

In Transcaucasia vegetable specialties usually include dishes similar to those of Near Eastern lands that are made with onions, tomatoes, zucchini, dried and fresh beans, artichokes, and okra, but the selection is much more varied.

Vegetables may be prepared and served as appetizers, in soups and stews, combined with eggs and cheese, cooked with meats and poultry, and used in some desserts. The recipes included here, however, are for dishes featuring vegetables that can be served as accompaniments to other foods or, in some cases, as entrées. Generally salads in the Caucasus are enjoyed either as an appetizer or with the main course.

The unmatchable freshness and flavor of the Caucasian vegetables are not easy to find elsewhere, for the sun and soil have long made them exceptional. Yet the age-old culinary techniques devised for the art of vegetable cookery are well worth emulating in any part of the world. Cooks will find this selection of a few of the many exceptional creations an extremely interesting and different one.

POTATO-MUSHROOM PATTIES

4 servings.

In the northern Caucasus potatoes are a staple food, used to make a number of simple but inviting specialties. Mashed cooked potatoes are combined with sautéed onions and mushrooms to make patties that can be enhanced with sour cream, mushroom, or tomato sauces. Here is a basic recipe for them.

2 tablespoons unsalted butter
1 medium yellow onion, minced
1 cup chopped mushrooms
2 cups warm mashed cooked potatoes
1 egg
Salt, freshly ground pepper
Fine dry bread crumbs
About 3 tablespoons unsalted butter or
 vegetable oil for frying

In a small skillet melt the butter over medium-high heat. Add the onion; sauté 4 minutes. Add the mushrooms; sauté 2 to 3 minutes. In a medium bowl combine the sautéed vegetables, mashed potatoes, and egg. Season with salt and pepper. With the hands, shape into flat round or oval patties. Roll in bread crumbs. In a medium skillet melt the butter or heat the oil over medium-high heat. Add the patties and fry, turning once or twice, until patties are golden and crisp, about 5 minutes.

VEGETABLES IN SOUR CREAM

4 servings

A characteristic Russian way of serving vegetables is to combine them, raw or cooked, with a sour cream sauce or mixture. Use this recipe with any cooked vegetables, such as beets, beans, carrots, eggplant, or potatoes.

3 cups sliced or cut-up cooked vegetables
About 1 cup sour cream at room temperature
1 tablespoon wine vinegar
2 tablespoons chopped fresh dill
Dash of sugar
Salt, freshly ground pepper

In a medium bowl combine the cooked vegetables, while still warm, with the sour cream, vinegar, dill, and sugar. Season with salt and pepper.

Note: Another way of preparing cooked vegetables is to arrange them in a buttered baking dish, top with sour cream, sprinkle with bread crumbs or grated cheese, dot with butter, and brown in a hot oven.

ANCHOVY-FLAVORED POTATOES

4 to 6 servings.

Exceptional anchovies from the Black Sea impart a distinctive and salty flavor to a number of Caucasian dishes, including those made with bland foods such as potatoes. This is a good accompaniment for fish.

> *1 pound (3 medium) waxy potatoes, washed*
> *Salt*
> *3 tablespoons olive oil*
> *2 tablespoons red wine vinegar*
> *6 scallions, sliced, with some green tops*
> *3 tablespoons chopped fresh parsley*
> *Freshly ground pepper*
> *1 can (2 ounces) anchovy fillets, drained*

In a medium saucepan cook the potatoes in boiling salted water to cover until tender, about 25 minutes. Peel. While still warm, cut into cubes. Turn into a medium bowl. Add the oil and vinegar; mash until smooth. Add scallions and parsley. Season with salt and pepper. Mash again. Spoon into a medium bowl. Refrigerate, covered, 2 hours, up to 4. To serve, unmold or form into a mound on a plate. Garnish the top and sides with anchovy fillets.

EGGPLANT DISHES

Throughout the Caucasus one of the most treasured vegetables is the eggplant, actually a fruit but eaten as a vegetable, and grown in different sizes and shapes. A staple food prepared in many dishes, it can be baked, fried, sautéed, broiled, stuffed, scalloped, and made into appetizers, purées, salads, sandwiches, and egg specialties. It goes especially well with onions, garlic, tomatoes, cheese, fresh and dried herbs, and olive oil. Here are instructions for making a few of them.

EGGPLANT CHIPS

This typical recipe is a simple dish that shows the delicate flavor of the eggplant, particularly enhanced by olive oil. In the Caucasus cooks always use this oil with the eggplant, for they learned years ago that the two are compatible.

Cut a washed and dried medium eggplant crosswise into $\frac{1}{4}$-inch slices or into finger-size rectangles. In a medium skillet heat olive oil, about $\frac{1}{2}$ inch deep, until hot over medium-high heat. Add the eggplant slices or rectangles and fry until golden on both sides, turning once. Drain on paper towels. Serve as appetizers or a vegetable.

FRIED EGGPLANT

6 to 8 servings.

2 medium eggplants
Salt, freshly ground pepper
Bread crumbs
1 egg, beaten
Olive oil for frying

Wash and dry the eggplants. Slice into rounds about ¼ inch thick. Season with salt and pepper. Dip into fine bread crumbs; dip into egg; dip again into bread crumbs. In a large skillet heat about ¼ inch olive oil over medium-high heat. Fry the slices on both sides until crisp. Drain on paper towels. Serve hot, and, with sour cream or yogurt, if desired.

EGGPLANTS IN OLIVE OIL

4 to 6 servings.

In some regions of Transcaucasia this dish is called by its Turkish name, The *Imam* Fainted (*Imam Bayeldi*), and there are many stories concerning its origin. One is about the young bride of an *Imam* (Mohammedan priest), known for his love of good food. As part of her dowry, he was given twelve jars, each large enough to hold a person, of olive oil. When married, every day she prepared a special dish for her husband but used so much oil that the entire supply was finished in twelve days. The *Imam* was so shocked that he fainted. And since that day, according to the story, his favorite dish has been known as The *Imam* Fainted.

½ cup plus 2 tablespoons extra-virgin olive oil
2 medium yellow onions, chopped
2 cloves garlic, crushed
2 medium tomatoes, peeled and chopped
3 tablespoons chopped fresh parsley
Salt, freshly ground pepper
2 medium eggplants
2 teaspoons sugar
3 tablespoons fresh lemon juice

Preheat oven to 350 degrees.

In a small skillet heat 2 tablespoons oil over medium-high heat. Add the onions and garlic; sauté 3 minutes. Add the tomatoes and parsley. Season with salt and pepper. Cook 5 minutes. Remove from the heat.

Wash the eggplants and cut the stem ends. With a sharp knife make 3 lengthwise slits, reaching almost from end to end, in each eggplant. Sprinkle salt inside the slits and over the eggplants. Put in a colander upside down to drain for 30 minutes. Wipe dry. With the hands spread apart the slits and spoon the onion-tomato mixture into them. Arrange eggplants in an oiled baking dish. Sprinkle with sugar, lemon juice and ½ cup oil. Bake, covered, for 40 minutes, until tender. Serve hot or cold with yogurt, if desired.

EGGPLANT-VEGETABLE STEW

8 servings.

In the Caucasus a favorite way of preparing vegetables is to cook one or more of them with seasonings to make a vegetable stew. This dish, cooked very slowly, has a rich thick sauce. It can also be prepared with green beans, okra, squash, or cauliflower and can be served hot or cold.

2 medium eggplants
1 cup olive oil
2 medium yellow onions, chopped
3 medium tomatoes, peeled and chopped
2 cloves garlic, crushed
¼ cup chopped fresh parsley
½ teaspoon dried marjoram
Salt, freshly ground pepper

Wash the eggplants and remove stems; cut into cubes. In a medium saucepan heat the oil over medium-high heat. Add the onions; sauté 4 minutes. Add eggplant cubes; sauté 2 minutes. Stir in tomatoes, garlic, parsley, and marjoram. Season with salt and pepper. Reduce the heat to medium-low. Cook slowly, covered, stirring occasionally, about 25 minutes, until eggplant is tender.

GARDENER'S STEW

4 to 6 servings.

This characteristic dish is made with a medley of fresh vegetables in season and served with crusty bread as a light evening dish.

⅓ cup olive oil
2 medium yellow onions, sliced
2 large carrots, scraped and thinly sliced
4 leeks, white parts only, sliced
4 medium zucchini, sliced
1 pound fresh green beans, stemmed and cut-up
½ pound fresh okra, stemmed and cut-up
4 large tomatoes, peeled and chopped
2 medium green bell peppers, chopped
4 medium potatoes, peeled and cubed
½ teaspoon dried thyme
¼ cup chopped fresh parsley
About ¾ cup chicken broth or water
Salt, freshly ground pepper

In a large saucepan heat the oil over medium-high heat. Add the onions, carrots, and leeks. Sauté 5 minutes. Add the zucchini, green beans, okra, tomatoes, bell peppers, potatoes, thyme, parsley, and ¾ cup broth or water. Season with salt and pepper. Mix well. Lower the heat to medium-low. Cook slowly, covered, about 35 minutes, until the vegetables are tender. Check during the cooking to see if a little more water is needed. Serve hot.

GEORGIAN GREEN BEANS

4 to 6 servings.

In Georgia fresh and dried beans of all kinds are beloved foods, eaten as appetizers and snacks as well as accompaniments for meat, poultry, and fish. Highly prized are fresh green beans in season that are cooked with a variety of flavorings. This typical dish is made with coriander-flavored walnut sauce and yogurt, an optional addition.

1 pound fresh green beans, stemmed
Salt
3 scallions, sliced, with some green tops
2 garlic cloves, crushed
½ cup finely chopped walnuts
½ teaspoon dried coriander
¼ cup chopped fresh parsley
Freshly ground pepper
1 cup plain yogurt (optional)

In a medium saucepan cook the green beans in a little salted boiling water over medium-high heat until just tender, about 12 minutes. Drain. Rinse in cold water. Cut into 1-inch pieces. Turn into a medium bowl. Add the scallions, garlic, walnuts, coriander, and parsley. Season with salt and pepper. Stir in the yogurt. Refrigerate, covered, 2 hours, up to 6.

BRAISED CARROTS WITH YOGURT

4 to 6 servings.

The colorful carrot, an important root vegetable native to southwestern Asia, was developed from an ancient weed to a vegetable of many varieties, and has been cultivated in the Caucasus long before the Christian era. Carrots are used to make soups, salads, pickles, relishes, and conserves, and are added to stews and grain dishes. Braised carrots, flavored with scallions and yogurt, are a good accompaniment for grilled lamb or poultry.

8 medium carrots, scraped and cut into ¼-inch slices
½ cup sliced scallions, with some green tops
¼ cup (½ stick) unsalted butter
1 teaspoon sugar
¼ teaspoon cayenne pepper
Salt, freshly ground pepper
1 cup plain yogurt, at room temperature
2 tablespoons chopped fresh coriander or dill

In a medium saucepan combine the carrot slices, scallions, butter, sugar, and cayenne over medium-high heat. Season with salt and pepper. Cook, covered, until tender, about 12 minutes. Add the yogurt and coriander or dill. Serve at once.

CHECHEN MUSHROOM-
PEPPER MEDLEY

4 servings.

The Chechens, an ancient mountain group with claims to antiquity, one of the Japhetic Caucasian tribes, live primarily in Chechnya in the North Caucasus where they have been waging bitter war with the Russians. Over the years they have withstood bitter conflicts and even deportation but are proud people who cherish their freedom. Whereas the capital is Grozy, the principal agricultural crops are grown in the Terek River valley. Farming is an important occupation in the lowlands and cattle raising in the mountain areas. This mushroom dish is a good accompaniment for meat and poultry.

> *1 pound fresh mushrooms*
> *⅓ cup vegetable oil*
> *1 tablespoon unsalted butter*
> *2 tablespoons fresh lemon juice*
> *¼ teaspoon paprika*
> *1 cup sliced scallions, with some green tops*
> *1½ cups chopped green bell peppers*
> *1½ cups chopped red bell peppers*
> *2 tablespoons wine vinegar*
> *½ cup sour cream*
> *1 tablespoon each chopped fresh dill,*
> * coriander, and parsley*

Clean mushrooms by rinsing quickly or wiping with wet paper towels to remove any dirt. Cut off any tough stem ends. Wipe dry and slice lengthwise. In a large skillet heat the oil and butter over medium-high heat. Add the lemon juice and paprika. Heat 1 minute. Add the scallions, green and red bell peppers; sauté 2 minutes. Stir in the sliced mushrooms; sauté 2 to 3 minutes. Add the vinegar, sour cream, dill, coriander, and parsley. Mix well. Remove from the heat. Serve at once.

STUFFED
VEGETABLES

Over the years ingenious Caucasian cooks have created an innovative variety of nourishing dishes by stuffing vegetables, or sometimes only their leaves, with savory mixtures. There's a saying that Caucasians will stuff any food and they do, including fruits as well as vegetables. The diverse flavors and textures of the vegetable and stuffing serve to complement each other in the dishes.

Excellent when served as an appetizer, a main course, or an accompaniment, the vegetables provide an interesting variation in everyday cooking. Easily prepared beforehand, and served either hot or cold, they are always appealing.

Very important to the success of these dishes is the careful selection of only the best vegetables, choosing those that are fresh, well colored, and firm. In some cases they should also be of uniform size and shape. In preparing the vegetables, remove the insides with care so the shells are not broken or cut. Once the vegetables are stuffed, they should be cooked, partially covered with liquid, on top of the stove or, with fats or liquids, in the oven. Either way they should not be overcooked as they will lose flavor and shape. Because vegetables can vary considerably in size, the precise cooking time in each case is difficult to predict. Consequently it is preferable to check the vegetables at least once or twice during cooking to be sure they will not be overdone.

ECHMIADZIN
RICE-FILLED TOMATOES

Makes about 12.

Echmiadzin, about twelve miles west of Yerevan, founded as Vargarsapat in A.D. 117, is one of the ancient capitals of Armenia and the seat of the Armenian Apostolic Orthodox faith. A place of pilgrimage for Christian Armenians from all over the world, the city is rich with various early churches and historic religious sites. The Cathedral of Echmiadzin (meaning "only-begotten descended") was built in 301. Today the city is also a busy market town in the center of an agricultural area known for its fruit and wine. A namesake dish is a combination of stuffed vegetables made with zucchini, eggplants, peppers, and tomatoes, usually served with a yogurt sauce.

> *12 to 14 medium tomatoes*
> *Salt*
> *½ cup olive oil*
> *1 cup finely chopped onions*
> *⅓ cup chopped pine nuts*
> *1 cup long-grain rice*
> *2 cups chicken broth*
> *⅓ cup dried currants*
> *½ teaspoon ground or grated nutmeg*
> *Freshly ground pepper*
> *⅓ cup chopped fresh parsley*

Cut a slice from the stem end of each unpeeled tomato. Set aside the slices. Carefully spoon out the pulp. Invert to drain. Sprinkle the insides with salt.

In a large skillet heat ¼ cup oil over medium-high heat. Add the onions; sauté 4 minutes. Add the pine nuts and rice; sauté until the grains are translucent and well coated with oil. Add the broth; bring to a boil. Mix in the currants and nutmeg. Season with salt and pepper. Cook, uncovered, briskly for 10 minutes, until just about all the liquid has been absorbed and the grains are tender. Remove from the heat; stir in the parsley. Spoon into the tomato shells, filling loosely. Cover with the stem slices. Place the filled tomatoes in a large kettle. Add ¼ cup olive oil and a little water. Cook, covered, over medium-low heat about 30 minutes, until tender. With a slotted spoon carefully remove the tomatoes. Cool. Serve cold.

Note: The exact number of stuffed tomatoes will depend on their size.

VEGETABLE-STUFFED GREEN PEPPERS

6 servings.

These peppers, filled with a flavorful vegetable medley, are topped with cheese.

> *6 large green peppers, uniform in size and shape*
> *5 tablespoons olive oil*
> *½ cup finely chopped yellow onions*
> *1 cup finely chopped scraped carrots*
> *4 cups finely chopped green cabbage*
>   *(about ½ firm head)*
> *Salt, freshly ground pepper*
> *⅓ cup finely chopped parsley*
> *1 cup grated yellow cheese*
> *1 cup tomato juice*

Preheat the oven to 375 degrees.

Cut off tops of the peppers; remove seeds and membranes. Rinse in cold water; drain. Bring a large saucepan of water to a boil over medium-high heat. Add peppers; parboil about 6 minutes. Drain. Meanwhile, heat the oil in a medium skillet over medium-high heat. Add onions, carrots, and cabbage. Season with salt and pepper. Cook, stirring frequently, until partially cooked and crisp, about 10 minutes. Stir in the parsley. Meanwhile, place the peppers upright in a deep round casserole. Spoon the vegetable mixture into the peppers, pressing down lightly. Sprinkle the top of each one with grated cheese. Pour in the tomato juice. Bake, covered, until ingredients are cooked, about 25 minutes. Serve hot.

SALADS

Although traditionally eaten as an element of the appetizer array, salads are also important accompaniments. They may range from a simple plate of herb-flavored raw vegetables to an elaborate presentation with garnishes.

VEGETABLE-WALNUT SALAD

4 servings.

This is another favorite Georgian dish that includes walnuts.

> 1 medium cucumber, peeled,
>   quartered lengthwise, thinly sliced
> 1 large tomato, peeled and diced
> ½ cup chopped celery
> 2 tablespoons chopped yellow onions
> Salt
> ½ cup chopped walnuts
> 1 garlic clove, crushed
> ⅛ teaspoon cayenne pepper
> 1 tablespoon wine vinegar
> 2 tablespoons finely chopped fresh coriander
> 2 tablespoons finely chopped parsley
> Crisp lettuce leaves

In a medium bowl combine the cucumber, tomato, celery, and onions. Season with salt. In a mortar with a pestle or food processor, grind together the walnuts, garlic, and cayenne. Add vinegar and enough cold water to blend well and form a paste. Add to the vegetables. Stir in the coriander and parsley. Mix to blend well. Refrigerate, covered, 2 hours, up to 6. Serve on lettuce leaves.

WINTER CABBAGE SALAD

8 to 10 servings.

This old-time specialty has unusual ingredients and seasonings that add luster to the basic cabbage.

> *½ firm large green cabbage, about 1 pound*
> *6 scallions, sliced, with some green tops*
> *1 large red apple, unpeeled, cored, and chopped*
> *½ cup plain yogurt*
> *¼ cup mayonnaise*
> *2 teaspoons sugar*
> *¼ teaspoon paprika*
> *Salt, freshly ground pepper*
> *½ cup chopped fresh parsley*
> *1 medium carrot, scraped and shaved with a vegetable*
> *   peeler*

Cut cabbage in half; cut out core. Remove and discard any wilted leaves. Cut cabbage into julienne strips or chop finely. In a large bowl combine the cabbage with the scallions and apple. In a small bowl combine the yogurt, mayonnaise, sugar, and paprika. Stir into cabbage mixture. Season with salt and pepper. Stir in parsley. Refrigerate, covered, 2 hours, up to 8. Serve garnished with the carrot shavings.

SEDA GELENIAN'S BEAN SALAD

Serves 10 to 12.

This bean salad, prepared by Seda Gelenian, was part of a cooking demonstration given by the Ladies' Guild of Soorp Khatch Church in Bethesda, Maryland. One of the area's primary Armenian churches, it is located in a suburb of Washington, D.C. The ladies participate in year-round events featuring their favorite Armenian dishes, which they make and share with the community.

> ¼ cup olive oil
> 4 cups sliced yellow onions
> 1 garlic clove, minced
> ½ cup diced carrots
> ½ cup diced celery
> ¾ cup diced, peeled, cooked potatoes
> ½ cup chopped fresh parsley
> ½ cup chopped fresh dill
> Juice of ½ lemon
> ½ cup tomato sauce or 1 cup canned tomatoes, chopped
> 1 tablespoon salt
> ½ teaspoon pepper
> ¼ teaspoon dried mint
> ½ teaspoon ground cinnamon (optional)
> 3 cups cooked or canned white beans, drained

In a large saucepan or pot heat a small amount of oil over medium-high heat. Add the onions; sauté until tender, about 5 minutes. Add the garlic, carrots, celery, potatoes, parsley, dill, lemon juice, tomato sauce or tomatoes, 2 cups water, salt, pepper, mint, cinnamon, and remaining oil. Mix well. Reduce the heat to medium-low. Cook about 5 minutes. Fold in the beans. Remove from the heat. Cool, covered, at room temperature. Refrigerate until ready to serve.

GARNISHED
CAULIFLOWER SALAD

4 to 6 servings.

The attractive cauliflower, a variety of cabbage developed centuries ago in the eastern Mediterranean lands, is an excellent vegetable to serve raw or cooked in salads. Its leaves, if tender, are good salad greens. The nutritious vegetable is highly prized by the cooks of the Caucasus who use it to make a number of interesting dishes, including this salad.

1 whole medium cauliflower (about 2 pounds)
Salt
1 tablespoon fresh lemon juice
1 large green pepper, chopped
12 pitted black olives, cut into halves
8 scallions, sliced, with some green tops
⅓ cup olive oil
2 tablespoons wine vinegar
½ teaspoon dried oregano or thyme
Freshly ground pepper
3 tablespoons chopped fresh dill or parsley

Cut off base and tough outer leaves of cauliflower. Wash into cold running water, holding upside down. In a large kettle heat 1 inch of salted water over medium-high heat. Add lemon juice and the cauliflower. Cook, uncovered, 5 minutes. Reduce heat to medium-low. Cover and cook until just tender, about 20 minutes. Drain and cool. Break into flowerets and placed in a salad bowl. Add peppers, olives, and scallions. In a small dish combine the oil, vinegar, and oregano or thyme. Season with salt and pepper. Pour over the salad ingredients. Toss. Serve sprinkled with dill or parsley.

EGGPLANT-YOGURT SALAD

4 to 6 servings.

Serve as an appetizer or accompaniment.

> 1 medium eggplant, about 1 1/4 pounds
> 1/2 cup minced onions
> 2 garlic cloves, crushed
> 2 tablespoons olive oil
> 1 tablespoon fresh lemon juice
> 1/2 cup plain yogurt
> Salt, freshly ground pepper
> 3 tablespoons chopped fresh coriander, dill, or parsley
> Paprika or cayenne pepper

Preheat broiler.

With a fork prick the eggplant in several places. Place on a small baking sheet. Put under the heated broiler and cook, turning several times, about 20 minutes, or until the skin becomes charcoal black on all sides. Remove from the oven. While still hot, peel off the skins and put pulp in a large bowl. With a wooden spoon mash thoroughly, pouring off any liquid. Add the onions, garlic, olive oil, lemon juice, and yogurt, beating after each addition. Season with salt and pepper. Refrigerate, covered, 2 hours, up to 6. Serve cold in a shallow dish or shaped into a mound on a plate, garnished with the chopped coriander, dill, or parsley, and paprika or cayenne.

BEET-YOGURT SALAD

6 to 8 servings.

The ruby red beet is much appreciated by Caucasians and appears on the table in many flavorful dishes, often enhanced with piquant flavorings such as sour cream. The adaptable and attractive root vegetable is a favorite salad ingredient, often served with piquant, sweet-sour flavorings, or yogurt.

> *¾ cup plain yogurt*
> *1 tablespoon fresh lemon juice or vinegar*
> *2 tablespoons chopped fresh dill or parsley*
> *Pinch of cayenne pepper*
> *Salt, freshly ground pepper*
> *2 cans (1 pound each) julienne beets,*
> *   drained and chilled*

In a medium bowl combine the yogurt, lemon juice or vinegar, dill or parsley, and cayenne. Season with salt and pepper. Mix to blend well. Refrigerate, covered, about 2 hours, up to 4. To serve, place beets in a shallow dish. Top with yogurt mixture.

RADISHES IN SOUR CREAM

4 servings.

The radish, a pungent fleshy root that comes in a number of shapes and may be white, black, purple, pink, or yellow, as well as red in color, is among the world's oldest vegetables. Radishes and sour cream are a favorite Russian specialty that is eaten as an appetizer or salad. This is one variation.

> *2 bunches cold crisp red radishes*
> *2 hard-cooked eggs*
> *⅔ cup sour cream*
> *½ teaspoon sugar*
> *Salt, freshly ground white pepper*
> *2 tablespoons chopped fresh dill*
> *Lettuce leaves, washed and dried*

Trim and thinly slice radishes. Put in a shallow serving dish. Cut eggs into halves; remove yolks; chop the whites. In a small bowl mix mashed yolks with the sour cream and sugar. Season with salt and pepper. Spoon over radish slices; toss to combine well. Sprinkle with chopped egg whites and dill. Refrigerate, covered, up to 2 hours. Serve in a mound surrounded with lettuce leaves.

CUCUMBER-RADISH SALAD

4 servings.

2 medium cucumbers, peeled and sliced thinly
12 red radishes, sliced
1 cup sliced scallions, with some tops
½ to ¾ cup plain yogurt
Pinch of sugar
Salt, freshly ground pepper
Chopped fresh mint, coriander, or parsley

In a medium bowl combine the cucumbers, radishes, and scallion slices. In a small dish combine the yogurt and sugar. Season with salt and pepper. Spoon over the vegetables; mix well. Refrigerate, covered, 1 to 2 hours. Serve garnished with the mint, coriander, or parsley.

SAUERKRAUT-CARROT SALAD

4 to 6 servings.

Tangy sauerkraut and carrots, flavored with herbs and sour cream, combine to make a nutritious winter dish.

1 pound (2 cups) bulk or canned sauerkraut, drained
1 cup sliced scallions, with some green tops
1½ cups shredded, scraped carrots (about 3 medium)
½ cup finely chopped fresh parsley or dill
2 tablespoons sour cream
2 tablespoons vegetable oil
1 teaspoon sugar
Salt, freshly ground pepper

In a large bowl combine the sauerkraut, scallions, carrots, parsley or dill. In a small dish mix the sour cream, oil, and sugar. Season with salt and pepper. Stir into the sauerkraut mixture. Refrigerate, covered, 2 hours, up to 6, stirring once or twice.

GRAINS AND LEGUMES

For generations, Caucasians have used flavorful grains and legumes as treasured basic foods and their culinary versatility is fully appreciated. Throughout the region a tremendously wide variety of delectable fare is created easily with fruits of the field, as grains are sometimes called, such as *kasha*, rice, bulgur, barley, millet, and to a lesser extent, corn.

Although considered by some persons to be humble and inexpensive fare, dishes made with these foods are beloved by everyone in the Caucasian lands. Even the simplest combination is made exciting by the addition of herbs and spices as well as other seasonings. Few foods can match grains and legumes for health-building power. Fortunately, these dishes provide not only nourishing daily sustenance but they are cherished national favorites.

From the beginning, Russian cookery was based on grains and cereals, but it necessarily relied primarily on those that could withstand the severe climate. Although wheat, barley, and millet were grown and used, the great favorite for making breads became the reliable rye. What would a Russian meal be like without large chunks of black bread?

It was another hardy, quickly grown grain, buckwheat, native to Siberia and Central Asia, which became so important to the everyday Russian diet that without it many people would not have survived. It can be easily grown, and is nourishing, flavorful and inexpensive. Although the corn of the New World did not gain general popularity in Russia and the Caucasus, it and cornmeal are used in southwestern Georgia where even corn on the cob and popcorn are enjoyed.

Bulgur, a staple grain in many areas of the Caucasus, particularly Armenia, consists of small brown kernels, actually hulled and pounded wheat. It has a delectable flavor, is used in many dishes, from appetizers and soups to pilafs and desserts, and especially as an accompaniment to roast meats and poultry.

For generations the people of Transcaucasia have used rice as a basic food, a beloved daily staple eaten at all meals. Of all the region's superb rice dishes those called *pilafs*, or variations of the name, are the best known. Certainly they are deserving of praise for the preparation, originally from Central Asia or Persia, has been treated in many variations that can be served as entrées or accompaniments and used as stuffing for meats, poultry, and vegetables. Although pilafs are customarily made with rice, they are sometimes prepared with other grains such as bulgur or barley.

Azerbaijanis are connoisseurs of rice, cultivated on the Caspian Sea coastal areas where several types are grown. Over the years cooks have developed the art of cooking the grain in a diverse number of national dishes. When the rice is cooked with other ingredients it becomes a *polo*, similar to a pilaf but usually more elaborate. In many of the specialties sweet and tart flavors are cleverly blended to make distinguished national dishes.

This characteristic and pleasing recipe collection reflects some of the goodness and versatility of the many ways that the fruits of the field may be used. Suffice it to say that they are a tribute to the cooks of yesteryear who created them.

RUSSIAN KASHA

Makes about 4 cups.

Kasha, a term referring to most kinds of grains, but usually buckwheat, when they are cooked to make a porridge, has been a staple Russian food for centuries, prepared in various forms for daily meals. It is eaten with milk for breakfast, served as an accompaniment for other foods, an ingredient in soups and stews, and as a stuffing or filling. Leftover *kasha* can be fried and served with melted butter or sour cream. A word that once meant "feast," *kasha* is also served for festivals and special celebrations. The basic recipe given below can be further enriched with sautéed onions and mushrooms or combined with sour cream and cottage cheese and baked. In the United States, buckwheat is packaged and sold as *kasha*: whole, coarse, medium, or fine.

> *1 cup* kasha
> *1 egg, slightly beaten*
> *2 cups chicken broth or water*
> *2 tablespoons unsalted butter*
> *Salt, freshly ground pepper*

In a medium bowl mix the *kasha* and egg to coat the kernels. In an ungreased medium skillet over medium-high heat add the egg-coated *kasha*. Cook about 3 minutes, stirring constantly, until egg has dried on the kernels and they are separate. Remove from heat. Meanwhile, in a medium saucepan heat the broth or water to boiling over medium-high heat. Add the butter. Season with salt and pepper. Stir in toasted egg-coated *kasha*. Reduce the heat to medium-low. Cook, covered, about 8 minutes, until the kernels are tender and liquid has been absorbed. Mix with a fork.

KASHA PILAF

4 to 6 servings.

This is a good accompaniment for meat, poultry, or game.

> *2 tablespoons unsalted butter*
> *½ cup chopped yellow onions*
> *¼ pound mushrooms, thinly sliced*
> *2 cups chicken broth*
> *Salt, freshly ground pepper*
> *1 cup* kasha
> *2 tablespoons chopped fresh coriander or parsley*

In a medium saucepan melt the butter over medium-high heat. Add the onions; sauté until tender, about 4 minutes. Add the mushrooms. Sauté for 3 minutes. Pour in chicken broth. Season with salt and pepper. Stir in the *kasha*. Bring to a boil. Lower the heat to medium-low. Cook, covered, about 10 minutes, until the grains are tender and the liquid has been absorbed. Stir in the coriander or parsley.

Cuisines of the Caucasus Mountains

BARLEY-MUSHROOM CASSEROLE

6 servings.

Barley, one of the world's oldest foods that ancients believed to have mystical and medicinal powers, is a nutritious grain with an appealing nutty flavor. Widely used in the Caucasus, barley makes marvelous soups and stuffings and, like this dish, is a common accompaniment for fish, meat, or poultry.

¼ cup (½ stick) unsalted butter
1 medium yellow onion, chopped
1 cup diced scraped carrots
½ pound fresh mushrooms, sliced
1 tablespoon fresh lemon juice
1 cup pearl barley
3 cups hot beef bouillon
Salt, freshly ground pepper
3 tablespoons chopped fresh coriander,
*   mint, or parsley*

In a medium saucepan melt the butter over medium-high heat. Add the onion and carrots; sauté 3 minutes. Add the mushrooms and lemon juice. Sauté 4 minutes. Stir in the barley. Add the bouillon. Season with salt and pepper. Mix well. Bring to a boil. Reduce the heat to medium-low. Cook, covered, until barley is tender and liquid is absorbed, about 45 minutes. Add the coriander, mint or parsley.

ARMENIAN BULGUR PILAF

4 servings.

Bulgur, one of the oldest forms of processed wheat that has been steamed, then dried before being crushed into various grinds, has been used for centuries in the Caucasus. Originally prepared by boiling the grain and spreading it in the sun to dry, the wheat is noted for its faintly nutty flavor and pleasing crunchy texture. The color varies from light to dark brown. It has exceptionally high nutritional value as it retains the bran and germ of the grain. In America it is sold in three different grain sizes: fine, medium, and coarse. While bulgur can be eaten after just a brief soaking in boiling or cold water, the grain takes on new dimensions when cooked with other foods and seasonings.

3 tablespoons unsalted butter
1 teaspoon olive oil
1 medium yellow onion, finely chopped
2 medium carrots, scraped and diced
1 medium green bell pepper, diced
2 medium tomatoes, peeled and chopped
1 cup medium bulgur
2 1/2 cups beef bouillon or chicken broth
Salt, freshly ground pepper
1 cup canned chickpeas, drained
2 tablespoons chopped fresh coriander or parsley

In a large saucepan melt 2 tablespoons butter and the oil over medium-high heat. Add the onion; sauté about 4 minutes. Add the carrots, bell pepper, and tomatoes. Cook uncovered 5 minutes. Stir in the bulgur. Sauté, tossing to coat the grains, for 1 to 2 minutes. Add the bouillon or broth. Season with salt and pepper. Mix well. Bring to a boil. Reduce the heat to medium-low. Cook, covered, about 25 minutes, until bulgur is tender and liquid has been absorbed. Stir in the chickpeas and remaining 1 tablespoon of butter. Serve sprinkled with coriander or parsley.

ARMENIAN LENTILS AND BULGUR

6 servings.

The lentil, a tiny disk-shaped seed, is one of man's most ancient and important foods and come in several kinds and colors. Marvelously nutritious, satisfying, and economical, lentils are rich in iron and other minerals as well as in vitamins B and A, and extremely high in protein. In the Caucasus they are used to make soups and salads and, in combination with other grains, casseroles, or other dishes such as this one. Known throughout the Near East as *megadarra*, usually made with lentils and rice, it has been called "poor man's dish," for it's inexpensive and nutritious, and may be served hot or cold, and accompanied by yogurt. In Armenia it is called *movjaddar* or *mudjadera*.

> 1 cup brown lentils, washed and picked over
> ½ teaspoon cayenne pepper
> 1 cup medium bulgur
> Salt, freshly ground pepper
> ¾ cup olive oil
> 1 cup finely chopped yellow onions
> Garnishes: Scallion strips, chopped fresh coriander or
>   parsley, freshly ground pepper

In a medium saucepan combine the lentils and 3 cups water over medium-high heat. Bring to a boil. Reduce the heat to medium-low. Cook, covered, 10 minutes, until lentils are partially tender. Add the cayenne pepper and bulgur. Season with salt and pepper. Cook, covered, about 20 minutes, until bulgur is just tender and liquid has been absorbed. Turn off the heat and let the pan stand, covered, for 10 minutes.

Meanwhile, in a small skillet heat the oil over medium-high heat. Add the onions; sauté about 4 minutes. Stir into the cooked lentils and bulgur. Season with salt and pepper. Serve with the garnishes.

MINTED BULGUR
WITH YOGURT

4 servings.

Fresh mint and yogurt add aroma and goodness to this unusual accompaniment for meats, poultry, or game.

> *3 tablespoons unsalted butter*
> *1 medium yellow onion, finely chopped*
> *1 cup diced fennel or celery*
> *1 cup medium bulgur*
> *2¼ cups chicken broth*
> *Salt, freshly ground pepper*
> *3 tablespoons chopped fresh mint*
> *1 cup plain yogurt*

In a medium saucepan melt the butter over medium-high heat. Add the onion and fennel or celery. Sauté 5 minutes. Add the bulgur. Sauté, tossing to coat the grains, about 2 minutes. Pour in the broth. Season with salt and pepper. Bring to a boil. Reduce the heat to medium-low. Cook, covered, about 20 minutes, until bulgur is tender and liquid has been absorbed. Remove from the heat. Stir in the mint and ½ cup yogurt. Serve topped with spoonfuls of the remaining yogurt.

Of all the Caucasus's superb grain dishes those called a pilaf or variations of the name are the best known. It is the festive national dish of the whole Near East. Basically a pilaf is a simple dish made by cooking rice in broth with butter to which other foods and seasonings may be added. More elaborate versions include herbs, spices, nuts, dried or fresh fruit, and perhaps vegetables, meat, and poultry. Staple fare for everyday and special occasion meals, there are so many versions of this creative dish that each cook has several favorite preparations. This is a basic pilaf made with long-grain rice to which other ingredients can be added.

> *4 tablespoons unsalted butter*
> *2 cups chicken broth*
> *1 cup long-grain rice*
> *Salt, freshly ground pepper*

In a medium saucepan melt 2 tablespoons butter over medium-high heat. Add the broth; bring to a boil. Stir in the rice. Season with salt and pepper. Reduce the heat to medium-low. Cook, covered, about 20 minutes, until rice is tender and liquid has been absorbed. Place a clean dish towel or cloth over the pan and top with the cover. Leave in a warm place for 15 minutes. This step is not necessary but it will absorb much of the starch. Stir in the remaining 2 tablespoons butter. Check the seasoning.

Other pilafs: After adding the rice, mix in pine nuts, currants, fresh herbs, or spices. Cook these ingredients with the rice. Or, after the pilaf is cooked, add to it cut-up cooked chicken or meat, seafood, or vegetables. Other suggestions are cooked red beans, chickpeas, or fava beans.

MOUNT ELBRUS
TOMATO PILAF

Mt. Elbrus, "the mountain soul of the Caucasus," as ancient as Mt. Ararat, is the highest point of the Caucasus and of Europe lying in the Greater Caucasus mountain range. It is capped by the conical peaks of two extinct volcanoes, the western one rising to 18,481 feet, and the eastern to 18,356 feet. In Persian the name means "Two Heads." To ancient Near Eastern and Mediterranean civilizations, Elbrus signified the end of the world, beyond which darkness prevailed. A major center for outdoor activities, in 1964 an extensive tourist and mountaineering base was opened with large scale sporting activities. While densely wooded in parts with great forests, grain is cultivated to a great height and the lower valleys produce other crops.

Add 2 peeled and chopped tomatoes or 2 tablespoons tomato purée to the butter before adding the broth in the basic pilaf recipe on page 185. Add 1 tablespoon of chopped fresh basil and 2 tablespoons chopped fresh parsley to the cooked rice.

GEORGIAN HOLIDAY PILAF

6 to 8 servings.

This special pilaf, flavored with nuts and raisins, is good to serve for a holiday or company meal.

3 tablespoons unsalted butter
2 medium yellow onions, chopped
½ cup chopped walnuts
⅓ cup chopped golden raisins
2 cups long-grain rice
4 cups chicken broth
2 large tomatoes, peeled and chopped
½ teaspoon dried basil
¼ teaspoon ground allspice
Salt, freshly ground pepper
¼ cup chopped fresh coriander or parsley

In a medium saucepan melt the butter over medium-high heat. Add the onions. Sauté about 4 minutes. Add the walnuts and raisins; sauté 1 minute. Add the rice; sauté 3 minutes. Pour in the broth. Add the tomatoes, basil, and allspice. Season with salt and pepper. Bring to a boil. Reduce the heat to medium-low. Cook, covered, about 20 minutes, until rice is tender. Stir in the coriander or parsley.

PILAF WITH NOODLES

4 to 6 servings.

A characteristic dish of the Caucasus is a pilaf made with rice and crumbled egg noodles. Sliced almonds or pine nuts, sautéed in butter, may be added, if desired.

> *2 tablespoons unsalted butter*
> *1 tablespoon olive oil*
> *½ cup crumbled fine noodles or vermicelli*
> *1 cup long-grain rice*
> *2 cups boiling chicken broth or water*
> *Salt, freshly ground pepper*
> *Ground allspice and / or cinnamon*

In a large saucepan melt the butter and heat the oil over medium-high heat. Add the noodles. Fry until golden brown. Add the rice; sauté 2 to 3 minutes to coat well with butter. Pour in the broth or water. Season with salt and pepper. Bring to a boil. Reduce the heat to medium-low. Cook, covered, about 20 minutes, until all the liquid is absorbed. Remove from heat. Stir once or twice. Leave, covered, for 10 to 15 minutes. Serve sprinkled with freshly ground pepper, allspice, and / or cinnamon.

KIZLYAR RICE WITH MUSHROOMS

4 to 6 servings.

Kizlyar, a Cossack region in the North Caucasus, bordered by North Ossetia in the west and by Dagestan in the east, is noted for its rice that is cultivated in the lower sections of the Terek River lands. Orchards and vineyards can be found in the higher areas of the valley.

> 6 tablespoons unsalted butter
> 3 tablespoons olive oil
> 1 large yellow onion, finely chopped
> 2 cups chicken broth
> 1 cup long-grain rice
> Pinch of cayenne pepper
> Salt, freshly ground pepper
> ½ pound fresh mushrooms, sliced thinly crosswise
> 2 tablespoons fresh lemon juice
> 2 tablespoons finely chopped chives or scallions
> 2 tablespoons chopped fresh dill or parsley

In a medium saucepan melt 3 tablespoons of butter and the oil over medium-high heat. Add the onion; sauté about 4 minutes. Add chicken broth; bring to a boil. Stir in rice. Season with cayenne, salt, and pepper. Reduce the heat to medium-low. Cook, covered, about 20 minutes, until the rice is tender and liquid has been absorbed.

Meanwhile, in a small skillet melt remaining 3 tablespoons butter over medium-high heat. Add mushrooms and lemon juice. Sauté 4 minutes. Stir, with the chives or scallions, and dill or parsley, into the cooked rice while it is still warm. Mix well.

HERBED BASMATI RICE PLOV

6 to 8 servings.

In Azerbaijan there are numerous rich rice dishes called *plov*, or variations of the name, which are similar to pilaf and equally variegated. Said to have originated in Central Asia, the dish is the pride of every household prepared as a work of art and served with respect as an important presentation for family and holiday celebrations.

Aromatic, delicate long-grain basmati rice from India, described as "needle shaped" because it is so narrow, is ideal for a *plov* as its grains stay separate and firm when cooked and tender. Readily available in America, it is similar to the kind of rice used in Azerbaijan. This and the next dish are made with packaged basmati rice.

> 2 cups basmati rice
> Salt
> 1 cup finely chopped scallions, with some green tops
> ½ cup chopped fresh dill
> ½ cup chopped fresh coriander
> 1 cup chopped fresh parsley
> 3 tablespoons unsalted butter, cut into pieces

Rinse the rice well under cold running water. In a large heavy saucepan bring 3½ cups water to a boil over medium-high heat. Season with salt. Add the rice. Stir. Bring to a boil again. Reduce heat to medium-low. Cook, covered, 15 minutes, until rice is tender and liquid has been absorbed. Stir in the scallions, dill, coriander, parsley, and butter. Stir to mix well. Remove from the heat and let stand 5 minutes.

AZERBAIJAN RICE WITH FRUIT

6 to 8 servings.

This rice dish is one of those called a "sweet one" as it's made with raisins, nuts, dried or fresh fruits, and sometimes honey. It may be served as an accompaniment or dessert.

> *1 cup dried apricots*
> *½ cup raisins*
> *¼ teaspoon ground saffron*
> *3 tablespoons unsalted butter.*
> *3 cups chicken broth*
> *1½ cups basmati rice*
> *Salt, freshly ground pepper*

In a small bowl cover the apricots and raisins with boiling water. Soak for about 2 hours. Drain; cut the apricots into bite-size pieces. In small dish steep saffron in 2 tablespoons hot water. In a medium saucepan melt the butter over medium-high heat. Add chicken broth. Bring to a boil. Stir in rice. Season with salt and pepper. Add apricots, raisins, and saffron. Mix well. Reduce the heat to medium-low. Cook, covered, about 20 minutes, until the rice is tender and liquid has been absorbed. Remove from the heat and let stand 5 minutes.

RICE STUFFING

*Makes about 4 cups, enough to fill
a 6- to 8-pound turkey.*

This pilaf of Turkish origin can be served by itself, as an accompaniment, or a stuffing for vegetables, meats, poultry, and game. In the spring it is particularly delectable as a filling for baby lamb.

> *3 tablespoons unsalted butter*
> *1 medium yellow onion, finely chopped*
> *6 scallions, minced, with some green tops*
> *⅓ cup pine nuts*
> *1 cup long-grain rice*
> *⅓ cup chopped currants or raisins*
> *2 cups hot chicken broth*
> *Salt, freshly ground pepper*
> *1 tablespoon sugar*
> *2 teaspoons ground cinnamon*
> *⅓ cup chopped fresh dill or parsley*

In a large skillet melt the butter over medium-high heat. Add the onion and scallions; sauté 4 minutes. Add pine nuts. Sauté 2 minutes. Stir in rice; sauté, stirring constantly, 5 minutes, or until rice is transparent and nuts are golden. Stir in the currants or raisins. Add the hot broth. Season with salt and pepper. Mix well. Reduce the heat to medium-low. Cook slowly, covered, until the rice is tender and all liquid has been absorbed. Add sugar, cinnamon, and dill or parsley. Cook another 1 or 2 minutes.

ARMENIAN BULGUR PILAF WITH FRUIT

6 servings.

Typical Armenian ingredients for pilafs include apricots, almonds, raisins, and cinnamon.

> *5 tablespoons unsalted butter*
> *½ cup slivered blanched almonds*
> *½ cup golden raisins*
> *1 cup coarsely chopped dried apricots*
> *½ teaspoon ground cinnamon*
> *½ cup sliced scallions, with some green tops*
> *1 cup medium bulgur*
> *1¾ cups chicken broth*
> *Salt*

In a medium skillet melt 2 tablespoons butter over medium-low heat. Add the almonds, raisins, apricots, and cinnamon. Sauté 2 to 3 minutes. Remove from the heat.

In a large saucepan melt 3 tablespoons butter over medium-high heat. Add the scallions; sauté 1 minute. Add bulgur; sauté about 2 minutes, until brown and toasted. Pour in the broth. Season with salt. Mix well. Bring to a boil. Reduce the heat to medium-low. Cook, covered, about 20 minutes, until bulgur is tender but still crunchy and liquid has been absorbed. Add the fruit mixture; mix well. Serve at once.

GEORGIAN GRITS
WITH CHEESE

Grits or groats, meaning hulled or ground cereal grains, are very old nutritious foods made from buckwheat, rye, oats, rice, and more recently, corn. They have long been eaten in various forms, particularly as a gruel or porridge or in soups. This is a variation of a dish prepared in western Georgia that is called *ghome*, sometimes prepared with white cornmeal.

> *1 cup stone-ground or old-fashioned grits*
> *Salt*
> *2 to 3 tablespoons unsalted butter*
> *¼ pound (¾ cup) fresh mozzarella, grated*

In a medium saucepan bring 4½ cups water to a boil over medium-high heat. Slowly stir in the grits. Add salt. Bring to a boil. Reduce the heat to medium-low. Cook, stirring frequently, about 20 minutes, until thickened and cooked. Remove from the heat. Let stand, covered, for 5 minutes. Stir in butter and grated cheese. Serve at once. 6 servings.

HONEY MILLET PORRIDGE

6 servings.

Millet, a grass cultivated for its tiny golden seeds, has a mild, sweet flavor and is very easy to digest. It also is especially nutritious, very rich in iron, calcium, B vitamins, phosphorous, and amino acids. Either by itself or in combination with other grains, millet is a versatile food that can be used to make all kinds of dishes, from soups to desserts.

2 teaspoons unsalted butter
1 cup millet
Salt
3 tablespoons honey
½ cup golden raisins
½ cup chopped walnuts

In a medium saucepan, melt the butter over medium-high heat. Add the millet. Cook, stirring constantly, until brown and toasted, 2 to 3 minutes. Pour in 2½ cups water. Season with salt. Stir. Reduce the heat to medium-low. Cook, covered, about 30 minutes, until the liquid is absorbed. Remove from the heat and fluff with a fork. Mix in the honey, raisins, and walnuts. Serve at once.

CHICKPEA MEDLEY

6 servings.

Plump and hard chickpeas, usually beige or golden and known by several names, are said to have been first cultivated in the Middle East. Relished for its rich, nutty flavor and high-protein content, the chickpea is cooked and eaten in a variety of ways. Freshly boiled dried chickpeas are recommended for a fuller flavored dish but canned ones make good substitutes. Serve this flavorful medley as a salad or accompaniment.

1 can (15½ ounces) chickpeas, drained and rinsed
½ cup diced scraped carrots
⅓ cup sliced scallions, with some green tops
½ cup finely chopped celery
12 pitted black olives, sliced
3 tablespoons olive oil
2 tablespoons wine vinegar
Salt, freshly ground pepper
1 tablespoon chopped fresh mint

In a large bowl combine the chickpeas, carrots, scallions, celery, and olives. Add the oil and vinegar. Season with salt and pepper. Mix in the mint. Refrigerate, covered, 2 hours, up to 8, to blend flavors.

BREADS, PASTAS, AND SAVORY PASTRIES

In the Caucasian culinary repertoire breads, pastas, and savory pastries play an important role in the daily menu and are made in fascinating varieties. Tasty, nourishing, inexpensive, and a pleasure to prepare, they are beloved by everyone. There are so many of the innovative specialties that here are only a few recipes for the gastronomic delights.

One of the great traditions of Russian and Caucasian cooking is the excellence of its bread, which takes many forms. Over the years homemakers have taken great pleasure in making freshly baked treats for everyday meals and especially holiday and family celebrations. Long regarded as a treasured "staff of life," bread plays a significant role in the religion and culture as well as the cuisine.

Russians love bread and regard it as almost sacred, an essential element of their daily living. Since ancient times bread and salt have been symbols of hospitality and friendship. To offer a person a piece of bread is a way to honor one's guest. Not only are the breads marvelous, noteworthy for their interesting variety, but they are eaten in great quantity, always enjoyed as a special pleasure.

Bakeries offer full-bodied dark brown or black breads made primarily with rye flour, caraway flavored crescents, poppy seed rolls, and a host of white kinds in various sizes and shapes from loaf to bun. There also are specialties as sweet as cake, served hot with butter and jam, especially with cups of teas.

Caucasians have a passion for bread, an essential part of every meal and eaten in between. They are justly famous for their satisfying innovative specialties, many of them unique. The moment you enter a home the aroma of freshly baked bread is like a symbol of welcome, and homemakers take great pride in demonstrating and explaining their bread-making techniques to guests.

One of the oldest breads known to man and often still made as it has been for centuries is what is called a flatbread, full of ancient origin. Thin or puffy, unleavened or leavened, sometimes fragrant with herbs or spices, they are simply prepared with a dough made from the flour of a grain, moistened with water, and formed into flat cakes. Traditionally flatbreads are baked in a cylindrical clay oven that resembles the *tandoor* of India, set outside the home, partially in the ground, and usually fired with wood. In Georgia it is called a *toné*, a *tonir* in Armenia, and *tandir* in Azerbaijan.

The most widely available and best known of all the flat breads is *pita* or *pide*, also called Arab, Armenian, or pocket bread. Made with wheat flour, it is a golden-to-dark brown soft, flat round that forms an internal pocket during the baking. One of the great things about the bread is that its two layers can be split easily to be covered with butter and honey or filled with various mixtures to make sandwiches. In the Caucasus the bread is commonly wrapped around pieces or slices of warm skewered meats, especially lamb. It also can be broken into pieces and used to scoop up dips and salads, or is very good buttered, cut into strips, and baked in the oven to become quite crisp and served like chips with soups or salads. Triangles of the bread are often fried in butter, toasted, and used as a basis for various dishes or to garnish entrées.

Another traditional bread, called *lavash* in Armenia and *lavishi* in Georgia, has survived for centuries because it's healthful and practical to make. Generally it comes in very thin, large sheets and is used for wrapping around food as well as eating. In Azerbaijan the most common bread, called *nan* or *non*, is leavened bread shaped like a circle with a flattened stamped center, or lines of ripples, and may contain yogurt or milk. Often it's flavored with onions, herbs, spices, or sesame seeds.

Among the favorite breads of Armenia is a sweet holiday specialty, *cheoreg* or *cheurek*, made in various sizes and shapes, sometimes sprinkled with sesame seeds. In Georgia it has long been the custom to bake bread, *puri*, daily in a *toné* over a very hot fire made from dried grapevines and in many locales this is still done, sometimes as a special treat for visitors. Particularly desirable is *deda's puri*, "mother's bread," long and slightly crooked with a distinctive flavor. Georgia is also known for its variety of cheese breads, made differently according to the region.

Russians and Caucasians are devotees of pasta that, since ancient times, has been an esteemed and basic food. Fortunately, they have a number of good and interesting dishes of great appeal that can be easily made with the creative pasta repertoire.

High on the list of Russian and Caucasian favorites are specialties made with filled dough and dumplings. One of the most interesting, called *khinkali*, is the staple food of the people in the higher mountainous regions of the Caucasus where the daily fare is hearty and satisfying. Believed to be of Tatar origin, the fresh and tasty creations are quite difficult to make but, nevertheless, are the pride of every housewife who prepare them especially to honor guests. For one variation, the dough is flattened with a long, narrow rolling pin, cut into dozens of symmetrical, square pieces or circles, each of which is filled with a ground meat mixture. To form the dumplings, the dough is drawn over the filling into small bundles and then pleated and pinched into stems or knots at the tops. When cooked in boiling salted water and drained, they are served steaming hot, sprinkled with freshly ground pepper, and with scallions, pickles, sprigs of fresh coriander and parsley, and especially ice cold *chacha* (vodka).

In *The Georgian Feast*, Darra Goldstein writes that a good place to enjoy the boiled dumplings is the village of Pasanauri, at the confluence of the two Aragvi rivers, the Black and the White. "Until the rivers finally mingle, they run within the same banks for a stretch, and the effect of their contrasting colors is striking. More people come to Pasanauri to eat than to gaze at the water, however. The town is a mecca for connoisseurs of *khinkali*, the Georgian version of the boiled dumplings found throughout Central Asia and the Orient. Some claim the special quality of the river waters makes Pasanauri *khinkali* so good; others believe the local flour makes the difference. Whatever the secret, the dumplings are the best appreciated legacy of the Mongol occupation."

Not to be overlooked are savory pastries, also among the most interesting specialties of the Caucasus and made in considerable variety with doughs and fillings that take a number of forms. No meal is complete without one of them.

This selection of recipes has been created to display the versatility of the many fine and diverse breads, pastas, and savory pastries.

BLINY

Makes about 3½ dozen.

Buckwheat yeast pancakes, called *bliny* or *blini*, are notable Russian favorites, usually eaten as appetizers. Although they may be served stuffed or folded over, the preferred way is to spread the small thin pancakes with melted butter, then with a piece or slice of smoked, salted, or pickled fish or caviar, topped with a dab of sour cream. Other widely used fillings or spreads include mushrooms and cottage cheese. Each year during *Maslenitsa*, or "butter festival," the carnival week before Lent, Russians consume the pancakes in great quantities, as snacks throughout the day or with meals. *Bliny* batter is made in several variations, but a common mixture is that of half buckwheat and half white flour.

> *1 package active dry yeast or 1 cake compressed yeast*
> *1 cup lukewarm water*
> *2 cups warm milk*
> *1½ cups sifted all-purpose white flour*
> *3 eggs, separated*
> *1 teaspoon sugar*
> *1 teaspoon salt*
> *3 tablespoons unsalted butter, melted*
> *2½ cups sifted buckwheat flour*
> *Unsalted butter or shortening for frying*

Into a large bowl sprinkle the dry yeast or crumble the cake yeast. Add water (use very warm water [110 to 115 degrees] for dry yeast and lukewarm for cake yeast). Let stand a minute or two and then stir to dissolve. Add milk and white flour. Beat well and put in a warm place. Cover with a clean light towel, and let dough rise until doubled in bulk, about 1 hour.

In another bowl beat the egg yolks until creamy. Add sugar, salt, melted butter, and buckwheat flour. Stir into the yeast mixture. Set again in a warm place, covered, to rise for 1 hour. In another bowl beat egg whites until stiff; fold into the yeast mixture.

To cook, pour a little batter onto a hot greased griddle or into a heavy skillet over medium-high heat. Cook until lightly browned on the bottom. Turn over and cook on the other side. Keep warm while cooking the others. Serve on a platter accompanied by a small bowl of melted butter, one of sour cream, and a plate of chopped salt herring, sliced smoked salmon, or caviar.

ONION BREAD FROM KUBA

Makes 12 to 14 rounds.

This flatbread called *nan* or *non* is named for Kuba, one of the most attractive places in northeastern Azerbaijan, bounded by the Great Caucasus mountains, Dagestan, and the Caspian Sea. It is known as the "Orchard Town" as over one hundred varieties of apples and pears are grown here. Famous for its carpets and architectural sites, including a nineteenth-century bathhouse with two egg-shaped domes, and mosques, as well as a handsome tree-shaded park, the town also is noted for its hospitality and dining establishments that serve flavorful breads.

> *6 tablespoons unsalted butter*
> *2 medium yellow onions (about 1½ cups),*
>   *finely chopped*
> *1 teaspoon salt*
> *¾ cup warm water (110 to 115 degrees)*
> *2½ to 3 cups all-purpose flour*

In a large skillet melt 2 tablespoons butter over medium-high heat. Add onions. Sauté 4 minutes. Remove to a large bowl; cool. Add remaining 4 tablespoons butter in the skillet. Melt the butter. Add the salt dissolved in warm water, and the cooled onions. Sift in flour, adding about ½ cup at a time, using enough to make a soft, smooth dough. Form into a large, compact ball, kneading a little while shaping it. Place in a large bowl. Let rest, covered with a clean towel, about 30 minutes. Turn out onto a lightly floured board. Tear off pieces of dough to form 12 to 14 balls, each 1½ to 2 inches in diameter. With a floured rolling pin, roll each ball into a thin circle about 8 inches in diameter. To cook, fry each one, in a hot 10- to 12-inch ungreased pan over medium-high heat for 3 minutes on each side. As cooked, remove and dry on a rack. Stack in a basket. If too dry, restore by placing on a baking sheet and warming in a preheated 250-degree oven for about 4 minutes.

ARMENIAN THIN BREAD

Makes 4 sheets.

These sheets of Armenian flatbread called *lavash* are used to wrap around cheese, herbs, or grilled meats. It is especially good when served fresh from the oven.

> 1 package active dry yeast
> 1 cup warm water (110 to 115 degrees)
> ¼ cup (½ stick) unsalted butter, melted and cooled to lukewarm
> 1 teaspoon sugar
> 1½ teaspoons salt
> About 3½ cups all-purpose flour

In a large bowl sprinkle the yeast over the warm water. Stir to dissolve. Add the lukewarm butter, sugar, and salt. Gradually add the flour, ½ cup at a time, beating as adding and using enough to make a stiff dough. Shape into a smooth ball. Turn out onto a lightly floured board. Knead until smooth and elastic, about 7 minutes. Place in a buttered bowl and turn to coat on all sides. Let rise, covered with a clean cloth, in a warm place until doubled in bulk.

Preheat oven to 350 degrees. Punch down the dough. Divide into 4 equal pieces. On a lightly floured surface roll each piece into a 10 by 14-inch rectangle. Place on ungreased baking sheets and bake about 20 minutes, until golden brown. Remove from oven. Cool on racks.

GEORGIAN CHEESE BREAD

10 to 12 servings.

Of all the Georgian breads, the favorite is a marvelous cheese bread called *khachapuri*, made in several shapes and sizes with different kinds of dough. While enjoyed throughout the country with meals, it also is a favorite snack, sometimes called the Georgian pizza. Interestingly, the bread has distinct regional versions. One, Adjarian cheese bread, made in western Georgia, is boat-shaped and served topped with a cooked egg nestled in the center.

The recipe for this bread yields a large round loaf filled with a mixture of cheese and eggs, and is cooked without yeast, using yogurt and baking soda as a substitute. It is adapted from a collection of recipes in a booklet, *The Classic Cuisine of Georgia* by Julienne Margvelashvili, written to honor a group of Georgian chefs when they toured the United States in 1988. In it the author says, "There are various types of cheese bread depending upon which region of Georgia one may come from. The most universal is Emeretian *khachapuri*—a leavened dough filled with Emeretian cheese and baked quickly in a hot oven or cooked on a cast iron griddle atop the stove. The traditional plate 'ketsi' was the usual baking plate for *khachapuri* in ancient times when cooking was done on an open fire.

<u>*Dough*</u>:
½ cup plain yogurt
1 tablespoon sunflower oil
1 teaspoon baking soda
1 cup unbleached flour

<u>*Filling*</u>:
1 egg
¾ pound grated yellow (Muenster-style) cheese

Preheat oven to 400 degrees.

In a medium bowl combine the yogurt, oil, and baking soda. Add flour and mix well to make a round soft dough. Shape into a ball. Turn out onto a lightly floured surface. Roll to a 12-to 14-inch circle about ⅛ inch thick. Let rest while preparing the filling.

Break the egg into a small dish. Beat lightly. Reserve 1 teaspoon for glazing the bread. In a medium bowl combine the remaining egg with the cheese. Put into center of the dough circle, spreading evenly within 2 inches of the edge. Pick up the edges like a drawstring bag, pressing out all the air. Pinch and seal the dough in the center. Pat with floured hands; then flip over onto a greased baking sheet. Glaze the top with reserved egg. Make a small round hole in the center to allow steam to escape while baking. Place in upper third of the oven. Bake 5 minutes. Reduce heat to 350 degrees. Bake 15 minutes. Serve hot, cut in wedges or slices, as an appetizer or snack.

Note: For stovetop cooking, do not glaze or make a hole in the center. Cook, covered, on medium heat for 5 to 8 minutes in a lightly oiled griddle or cast-iron pan. Turn to cook on the other side until golden.

PITA POCKETS

A recipe for the familiar pita or pocket bread is not given in this book as top-quality kinds are readily available in American stores. As mentioned above, the bread can be used in many ways. For an easy-to-prepare specialty, brush the cut side of the bread with olive oil and sprinkle with a mixture of herbs and spices such as *za'atar*, a blend that generally includes thyme, sesame seeds, sumac, and hyssop. Made in several varieties, it is sold ready-made in Near Eastern stores.

Pita's hollow shape and mild flavor make it ideal as a pocket bread for sandwich ingredients. Split a pita round in half. Open the cut edge, leaving space for a filling. Here are a few filling suggestions.

1. Spread the bread with mustard; add thinly sliced cooked lamb and thin slices of cucumber. 2. Spread the bread with olive oil; fill with a chickpea salad or prepared hummus and sliced radishes. 3. Spread the bread with softened butter; fill with a mixture of feta cheese, chopped dates, and walnuts.

KUTASHI CORN BREAD

Makes 6.

In Imereti, a region of West Georgia, a staple bread called *mchadi* is made from a moist dough of finely ground yellow cornmeal and water that is shaped into flat, round cakes and baked in a clay dish, set in the fireplace or over an open fire. Eaten hot it is soft and moist, but when cold, it becomes hard and not palatable.

Kutasi, Georgia's second largest city in the province of Imereti, located along the Rioni River on the Tbilisi-Sukumi highway, was one of the main centers of ancient Colchis and also capital of the region. Today it is known for its attractive gardens, Bagrati Cathedral, museums, scenic views, thriving marketplace, and hospitable guest houses offering Georgian specialties.

> *1 cup stone-ground white cornmeal*
> *¼ teaspoon salt*

In a large bowl combine the cornmeal and salt. Gradually add about ½ cup cold water, enough to form a moist dough. Mix well. Leave for ½ hour. Shape into 6 flat oval cakes. Put in a lightly oiled 10-inch skillet over medium-high heat. Cook, covered, 8 minutes, until golden and crisp. Turn over and cook another 8 minutes. Serve at once.

YOGURT PANCAKES

6 to 8 servings.

Prepare these pancakes beforehand and keep refrigerated to use for breakfast.

> *2 cups plain yogurt*
> *½ cup milk*
> *2 eggs, slightly beaten*
> *2 cups all-purpose flour*
> *1 teaspoon baking powder*
> *½ teaspoon baking soda*
> *½ teaspoon salt*
> *2 teaspoons sugar*
> *2 tablespoons unsalted butter, melted*
> *Fat for frying*

In a large bowl combine the yogurt, milk, and eggs. Mix well. Sift in the flour, baking powder and soda, salt, and sugar. Mix well. Stir in the butter; mix again. To cook, pour 3 tablespoons batter onto a hot greased griddle or in a frying pan. When bubbles form on the top of the pancakes, turn over and cook on the other side. Keep warm in a preheated very slow oven (200 degrees) while frying the others. Serve with butter and a sweet syrup.

CHEESE-FILLED PASTA

Makes about 16.

Although traditionally associated with the Ukraine, a beloved all-purpose dumpling filled with cheese, fruit, or vegetables and called *varenky* or *varenik* also is a favorite in the Caucasus. A common filling consists of a sweetened white-cheese mixture. Serve as an accompaniment or dessert.

Cheese Filling:
1 pound (2 cups) farmer cheese, strained
1 egg yolk
2 tablespoons sugar
Salt

Dough:
2 cups all-purpose flour
1 teaspoon salt
2 eggs, slightly beaten
1 egg white, slightly beaten
Sour cream
Confectioners' sugar, optional

For the filling, in a medium bowl combine the cheese, egg yolk, and sugar. Add salt. Mix to blend well. Set aside.

For the dough, in a large bowl combine the flour and salt. Make a well in the center of the mixture and break the eggs into it. Stir in enough cold water (about ½ cup) to make a stiff dough. Turn out on a floured surface and knead about 1 minute, until smooth and elastic. Shape into a ball and let stand 1 hour. Roll out very thin on a floured board. Cut into small rounds, about 4 inches in diameter, rerolling any scraps of dough.

Place a spoonful of the cheese filling on lower half of each circle. Brush edges with egg white. Fold pastry over to form a half-circle; press edges together. Drop, a few at a time, into a large kettle of boiling water over medium-high heat. Cook briskly about 15 minutes, or until dumplings rise to the surface. With a slotted spoon remove and drain. Serve warm with sour cream, sweetened with confectioners' sugar, if desired.

NOODLES WITH SOUR CREAM

4 servings.

In the northern Caucasus noodles, called by different names, are made with a simple egg dough, sometimes flavored with cottage cheese or sour cream. The noodles are served in soups, baked in casseroles with cheese, or, as in this dish, garnished with sour cream and dill. Mushrooms are added for extra flavor. Serve with grilled lamb or chicken or meatballs.

> *8 ounces medium egg noodles, broken*
> *Salt*
> *3 tablespoons unsalted butter*
> *2 tablespoons fresh lemon juice*
> *1 cup sliced mushrooms*
> *1½ cups sour cream, at room temperature*
> *⅛ teaspoon paprika*
> *Freshly ground pepper*
> *2 tablespoons chopped fresh dill or parsley*

In a large saucepan cook the noodles in boiling salted water to cover over medium-high heat until tender. Drain. Keep warm. In a large saucepan melt the butter over medium-high heat. Add the lemon juice and mushrooms. Sauté 4 minutes. Stir in the sour cream and paprika. Season with salt and pepper. Reduce the heat to medium-low. Heat 2 to 3 minutes, until hot. Add the warm cooked noodles. Toss to combine the ingredients. Spoon into a bowl. Serve garnished with the dill or parsley.

Filled dough or dumplings are basic to Russian cookery, and there are a fascinating number of them, which vary from region to region. The most popular are *pelmeny*, or *pelmeni*, stuffed triangles or half-circles. Although Russian in origin, they are associated with Siberia where housewives in the large cold northern expanse once made them in great quantities to be used throughout the winter. Introduced to the Caucasus by the Tatars, the dumplings are commonly filled with a coriander-flavored ground lamb mixture. Given here are two fillings for the dumplings.

> *Cheese Filling:*
> *1½ cups pot or dry cottage cheese*
> *1 egg, beaten*
> *¼ cup sour cream, at room temperature*
> *2 tablespoons chopped fresh dill or parsley*
> *Salt, freshly ground pepper*

In a large bowl combine the cheese, egg, sour cream, and dill or parsley. Season with salt and pepper. Mix well.

> *Lamb Filling:*
> *1 tablespoon unsalted butter*
> *⅓ cup finely chopped onions*
> *½ pound lean ground lamb*
> *1 egg, beaten*
> *2 tablespoons chopped fresh coriander or parsley*
> *Salt, freshly ground pepper*

In a small skillet melt the butter over medium-high heat. Add the onions. Sauté 3 minutes. Add the lamb and cook, stirring, until the redness disappears. Spoon off any fat. Remove from the heat and cool. Stir in the egg and coriander or parsley. Season with salt and pepper.

Dough:
1½ *cups all-purpose flour*
1 *egg, at room temperature*
½ *teaspoon salt*
Unsalted butter, melted
Sour cream

In a large bowl put the flour in the center to form a mound. Make a well in the center; break the egg into it. Add the salt and 2 tablespoons water. With the tips of the fingers, mix the flour with the egg and salt. Add the water, a little at a time as needed, to form a stiff and compact ball of dough. Turn out on a floured surface and knead 5 to 10 minutes, or until dough is smooth and elastic. Cut dough into 2 portions. Roll out each portion as thin as possible. With a tumbler or cookie cutter, cut the dough into 3-inch circles. Place a small spoonful of the filling in the center of each circle. Dip the tip of a finger in cold water; rub around the edge of the dough. Fold over to form a crescent; pinch the edges to enclose the filling. When ready to cook, drop the filled dumplings, several at a time, into a large kettle of boiling salted water. Keeping the water at a steady boil, cook about 10 minutes, until the dough is cooked. With a slotted spoon remove and drain. Serve warm with melted butter and sour cream.

PASTA WITH EGGPLANT

6 to 8 servings.

Serve this flavorful duet as an accompaniment to any lamb or poultry dish.

> *1 medium eggplant, about 1¼ pounds*
> *Salt*
> *About ½ cup olive oil*
> *6 scallions, sliced, with some green tops*
> *1 garlic clove, crushed*
> *⅓ cup pine nuts or almond slivers*
> *3 tablespoons wine vinegar*
> *½ teaspoon cayenne pepper*
> *Salt, freshly ground pepper*
> *8 ounces seashells or other small pasta, cooked and*
>   *drained*
> *2 cups plain yogurt*
> *½ cup chopped fresh coriander or parsley*

Remove the stem end from the eggplant. Cut, unpeeled, into small cubes. Turn into a colander. Sprinkle with salt. Leave to drain for 30 minutes. Shake well to drain off any liquid. Wipe dry. In a large skillet heat 2 tablespoons oil over medium-high heat. Add the scallions, garlic, and pine nuts or almonds. Sauté 1 minute. Add eggplant cubes. Cook, stirring, and adding oil as needed, until soft. Stir in the vinegar and cayenne. Season with salt and pepper. Reduce the heat to medium-low. Cook slowly, covered, for 10 minutes, or until eggplant is cooked. Add the cooked pasta and heat through. Stir in the yogurt and coriander or parsley. Stir well and heat gently.

NOODLES WITH YOGURT SAUCE

6 servings.

Egg noodles are covered with a flavorful sauce enhanced by cheese and tomato paste. It's a good accompaniment for fish, meat, or poultry.

> *8 ounces egg noodles*
> *5 tablespoons unsalted butter*
> *1 large yellow onion, finely chopped*
> *1 to 2 garlic cloves, crushed*
> *3 tablespoons tomato paste*
> *3 tablespoons grated yellow cheese*
> *1 cup plain yogurt, at room temperature*
> *Dash of cayenne pepper*
> *Salt, freshly ground pepper*
> *1 teaspoon paprika*

Cook the noodles according to package directions and drain. Keep warm.

In a small skillet melt 3 tablespoons of butter over medium-high. Add the onion and garlic. Sauté 4 minutes. Stir in the tomato paste, cheese, yogurt, and cayenne. Season with salt and pepper. Mix well. Reduce the heat to medium-low. Heat about 2 minutes. Mix with the warm noodles in a serving dish. Meanwhile, in a small saucepan melt the remaining 2 tablespoons butter. Add paprika; mix well. Spoon over the noodles. Serve at once

MUSHROOM-FILLED PIROZHKI

Makes about 3½ dozen.

Small oval or round plump pastries made with nonsweet dough and filled with various food combinations are called *pirozhki*. The term is derived from an old Russian word *pir*, meaning "feast." *Pirozhki* are made with both raised dough and plain pastry, and can be filled with mixtures based on mushrooms, cabbage, chicken, ground beef, or fish. They are popular appetizers and also are served with soups. Generally those that will be used with soups are made a little larger, about 5 inches in diameter.

Dough:
1 envelope active dry yeast or 1 cake compressed yeast
¼ cup lukewarm water
½ cup (1 stick) unsalted butter
1 cup lukewarm milk
1 teaspoon salt
2 teaspoons sugar
4½ to 5 cups all-purpose flour
3 eggs
1 egg yolk

Mushroom Filling:
½ pound fresh mushrooms
3 tablespoons unsalted butter
½ cup finely chopped scallions, with some green tops
⅛ teaspoon freshly grated nutmeg
Salt, freshly ground pepper
3 tablespoons chopped fresh dill or parsley
¼ cup sour cream, at room temperature

Into a large bowl sprinkle the yeast or crumble the cake. Add the water. (Use very warm water for dry yeast and lukewarm for cake yeast.) After a minute or two, stir to dissolve. In another bowl put butter in the warm milk. Leave until melted. Add, with salt and sugar, to the yeast. Stir in 1 cup of flour and then the eggs, beating well after each addition. Add the remaining flour, enough to make a soft dough. Turn out on a floured board. Knead dough until smooth and elastic. Form into a large ball and put in a large buttered bowl. Turn the dough over so it becomes greased on all sides. Leave in a warm place, covered with a clean towel, until doubled in bulk, about 1½ hours.

Meanwhile, make the mushroom filling. Clean mushrooms by rinsing quickly or wiping with wet paper towels. Cut off any tough stem ends. Chop finely. In a small skillet melt butter over medium-high heat. Add scallions. Sauté 2 minutes. Add mushrooms. Sauté 4 minutes. Season with nutmeg, salt, and pepper. Remove from heat. Stir in dill or parsley and sour cream. Let cool.

Punch down dough. Turn out on a floured board. Knead until smooth and elastic. Heat oven to 400 degrees. Cut off small pieces of dough and flatten into thin circles, about 2½ inches in diameter. Place about 1 teaspoon mushroom filling in the center of each circle. Bring up the dough around the filling to secure completely. Shape into a smooth round. Place on a greased baking sheet. Let rise, covered with a light cloth or towel, in a warm place for 20 minutes, or somewhat larger. Meanwhile, in a small bowl mix the egg yolk and 2 tablespoons cold water. Brush tops of pastries with it. Bake for about 20 minutes, or until tops are golden and dough is baked. Serve warm.

This delectable filled dough called *kulebiaka*, which can be made with a short pastry or yeast dough, may be filled with white fish or salmon or a combination of the two, and can include *kasha* instead of rice. Serve as an appetizer, first course, or buffet dish.

Dough:
1 package active dry yeast or 1 cake compressed yeast
⅔ cup lukewarm milk
¼ cup (½ stick) unsalted butter, melted
4 eggs
1 tablespoon sugar
Pinch of salt
3 ½ cups (about) sifted all-purpose flour
2 cups cold cooked rice
3 hard-cooked eggs, sliced

Salmon Filling:
¼ cup (½ stick) unsalted butter
2 medium yellow onions, finely chopped
1 cup chopped mushrooms
2 tablespoons fresh lemon juice
3 cups flaked cooked red salmon
¼ cup chopped fresh dill
Salt, freshly ground pepper

Into a large bowl sprinkle or crumble the yeast. Add some of the milk. (It should be slightly warmer for dry yeast). After a minute or two, stir to dissolve. Add remaining milk, melted butter, 3 eggs (one at a time), sugar, and salt. Mix well. Add 1½ cups flour and beat well to combine ingredients. Add remaining flour, enough to make a soft dough. Beat well again. Turn dough onto a floured board; knead until smooth and elastic. Form into a large ball and place in a greased bowl, turning dough over once to grease the other side. Leave in a warm place, covered with a towel, until doubled in bulk, about 1½ hours.

Meanwhile make the salmon filling. In a medium saucepan melt the butter over medium-high heat. Add the onions. Sauté for 3 minutes. Add mushrooms and lemon juice. Sauté 4 minutes. In a large bowl combine the sautéed vegetables with the salmon and dill. Season with salt and pepper. Mix well. Cool.

Punch down dough and turn out onto a floured board. Knead again. Roll into a rectangle, 20 inches by 14 inches. Spread ½ of the salmon filling lengthwise along the center of the rectangle, leaving a 4-inch border on all sides. Place layers of rice, egg slices, and remaining salmon filling over the dough. Bring the long sides of the dough together and pinch. Fold the two short sides over and pinch. Seal the edges with water; press to close firmly.

Butter and flour a baking sheet. Carefully place the filled dough on it so that the sealed edges are down. Make several small slashes in the top of the dough. Cover with a cloth. Let rise in a warm place for about 30 minutes, until light and enlarged. Preheat oven to 375 degrees. In a small dish beat the remaining egg slightly. Brush over the top. Bake about 30 minutes, until the dough is crisp and golden. To serve, slice crosswise.

Note: The top may be decorated with pastry leaves cut from the dough, if desired.

BOEREKS

One of the most versatile savory pastries is a fried or baked crisp, filled del-icacy called *boerek* or similar names, which takes many forms. Made with sheets of thin pastry, and filled with cheese or meat mixtures, how it is served depends on its size, shape, and filling. The little ones, made into very small rolls, triangles, or other shapes, are eaten as appetizers, while more substantial varieties are served as or with the meal itself. One example is the tray *boerek*. Of enormous size, it is comprised of several sheets of pas-try, each brushed with milk and melted butter. Its center filling is a spicy ground meat or spinach mixture. Baked until golden and crisp, it is cut into large squares and eaten piping hot.

CHEESE-FILLED PASTRY

6 to 8 servings.

This so-called pie may be served as a main course.

> *1 pound small curd cottage cheese*
> *½ pound feta or Muenster cheese, crumbled or grated*
> *½ cup minced yellow onions*
> *1 cup plain yogurt*
> *2 eggs, beaten*
> *Salt, freshly ground pepper*
> *½ pound (about 25 sheets) phyllo*
> *About ¾ cup (1½ sticks) unsalted butter, melted*

Preheat oven to 350 degrees.

In a large bowl combine the cheeses, onions, yogurt, and eggs. Season with salt and pepper. Mix to combine well. In a buttered 12 by 9 by 3-inch bak-ing dish, place ⅓ of the pastry sheets, each brushed with melted butter and folded over, in the dish. Brush just before putting in the dish. Spread half the cheese mixture over the pastry sheets. Repeat the brushing of another ⅓ of the sheets and place them, another layer of the cheese mixture, and the remaining ⅓ of the sheets in a dish. Brush the top generously with melted butter. Bake for 1 to 1¼ hours, until golden and crisp on top. To serve, cut into squares or rectangles. Serve warm.

Note: Keep the pastry sheets covered with a moistened cloth while preparing the dish. Otherwise, the sheets will become dry and crumble.

LAMB-FILLED
NOODLE CRESCENTS

Makes about 36.

These are a good main dish for an outdoor meal.

> *Filling:*
> *1¼ cups cooked ground lamb,*
> *drained of any fat*
> *2 tablespoons minced scallions,*
> *with some green tops*
> *¼ cup plain yogurt*
> *1 egg, slightly beaten*
> *2 tablespoons chopped fresh coriander,*
> *dill, or parsley*
> *Dash of cayenne pepper*
> *Salt, freshly ground pepper*
>
> *Dough:*
> *1½ cups all-purpose flour*
> *1 egg, at room temperature*
> *½ teaspoon salt*
> *Plain yogurt*
> *Unsalted butter, melted*
> *Cayenne pepper*

In a large bowl combine the lamb, scallions, yogurt, egg, and coriander, dill, or parsley. Add the cayenne, salt, and pepper. Mix thoroughly. Set aside.

In a large bowl spoon the flour into a mound. Make a depression in the center. Break the egg into it. Add the salt and 2 tablespoons of water. Working with the tips of the fingers, mix the flour with the egg and water to combine well. Gradually add more water, a little at a time, as needed, to form a stiff and compact ball of dough. Turn out on a floured surface. Knead about 5 minutes, until the dough is smooth and elastic. Divide the dough

Cuisines of the Caucasus Mountains

into 2 portions. Roll out each portion, turning over and rolling several times, on a floured board until as thin as possible. With a tumbler or cookie cutter cut into 3-inch rounds. Put a small spoonful of the lamb filling on each round. Dip the tip of a finger in water, and rub around the edge of the dough. Fold over to form a crescent, and pinch the edges together.

In a large saucepan of boiling salted water over medium-high heat drop several of the filled noodles at a time. Cook about 8 minutes, or until cooked. Drain. Serve warm with yogurt, melted butter, and a sprinkling of cayenne powder.

DESSERTS
AND SWEETS

When traveling in the Caucasus it is interesting to note that the number of dessert selections on most restaurant menus is generally quite limited. In fact very often there are only a few tempting items that are apt to be the same wherever you wander. Yet this is not to say that there is a lack of marvelous toothsome sweets. For one suddenly discovers that bakeries, pastry shops, and confectioners' stores are simply aglow with calorie-laden delights.

It soon becomes quite apparent in these lands that desserts are rather simple ones, especially fresh fruits of many kinds, cheese, ice cream, or a light pudding. The luscious sweets, like thick syrup pastries, jams, preserves, rich puddings and creams, are generally in-between delights, consumed in enviable quantities throughout the day and evening. A most popular pastime is to visit an indoor milk shop or outdoor café for a sampling of a favorite taste-tempter.

The offering of sweets in the home is a pleasurable Caucasus symbol of hospitality, for a guest is generally welcomed with a spoonful of preserves and a glass of water, a slice of gooey pastry, plateful of dates, honey almonds, or walnut confections.

Since ancient times honey has been the favorite sweetener in the Caucasus and, despite the contemporary generous consumption of sugar, is still used profusely in making sweets, many of them similar to those of the Near East. Of the many varieties, *baklava*, oozing with syrup and nuts, is perhaps the best known. Others are fried dough, cakes, and pastries, some with such tantalizing appellations as sweetheart's lips, lady's navel, women's dimples, or glad-eyes.

Caucasian fruits are especially luscious and the great number of orchards and favorable climatic conditions ensure an inviting supply of some variety during each season of the year. With fascinating anticipation the arrival of apples, pears, all kinds of berries, and especially glorious figs, grapes, melons, peaches, quinces, apricots, grapes, pomegranates, persimmons, red currants, and cherries, to name only a few, is eagerly awaited. Caucasians are particularly fond of the Cornelian cherry, not a true cherry but rather the fruit of the dogwood family that is used in all kinds of dishes, including sweets.

Although treasured fresh and placed as a dining table centerpiece at most meals, the fruit also is made into compotes, pastries, and confections. Candied fruits are special treats and the peels of some, such as the orange and lemon, are utilized extensively in the cookery. Favorite flavorings are flower waters, particular rose and orange flower.

Russians and Caucasians are extremely fond of sherbets and ice creams. Visitors to the area always are delighted with the availability and quality of the "frozen stuff," made with a fascinating range of fruits and flavorings. It's a traditional family outing to drop in at a café for a local favorite. Another popular custom is to visit a milk shop, a tiny place buzzing with activity, for a bowl of yogurt, yogurt drink, or milk pudding—a chalk-white, gelatinous dish fancily decorated with a sprinkling of spices and ground nuts and flavored with flower water.

Recipes for some of the best of the traditional dishes that can be easily prepared in Western kitchens are included here.

KISSEL

4 to 6 servings.

One of the oldest and most widely enjoyed Russian desserts is a simple fruit gelatin-like pudding called *kissel*, made by thickening puréed cooked fruit with cornstarch. Its name derives from the word *kisley*, "sour," and the preferred fruits are those with tart flavors, such as cranberries, rhubarb, sour cherries, or apples, as well as all kinds of berries. The thickness of the dessert can vary from that of jelly to a bit more runny consistency. Customarily it is served with thick cream.

> *2 cups fruit purée*
> *3 to 6 tablespoons sugar, depending on the tartness of*
> *the fruit*
> *2 to 3 tablespoons cornstarch*

In a medium saucepan heat the purée over medium-high heat. Add the sugar. Bring to a boil, stirring. Reduce the heat to medium-low. Cook, stirring, 2 to 3 minutes, until sugar is dissolved. Meanwhile, in a small dish blend the cornstarch, the amount varying according to the desired consistency, with a little cold water to make a smooth paste. Stir into fruit mixture. Cook, stirring constantly, about 3 minutes, or until mixture thickens. Remove from heat and cool, stirring occasionally. Spoon into serving dishes. Refrigerate, covered, up to 4 hours. Serve with whipped cream, if desired.

HONEY MOUSSE

4 servings.

Some of the simple Russian desserts like this one, made with honey and eggs, are called by the French term, mousse or *muss*.

> *4 eggs, separated*
> *1 cup honey*
> *1 teaspoon grated lemon rind*

In a medium saucepan combine the egg yolks, honey, and lemon rind over medium-low heat. Cook, stirring constantly, until mixture thickens. Remove from heat. Cool at room temperature. Meanwhile, in a large bowl whip eggs whites until stiff. Fold into honey mixture. Spoon into dessert dishes. Refrigerate, covered, up to 4 hours. Serve with whipped cream, if desired.

EASTER PASKHA

12 servings.

Paskha is the Russian word for Easter as well as for a marvelous traditional rich dessert to honor that very special holiday. The dessert is a splendid, gaily decorated tall, round or pyramid creation made with pot cheese, nuts, and candied fruits. Her *paskha* is the pride of every Russian housewife. In the old days most households had a special four-sided wooden mold in the shape of a pyramid, which was carved inside with a cross and the letters XB (*Khristos voskrese*: Christ is risen). Otherwise an ordinary two-quart flowerpot with a hole in the center for drainage may be used. Very important to the preparation of *paskha* is the firmness of the dessert, as it must be able to maintain its shape after unmolding. On the Easter table the dessert is served with *kulich*, a raisin-studded yeast bread.

> *3 pounds farmer or pot cheese*
> *1 cup (2 sticks) unsalted butter, softened*
> *1 cup sugar*
> *3 egg yolks, beaten*
> *1 cup heavy cream*
> *½ cup chopped blanched almonds, plus additional for garnish*
> *½ cup mixed candied fruits, plus additional for garnish*

To be sure the cheese is completely dry, wrap it in cheesecloth and place in a colander to drain off any liquid. Put cheese through a fine sieve into a large bowl. Add butter; mix well. In a small dish combine the sugar and egg yolks; mix well. Add, with the cream, almonds, and fruit, beating after each addition and stirring while adding, to the cheese mixture. Blend to make as smooth as possible. Line a *paskha* mold or ordinary flowerpot that has a hole in the bottom for drainage with fine cheesecloth that has been rinsed in cold water and wrung out. Pour cheese mixture into the mold or pot and bring the cheesecloth up around the mixture to cover it. Put a weight on top of the cheesecloth-wrapped mixture. Leave at room temperature for 24 hours to drain. Unmold onto a serving plate. Decorate the sides and top with candied fruits and almonds. Place fresh flowers and green leaves on the plate around the dessert, if desired. The dessert will keep in the refrigerator for several days.

PISTACHIO MILK PUDDING

6 servings.

In the Caucasus cold solid milk puddings made with cooked rice and milk or milk thickened with rice flour, and garnished with finely chopped nuts or ground spices, are favorite desserts and snacks. Many of them are garnished with chopped pistachios, a pale green nut with a fine texture and distinctive pleasing flavor, native to the Near East and/or Central Asia where they have been flourishing for centuries. The beloved foods are eaten out of the shell, or salted, as snacks, and used for flavoring pastries, desserts, and confections, as well as a garnish. While the pistachio shell is ivory, the kernel inside comes in a marvelous range of greens, making it one of the world's most attractive nuts. This is a short-cut method for making a classic pudding.

> *½ cup cornstarch*
> *4 cups cold milk*
> *⅓ cup sugar*
> *1 teaspoon rose water or vanilla extract*
> *1 teaspoon ground cinnamon*
> *Finely chopped pistachios*

In a small bowl dissolve the cornstarch in 1 cup of milk. In a medium saucepan combine the remaining 3 cups milk and sugar over medium-high heat. Bring to a boil. Cook, stirring, 2 to 3 minutes, until sugar is dissolved. Reduce the heat to medium-low. Add the dissolved cornstarch mixture. Cook, stirring, about 10 minutes, until mixture is thickened. Stir in rose water or vanilla. Spoon into a shallow serving dish or individual bowls. Sprinkle with cinnamon and pistachios. Refrigerate, covered, 1 hour, up to 6.

ARMENIAN BAKED APRICOTS

6 servings.

The luscious apricot is a fruit belonging to the rose family that is rich in iron and calcium and "keeps you looking, thinking, feeling calm and lovable." A beloved Armenian food, it's widely used in the cookery. The fruit goes particularly well with lamb and is included in rice dishes, stews, vegetable casseroles, desserts, and confections. Sometimes called the Golden Gift of Armenia, it was believed by the ancients to have originated in that country as its scientific name is *Prunus armeniaca*. Naturally sweet and fragrant, fresh and dried apricots are widely eaten and used in the cookery of the Caucasus. Some of the people believe that a major reason for their longevity is because they eat so much of the fruit.

14 (about 2 pounds) firm fresh apricots
Fresh lemon juice
¾ cup sugar
1 teaspoon vanilla extract
Whipped cream

Preheat oven to 375 degrees.

Wash and peel the apricots. Cut into halves along their natural lines. Remove the pits. In a shallow baking dish arrange the apricots and sprinkle with a little lemon juice. Meanwhile, in a small saucepan combine the sugar, 1 cup water, and vanilla over medium-high heat. Bring to a boil. Reduce the heat to medium-low. Cook 5 minutes. Pour over the apricots. Bake about 25 minutes, or until apricots are soft. Serve warm. Or cool and refrigerate. Serve cold with whipped cream.

APRICOT-RAISIN CONFECTION

Makes about 48.

One of the traditional foods of the Armenian Christmas, celebrated on the sixth of January, is a confection made with apricots, raisins, and walnuts.

> 2 cups golden raisins
> 1 cup dried apricots
> ½ cup shelled walnuts
> ½ cup confectioners' or granulated sugar,
>   plus additional for rolling
> 1 teaspoon vanilla extract

In a food processor, using the steel blade, chop the raisins, apricots, and walnuts. Add ½ cup sugar and vanilla. Process to make a fine mixture. Shape into ¾-inch balls. Roll in sugar. Store in single layers between wax paper in an airtight container. Keep in a cool dry place.

MOUNT ARARAT PUDDING

6 servings.

Legend has it that when Noah's ark came to rest on Mount Ararat in what is now northeastern Turkey, rising majestically across the border from Armenia, the occupants realized that a feast of celebration was called for but their supplies were almost exhausted. Noah ordered everyone to collect whatever was available and put them together. So they did as he directed and prepared a pudding made of nuts, fruits, raisins, grains, and spices. Over the years it became known by various names in the Near East and Caucasus where the basic ingredient is rice or bulgur. This is one of many versions.

> *5 tablespoons unsalted butter*
> *½ cup slivered blanched almonds*
> *½ cup golden raisins*
> *1 cup coarsely chopped walnuts*
> *½ teaspoon ground cinnamon*
> *1 cup medium bulgur*
> *1 ¾ cups orange juice*
> *Salt*

In a medium skillet melt 2 tablespoons butter over medium-high heat. Add the almonds, raisins, walnuts, and cinnamon. Sauté 2 to 3 minutes. Remove from the heat.

In a large saucepan, melt the remaining 3 tablespoons butter over medium-high heat. Add the bulgur; sauté about 4 minutes, until brown and toasted. Pour in the orange juice. Season with salt. Mix well. Bring to a boil. Reduce the heat to medium-low. Cook, covered, about 25 minutes, until bulgur is tender but still crunchy and liquid has been absorbed. Add the fruit mixture. Stir well. Serve at once.

PUMPKIN-NUT PUDDING

6 servings.

The New World pumpkin became a common dessert food in the cuisines of the Caucasus where one favorite way of serving it is as a pudding such as this one.

> *2 pounds pumpkin, peeled and*
>   *cut into 1½-inch pieces*
> *About 1 cup sugar*
> *1 teaspoon ground cinnamon (optional)*
> *1½ cups finely chopped walnuts or hazelnuts*
> *Heavy or clotted cream*

Remove any stringy fibers from the pumpkin pieces. In a large saucepan combine the pumpkin and about 1 cup water over medium-low heat. Cook, covered, about 20 minutes, or until just tender. Add the sugar and continue cooking another 10 minutes. Remove from the stove and cool in the saucepan. Stir in the cinnamon. Turn into a large bowl. Serve at room temperature or refrigerate and serve cold sprinkled with the nuts and accompanied with cream.

FIGS IN WINE

6 servings.

One of the oldest and best Caucasian fruits is the wholesome small pear-shaped fig, grown in several varieties and colors and enjoyed fresh or dried. For dessert, fresh figs are eaten out of hand, served sliced with cream or a squeeze of lemon juice, or paired with green grapes. They also may be stuffed with nuts or served in red wine or honey. Dried figs can be cooked with other fruits as compotes, candied, made into preserves, or eaten plain. This and the next recipe are for two fig specialties.

18 fresh ripe figs
½ cup dry red wine
2 to 3 tablespoons honey
½ cup heavy cream, whipped
⅓ cup slivered blanched almonds

Preheat oven to 350 degrees.

Put the figs in a shallow baking dish. Cover with wine. Bake, covered, basting occasionally with the wine, for 30 minutes, or until the figs are hot and plump. Remove from the stove. Spoon figs into a serving dish. Drizzle with the wine drippings and honey. Top with whipped cream. Sprinkle with almonds.

NUT-STUFFED FIGS

Makes 12.

12 large dried figs
4 tablespoons finely chopped walnuts
2 tablespoons honey
12 large almond slivers

Preheat oven to 350 degrees.

With scissors or a small sharp knife, cut the stems off the figs. With a small finger or tip of a small knife, make a deep depression in the stem end of each fig. Stuff 1 teaspoon of the walnuts and a little honey into each depression, packing tightly. Pinch openings firmly closed. Arrange figs, pinched sides up, on an ungreased baking sheet. Bake 15 minutes, turning once. Remove from the oven. Press an almond into the outside of each fig. Serve warm.

NUT-FILLED SHREDDED PASTRY

6 servings.

In the Caucasus, particularly Armenia, a favorite dessert called *kadaif* is made with soft, white uncooked dough or pastry strands shaped into small oblong rolls stuffed with spices and nuts, then baked, and while still warm, moistened with a light syrup. While the shredded pastry dough can be bought fresh or frozen, some cooks in America use the breakfast cereal, shredded wheat, as a substitute.

> *6 shredded wheat biscuits*
> *2 cups sugar*
> *1 tablespoon rose water, orange-flower water or*
> *   1 teaspoon vanilla*
> *1 cup chopped walnuts*
> *1½ cups heavy cream, whipped*

Preheat oven to 425 degrees.

Crush shredded wheat into a shallow baking dish. Toast in oven about 20 minutes. Meanwhile, in a medium saucepan combine the sugar and 1 cup water over medium-high heat. Boil about 4 minutes, until the consistency of a thick syrup. Add the flower water or vanilla. Remove from the heat. Place toasted shredded wheat on 6 individual small serving plates. Cover with the syrup. Let cool at room temperature. Sprinkle each serving with chopped walnuts. Top with whipped cream.

Caucasians are extremely fond of compotes made with their great variety of fresh fruit, prepared and eaten in season. Cooked in sweetened water and served cold, sometimes topped with a spoonful of *kaymak* (thickened cream) or ground nuts, they are customarily flavored with spices, wines, liqueurs, or fruit rinds, and sometimes include chopped nuts. The amount of sugar required varies according to the type of fruit and according to individual tastes. Some of the compotes are made with a combination of fruits, which are cooked separately. This is a general recipe that can be varied to taste with apricots, berries, oranges, figs, plums, peaches, pears, and quinces.

> *2 pounds fresh fruit*
> *1½ to 2 cups sugar*
> *1 tablespoon fresh lemon juice or wine*
> *1 cinnamon stick*
> *Whipped cream (optional)*

Prepare fruit by washing, peeling, coring or removing any pits. Cut into halves or quarters. In a medium saucepan combine the sugar, lemon juice or wine, cinnamon stick, and fruit with water to cover over medium-high heat. Bring to a boil. Reduce heat to medium-low. Cook, covered, until fruit is tender but not mushy. The time will depend on the kind of fruit. Remove from the heat. Take out and discard the cinnamon stick. Cool. Refrigerate to chill. Serve cold with fresh or whipped cream, if desired.

BAKED QUINCES

4 to 6 servings.

The aromatic hard, acid apple-like rich yellow or greenish yellow quince, noted for its appealing rich flavor, is a favorite food in the Caucasus where it has long had mythological significance. Not only was it used in love potions but also to make savory and sweet dishes including jams, preserves, and desserts, some reserved for festival and holiday celebrations. The quince has to be cooked before it can be eaten.

> *4 medium quinces, about 2 pounds*
> *⅓ cup honey*
> *2 tablespoons lemon juice*
> *½ teaspoon ground allspice*

Preheat oven to 425 degrees.

Wash quinces. Cut into halves, peel and core, removing seeds. Cut into slices. Arrange in a shallow baking dish. Top with the honey, lemon juice, allspice, and 2 to 3 tablespoons water. Bake, covered, about 45 minutes, until fruit is tender and syrup is slightly thickened.

YOGURT FRITTERS IN SYRUP

8 servings.

This is a typical sweet snack or dessert that one finds in pastry shops throughout the Caucasus. The fritters also are enjoyed with tea or coffee in the home.

> *Syrup:*
> *1 cup sugar*
> *1 teaspoon strained fresh lemon juice*
> *⅛ teaspoon ground cinnamon*
> *¼ cup honey*
>
> *Fritters:*
> *4 eggs*
> *1 cup plain yogurt*
> *2 cups all-purpose flour*
> *2 teaspoons sugar*
> *1 tablespoon baking powder*
> *1 teaspoon baking soda*
> *Vegetable oil for deep frying*
> *Garnish: ¼ cup finely chopped walnuts or pistachios*

For the syrup, in a small saucepan combine the sugar, ⅔ cup water, lemon juice, and cinnamon over medium-high heat. Bring to a boil. Cook, stirring, 2 or 3 minutes, or until sugar is dissolved. Stir in honey. Reduce the heat to medium-low. Cook, uncovered, for 10 minutes. Remove from the heat and cool.

For the fritters, in a large bowl combine the eggs and yogurt. Whisk to blend well. In another bowl combine the flour, sugar, baking powder, and baking soda. Add to yogurt mixture. Blend well.

In a deep fryer or heavy saucepan heat 4 inches oil over moderate-high heat. Drop 1 tablespoon of the batter at a time, into hot oil. Fry until evenly browned on all sides. With a slotted spoon remove from the oil. Drain on paper towels. To serve, mound fritters on a serving plate. Pour syrup over them. Sprinkle with nuts.

BAKLAVA

Makes about 20 pieces

Baklava, or *paklava*, a crisp, wonderfully rich sweet made from thin pastry sheets, chopped nuts, and a thick syrup, is an internationally known dessert that is well-liked in the Caucasus where the recipes vary from one household to another. Although the paper-thin pastry was once prepared in the home, the process is very difficult so it's usually purchased. Nobody knows the origin of the sweet but it has been prepared in the Near Eastern countries for centuries. This is one of many variations.

> *1 pound phyllo pastry sheets*
> *About 1 cup (2 sticks) unsalted butter, melted*
> *1 pound (4 cups) shelled walnuts, coarsely chopped*
> *½ cup chopped blanched almonds*
> *2 cups sugar*
> *1 teaspoon ground cinnamon*
> *¼ cup honey*
> *3 tablespoons fresh lemon juice*

Preheat oven to 375 degrees.

Arrange ⅓ of the pastry sheets, each one brushed with melted butter, in a buttered baking dish (13 by 9 by 2-inches). In a small bowl combine the walnuts, almonds, ½ cup sugar, and cinnamon. Sprinkle ½ of mixture over pastry sheets. Place another third of the sheets, each one brushed with melted butter, over nut mixture. Repeat with another layer of nut mixture and remaining ⅓ of pastry sheets. With a sharp knife, cut into diamond-shaped pieces. Bake 1 hour, or until the top is golden and crisp. Remove from oven; cool a little.

Meanwhile, in a medium saucepan combine remaining 1½ cups sugar, 1½ cups water, honey, and lemon juice over medium-high heat. Bring to a boil. Reduce heat to medium-low. Cook, uncovered, about 10 minutes, until mixture thickens. While still warm pour over the *baklava*. Leave at room temperature until ready to serve.

WALNUT CAKE

Makes about 16 pieces.

Caucasians are very fond of either a plain or nut-flavored cake, which is covered with a sweet syrup. This version is flavored with lemon rind and one of the region's most widely used foods, walnuts.

> ½ cup (1 stick) unsalted butter, softened
> 2½ cups sugar
> 2 eggs, slightly beaten
> 2 cups sifted all-purpose flour
> 1 teaspoon baking powder
> 1 teaspoon baking soda
> ½ teaspoon ground cinnamon
> ⅔ cup sour milk
> 1 cup chopped walnuts
> Grated rind of 1 lemon

Preheat oven to 350 degrees.

In a large bowl cream the butter. Add 1 cup of sugar and eggs, 1 at a time. Cream until light and fluffy. Sift in the flour, baking powder, baking soda, and cinnamon, adding alternately with sour milk. Mix in the walnuts and lemon rind. Blend well. Spoon the batter into a greased rectangular baking dish (13 by 9 by 2 inches). Bake for 45 minutes, until tester inserted into the center comes out clean.

Meanwhile, in a medium saucepan combine 1½ cups sugar with 1 cup water over medium-high heat. Cook, uncovered, about 12 minutes, until thickened. When cake is cooked, remove from the oven. While still warm, cover with the syrup. Turn off the oven. Put the cake back in the oven for 5 minutes. Cut into diamond shapes. Serve warm or cool.

LEMON YOGURT CAKE

Makes about 10 servings.

This is a traditional Near Eastern dessert that has an exceptional tangy flavor derived from the combination of fresh lemon juice and yogurt. It's easy to make and ideal to serve with afternoon tea.

½ cup (1 stick) unsalted butter, softened
⅔ cup sugar
2 eggs, beaten
2 teaspoons grated lemon rind
1 cup plain yogurt
2 cups sifted all-purpose flour
2 teaspoons baking powder
½ teaspoon baking soda
½ teaspoon salt
Confectioners' sugar

Preheat oven to 350 degrees. Grease and lightly flour a 9-inch square baking dish.

In a large bowl cream the butter with the sugar until light and fluffy. Add eggs, one at a time. Stir in lemon rind and yogurt. Mix well. Sift in flour, baking powder, baking soda, and salt. Beat until smooth. Turn into prepared dish. Bake about 35 minutes, until a tester inserted into center comes out clean. Remove to a rack. Cool in pan for 5 minutes. Turn out on a rack. Sprinkle with confectioners' sugar. Cut into squares. Serve warm or cool.

TWIGS

Makes about 3 dozen.

These deep-fried cookies take their name, *khvorost*, from the Russian word for firewood kindling—twigs or branches—which they somewhat resemble.

> ½ cup milk
> 2 eggs, beaten
> 2 tablespoons brandy
> ¼ cup sugar
> ½ teaspoon salt
> 2½ to 3 cups sifted all-purpose flour
> Vegetable oil for deep-frying
> Confectioners' sugar
> Ground cinnamon

In a large bowl combine the milk, eggs, brandy, sugar, and salt. Mix well. Gradually add flour, enough to make a stiff dough. Turn out on a floured board. Knead until smooth. With a rolling pin roll out thinly. Cut into 5 by 1-inch strips. Make a lengthwise slit down the center of each strip, allowing 1 inch on each end uncut. Put one end of the dough through the slit to form a sort of loop. Deep-fry a few at a time in hot oil (375 degrees on a frying thermometer) about 3 minutes, until golden. With a slotted spoon remove from the oil. Drain on paper towels. Sprinkle with confectioners' sugar and cinnamon. Cool.

CINNAMON COOKIES

Makes about 6 dozen.

Cinnamon, one of the world's oldest spices, thought in ancient times to inspire love, is a beloved flavoring in the Caucasus, especially in Armenia where it is widely used in vegetable and meat dishes as well as desserts and baked goods.

> *2 eggs, beaten*
> *1 cup sugar*
> *1⅔ cups sifted all-purpose flour*
> *1 teaspoon ground cinnamon*
> *⅓ cup blanched almond slivers*
> *1 tablespoons fresh lemon juice*
> *2 teaspoons grated lemon rind*

Preheat oven to 350 degrees.

In a large bowl combine the eggs and sugar; mix well. Add the flour and cinnamon; mix again. Stir in almonds, lemon juice, and lemon rind. Mix to thoroughly combine ingredients. Chill in refrigerator 1 hour. Turn out on a floured board. Roll to a thickness of ¼ inch. Cut into 3 by ½-inch strips. Arrange on a lightly floured greased baking sheet. Bake about 15 minutes, until cooked. Remove to a rack and cool.

GEORGIAN WALNUT SWEET

*Makes about 20 pieces,
depending on the shapes.*

One of Georgia's favorite confections is a honey-walnut confection called *gozinaki* that is prepared traditionally for the New Year. This is a typical recipe for it.

> *1½ cups honey*
> *⅓ cup sugar*
> *1 pound walnuts, shelled and finely chopped*

Chill a baking sheet in the refrigerator. In a small saucepan combine the honey and sugar over medium-high heat. Bring to a boil, stirring constantly, until sugar is dissolved. Reduce heat to medium-low. Add walnuts. Cook about 12 minutes, until thickened. Pour onto the chilled baking sheet, spreading evenly. Cool. Cut into small squares or diamond shapes.

MOUNT KAZBEK
HONEY WALNUTS

Makes about 4 cups.

One of the most acclaimed places in the Caucasus is snow-capped Mt. Kazbek, an extinct volcano of 16,541 feet, in the magnificent mountain region of northern Georgia reached along the Military Highway. Of the many myths connected with the mountain, the most famous is that it's where the angry gods of Greek mythology banished Promethus for stealing fire from heaven and sharing its secrets with mortals. For doing so he was chained to a rock and tortured by an eagle picking at his liver until Hercules killed the eagle and rescued him. The nearest place to stay while visiting the mountain is in the town of Kazbegi, dominated by a glorious view of Kazbek to the northwest.

Honey walnuts are a healthful snack for mountaineers or for any at home who wish to have a delicious treat made with two favorite Georgian foods, walnuts and honey.

> 2 tablespoons unsalted butter, melted
> ½ cup honey
> ½ teaspoon grated lemon rind
> ¼ teaspoon ground cinnamon
> 4 cups shelled walnuts

In a medium saucepan combine the butter, honey, lemon rind, and cinnamon over medium-high heat. Bring to a boil. Add the walnuts. Reduce the heat to medium-low. Cook, stirring occasionally, about 12 minutes, until walnuts are well coated with the honey mixture. Remove from the heat and spread on foil. Cool. Store in an airtight container.

NUT-STUFFED DATES

Makes 1 pound.

The dark brown shiny date with a high sugar content is a revered food, accorded a place of honor on the tables of many Caucasian homes, particularly in Azerbaijan. A plateful of dates is traditionally served as a welcome or congratulatory gesture. The fruit is eaten as an appetizer and snack, included in many dishes, and served as a special finale for many special meals. For dessert, dates are baked in cookies, mixed with fruits, or sweetened with honey, and made into a confection known by the Persian word *halva*, customarily served as a ceremonial food. Special treats are dates filled with ground pistachios, almonds, or pine nuts, flavored with sugar and rose water.

> *½ cup finely chopped almonds*
> *½ cup chopped walnuts*
> *¼ cup chopped pistachios*
> *1 pound pitted dates*
> *Confectioners' sugar*

In a small bowl combine the almonds, walnuts, and pistachios. Stuff each date with a little of the mixture. Roll in confectioners' sugar. Store in an airtight container.

BEVERAGES, DRINKS, AND WINES

In the realm of Caucasian dining, beverages, drinks, and wines are of great importance. For the success of a family celebration, social event, and sometimes even a business transaction may depend on the choice, preparation, and serving of the liquid refreshment.

Russians are renowned tea drinkers who love their strong *chay* or *chai*, served throughout the day at every meal and in between wherever they happen to be—on a train, at work, and, particularly, relaxing with friends. Tea is offered to guests as a welcome gesture, often ceremoniously, and enjoyed in teahouses as well as homes. Traditionally, the beverage is drunk by women in a cup and by men in a glass set in a filigreed or engraved metal holder with a handle. Usually sweetened with sugar, or perhaps honey, the tea is sometimes accompanied by homemade preserves. In Azerbaijan, however, it is flavored with cinnamon or ginger and, perhaps, lemon slices, and served in tulip-shaped clear glasses.

Very important to the serving of tea is the samovar, an ornate urn used to boil water for making the beverage, and a traditional symbol of hospitality. Introduced to Russia by the Mongols, it is a treasured feature of the home, standing as a centerpiece on a table around which conversation and discussions take place. Customarily the hostess makes a cup of tea simply by adding boiling water from the samovar to the strong tea poured from the teapot, set over the samovar to keep it hot. In this way the strength of the tea can be made according to taste. Traditional accompaniments are an attractive assortment of breads, buns, cookies, cakes, pastries, and perhaps cheese and fish dishes.

A great deal of the tea drunk in the Caucasus comes from the mountain slopes and river valleys, especially those in western Georgia where there are extensive plantations. Those just north of Sochi, a renowned seaside resort at the foot of the Caucasus Mountains, in the area around Dagomis are the world's most northerly, producing high quality Krasnodarsky tea. At the Dagomis Tea Farm visitors may take a tour of the grounds and enjoy cups of tea in the tropical gardens.

From the Turks, Caucasians acquired a fondness for strong dark coffee, the traditional social drink, enjoyed in homes, restaurants, and cafés to "seal the bonds of a long friendship." It's even offered by merchants, usually with a glass of water, to potential customers before prices are discussed and bargaining begins. As the saying goes, "Serious conversation does not begin before coffee starts the flow of words."

Commonly called Turkish coffee, each person has a strong opinion about its preparation, sweetness, and service. Made with ground roasted green beans, the coffee is brewed in a special utensil called a *jezve* or *cezve*, made of brass or copper with a long handle, no spout, and no cover. Once brought to a boil, it's poured into a tiny cup, and should be foamy on top, a sign of good luck. The amount of sugar is a matter of taste and one is asked whether it is to be without sugar, medium, or sweet. According to an old adage, the coffee should be as "black as night, hot as fire, and as sweet as love." Although the beverage is sipped, slurping is an accepted custom. Making a great deal of noise while drinking coffee is a way of indicating how good the drink is.

A favorite diversion in the Caucasus is fortune telling by coffee cups. When the coffee is drunk, you put the saucer over the cup, turn them three times around, and quickly turn the cup upside down. Leave until the cup is cooled and the grounds are settled into strange patterns from which the seer interprets one's future.

While Caucasians do enjoy refreshing beverages made with fruit juices, flower waters, yogurt, chocolate, and honey, the drinking of alcoholic libations has always been a national joy as well as a sorrow during good and bad times. The tradition of imbibing continues unabated, a subject mentioned prominently in the novels and books about the area. While Russians and North Caucasians have long favored old-time homemade brews like honey-based mead and the lightly fermented *kvass*, also used in cookery, the preferred drink is vodka.

Known in Russia since the fourteenth century, vodka, meaning "dear little water," is a clear, potent drink distilled from grain, rye, or wheat, or perhaps potatoes or sugar beets. While generally colorless, vodka also comes in several colors and flavors made from various kinds of herbs, spices, fruit, tea, and aromatics. One pink variety is infused with berries, and a yellowish type, called *zubrovka*, is colored with buffalo grass. A unique form of vodka called *chacha* is made in Georgia from grape skins.

Vodka introduces all meals. Drunk chilled and straight, customarily taken in one quick gulp or swallow from a small glass, it is followed by a bite of food or accompanied by appetizers, *zakuski*. In Transcaucasia, however, a traditional drink before meals, as well as in between, particularly in cafés, is a distinctive anise-flavored colorless potent libation called *raki* or *arak*, distilled chiefly from grapes. Sometimes called "lion's milk," usually drunk neat, it turns milky white when diluted with water.

The basic and beloved drink of the Caucasus, however, is wine, a local product that has been important in the culture for centuries. From earliest times, the delicate balance of soil and sunshine, slope and moisture that are needed to produce fine wine grapes are found in many parts of the region, especially Georgia and Armenia. Traces of viticulture have been found in the Armenian plain and the southern part of Transcaucasia. Homer praised the "perfumed, sprightly wines of Colchis, land of the golden grape." Today the vine is still a leading product that fuels the economy, daily life, vision, and character of the people. It also is a symbol of both spiritual and economic wealth.

Caucasians are heirs to the ancient tradition of making wine. According to the Old Testament one of the first things Noah did after his ark landed on Mt. Ararat was to plant a vineyard and some of the earliest recorded accounts of grape growing come from Armenia. Georgia, a principle area for grape cultivation and the production of wines also is rich in historic wine lore. When a young missionary named Saint Nino brought Christianity to Georgia from Cappadocia in Asia Minor she is said to have carried a cross plaited from dried vines and bound with her own hair. Thus the grapevine and cross have been inextricably entwined and wine is an integral part of the daily life.

One of the best places to learn about and enjoy excellent wine is Kakheti, the easternmost region of Georgia, a beautiful and bountiful land of vineyards that stretch all along the highways, throughout the valleys, and around the villages. It is called the homeland of vine growing that can be traced back to about 6,000 B.C., and is the center of the country's thriving wine industry. As mentioned in the preface, a good place for visitors to begin their regional tour is in the capital of Telavi. Situated in the lovely valley of the

Alazani River at the foothills of the Caucasus Mountains, it is dominated by the Batonistsikhe Castle, a massive fortified compound, the former residence of Kakhetian kings.

Although commercial production of wine is significant in Kakheti, almost every village family has its own specialty, made with grapes lovingly cared for and with an age-old method that includes seeds, skins, and stems with the juice as it ferments. Not only does it yield a full-bodied wine with a fine bouquet and hue, believed to be full of vitamins and good for the health, but is touted as a primary reason for the Georgians' longevity.

Kakhetians have a particular flair for making merry with wine that even includes its storage in a large red clay amphora, called a *khevri*, buried ceremoniously underground in a *marani*, or "sacred" garden area. Weeks later, when the jug is unearthed, the seal broken, and the fresh wine poured out, it's a joyous celebration, a gathering of family and friends for feasting and drinking. Certainly one of the best times to be with the hospitable wine lovers is in the glorious autumn during the grape harvest, *rtveli*, enlivened with dancing, singing, feasting, and, of course, imbibing wine.

In Kakheti one finds that red wines are a real discovery and there are a number of outstanding whites, produced in districts that bear their names. Among them are Kindzmarauli, a smooth aromatic red; Mukuzani, a dark, dry strong red, made from Saperavi grapes; and Gurdzhaani, a pale golden white made from Rkatsiteli and Mtsvane grapes. The most popular and notable dry white wine, however, is Tsinandali, produced from Rkatsiteli and Mtsvane grapes at a famous winery on the restored family estate of Prince Alexander Chavchavadze in the village of Tsinandali, located several miles southeast of Telavi.

Now a museum, the house and estate, entered through a pair of handsome wrought-iron gates, have been preserved just as they were in memory of the prince, a nineteenth-century poet, to give visitors an idea of royal Georgian life during his time. Surrounding the pink-grey sandstone house is a handsome park full of domestic and exotic trees and plants, and in the rear, the Tsinandali Winery offering tours and wine-tasting.

Kvareli, northeast of Telavi at the foot of the greater Caucasus Mountains, is famous for its sweetish red wine, Kindsmaruli, produced at a local winery. The town is also the birthplace of the nineteenth-century poet and reformer, Ilia Chavchavadze, whose house, fortified with a tower, has a spacious *marani* and a museum. Both the winery and the home are open to the public and local cafés serve regional specialties and wines.

As previously mentioned, no occasion is complete in Kakheti without wine, and when enjoyed as an accompaniment to food for a joyous meal, Georgians observe an ancient ritual called *supra* that a has a long history, intertwined with that of the country. When you sit down to dine, along with eating one joins in a fixed pattern of toasting in which Georgians pay tribute to the past, present, and future, to honor families and friends, and, perhaps delve into historic or current events. The only restriction to the subject is that one may not drink to anything negative, and, while it is customary to say something about everyone at the table, whether you like them or not, you enunciate something nice.

While wine is served in glasses, held properly only with the right hand, for centuries Georgians drank and in some areas still drink it from skins and horns specially treated for the purpose. These drinking implements came from their herd animals and were cleaned, boiled, and polished, creating a unique durable and quite stylish vessel, sought-after purchases for those who traveled in the Caucasus. What is called the traditional drinking cup or horn, *kanzi*, is conch-shaped and comes in different sizes, often decorated with silver. Because Georgians are famously hospitable people, an essential feature of the horn is that once filled with an appropriate libation, usually wine, it requires drinking to the bottom (*bolomde*) on each toast. Practically, it can't be put down until empty or the liquid will spill. Occasionally, after emptying the horn or a glass, a person will say, "may you be emptied of enemies as this glass has been emptied of wine." In Kakheti the drinking and enjoyment of wine takes on a new meaning.

In her book, *Flying Time*, Elisavietta Ritchie, one of my traveling companions in Kakheti, has a memorable account of a *supra* in an essay entitled, ZURAB, the name of a young man she met at a *supra*.

"He stands like a prince in the State-owned vineyard. In the meadows calves are grazing on chicory and Queen Anne's Lace. Beyond, the peaks of the Caucasus catch the afternoon sun... Here in this flat valley, pomegranates, figs, grape and raspberry vines overhang stone walls painted blue.

At the head of the table sits the *tamada*, toast-master. The tips of his black moustaches reach almost to his ears. He picks up his glass and toasts the strangers God sends. Then with five kinds of wine, we drink to the harvest, the vintage, the collective farm, to the Caucasus mountains Elbruz and Ararat, to the strangers again.

'This wine is the best.' Zurab pours from a bottle studded with medals. 'It won't spoil for one hundred years. Think what it survived! In the tenth century, Persian soldiers surrounded our village. The wine casks were sealed and hidden under layers of clay beneath the cathedral floor. The Persians rode through the portals, camped in the nave, damaged the frescoes, stole whatever gold they could fine. But four years ago a workman repairing the floor of the nave unearthed the casks. Archaeologists flocked, tested the wine—this very kind—and pronounced it superb."

"It is superb," I echo. "Like melted garnets and honey."

Although wine is the preferred Georgian drink, the country also produces good quality brandies such as Egrisi, Vartsikhe, Gremi, Kazbegi, Abkhazeti, Tbilisi, and Sakartvelo, as well as beer, mineral waters, and champagne.

ARMENIA

Wine has always been a fundamental product in Armenia and the country has been called "Fatherland of the Vine." The grape is a part of the national culture. One region of cultivation is around Lake Sevan where in the volcanic soil there are vineyards producing dry white table wines, as well as champagne-style and fortified wines. Another region known for its wine is Areni, southeast of Yerevan.

Armenia is justly proud of its brandy, "the beverage that feeds the soul," produced for over a hundred years. Today the country boasts a wide range of fine brandy, especially the renowned colorless and mildly flavored Ararat, very smooth with a high alcoholic content. In production since 1887, it is aged in oak barrels for three or five years, or for six finer brands, seven to twenty years, at the Yerevan Brandy company where visitors are welcome to take tours and see a video presentation. There's also a museum.

In Armenia brandy is drunk chilled with slices of lemon to complement the rich, smooth flavor. Enjoyed as an aperitif as well as an after-dinner drink, it is also drunk with the meal as Armenians believe the taste of the brandy goes well with food.

Armenia has 700 natural springs producing high-quality mineral waters, prized for their medicinal qualities and also important exports. The most famous are at Jermuk, Arzni, Dilijan, Bjni, Hankavan, and Svan.

Cuisines of the Caucasus Mountains

Although Azerbaijan is primarily a Moslem nation where soft drinks and fruit beverages are commonly enjoyed and tea is the national drink, the people do consume a number of alcoholic drinks, especially vodka and *kvass*, as well as a strong local brew called *tutovka*, distilled from mulberries. Table wines are produced in the areas around Kirovabad as well as Kuramirsk, Chemakhinsk, and Geokchai. Some dessert and fortified wines are also made in the region.

In modern times Caucasian wines and spirits have been little known outside of the area and Russia because of limited production and distribution but they have gained a favorable reputation in Europe and are becoming better known in America.

Here are recipes for a few of the beverages.

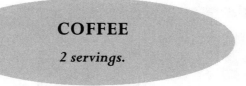

COFFEE

2 servings.

3 to 5 teaspoons sugar
2 teaspoons pulverized coffee

Put ½ cup cold water in a cylindrical pot with a long handle or small saucepan. Add sugar, according to taste, and coffee. Stir well. Place over medium-low heat. Bring to a full boil. Remove from heat; pour off froth into 2 demitasse cups. Bring to a boil again. Remove from heat. Pour coffee over froth to fill the cups.

COLD YOGURT DRINK

1 serving.

This typical Caucasian beverage is a soothing, creamy drink to serve with meals or in between as a snack. It's simple to make and good for the health, particularly during warm weather.

> ½ cup plain yogurt
> Salt to taste
> 2 fresh mint leaves

In a medium bowl or electric blender combine the yogurt, ½ cup cold water, and salt. Mix or blend until smooth and creamy. Pour into a tall glass. Refrigerate or add ice cubes. Serve garnished with mint leaves.

MINT TEA

6 servings.

This is a refreshing drink for a summer get-together.

> 1 tablespoon green tea
> 1 large bunch fresh mint leaves
> About ¼ cup sugar

Preheat a teapot by rinsing with ½ cup hot water. Put tea into pot; add mint leaves and sugar. Cover with boiling water (about 4 cups) and let steep 3 to 5 minutes, stirring a little at the end. Pour into glasses.

BIBLIOGRAPHY

Agayev, Emil. *Baku: A Guide*. Moscow: Raduga Publishers, 1987.

Army, Department of the. *Armenia, Azerbaijan, and Georgia, County Studies*. Washington, DC: Government Printing Office, 1995.

Cressey, George B. *The Basis of Soviet Strength*. New York: McGraw Hill, 1945.

Davidson, Alan. *The Oxford Companion to Food*. New York: Oxford University Press, 1999.

Goldstein, Darra. *A La Russe*. New York: Random House, 1983. *The Georgian Feast*. Berkeley: University of California Press, 1999.

Kaplan, Robert D. *Eastward to Tartary*. New York: Random House, 2000.

Karny, Yo'av. *Highlanders: A Journey to the Caucasus in Quest of Memory*. New York: Farrar, Straus & Giroux, 2000.

Lermontov, Mikhail. *A Hero of our Time*. London: J.M. Dent, 1995.

Maclean, Fitzroy. *Eastern Approaches*. London: Jonathan Cape, 1949. *To Caucasus, the End of all the Earth*. Boston: Little Brown & Co., 1976.

Margvelashvili, Julianne, *The Classic Cuisine of Georgia*. New York: Prentice Hall, 1991.

Nelson, Kay Shaw. *The Eastern European Cookbook*. Chicago: Henry Regnery Co., 1973. *Mediterranean Cooking for Everyone*. New York: Dover, 1979.

Norman, Barbara. *The Russian Cookbook*. New York: Atheneum, 1967.

Ritchie, Elisavietta. *Flying Time*. Carrboro, NC: Signal Books, 1996.

Shoemaker, M. Wesley. *Russia, Eurasian States and Eastern Europe*. Styker-Post Publications, 1999.

Spector, Ivan. *An Introduction to Russian History & Culture*. Princeton, NJ: D. VanNostrand Co. Inc., 1949.

Taplin, Mark. *Open Lands: Travels Through Russia's Once Forbidden Places*. South Royalton, VT: Steeforth Press, 1997.

VonBremzen, Anya, and Welchman, John. *Please to the Table*. New York: Workman, 1990.

Wilson, Neil; Potter, Beth; Rowson, David; and Japaridze, Keti. *Georgia, Armenia & Azerbaijan*. Melbourne: Lonely Planet Publications, 2000.

RECIPE INDEX

A

A Centerpiece of Fresh Herbs, 25
A Garnished Herring Platter, 31
Almond (s)
  Appetizer, Sesame-, 35
  Salted, 27
Anchovy (ies)
  -Flavored Potatoes, 155
  -Pepper Relish from Shekki, 37
  Purée, 36
A Pink Cabbage "Rose," 41
Appetizer (s)
  A Centerpiece of Fresh Herbs, 25
  A Garnished Herring Platter, 31
  Anchovy-Pepper Relish from Shekki, 37
  Anchovy Purée, 36
  A Pink Cabbage "Rose," 41
  Armenian Bulgur-Vegetable Dip, 39
  Caspian Sea Caviar, 28
  Cucumber Pickles, 46
  Eggplant with Walnut Sauce, 38
  Eugenia's Cold White Beans, 40
  from Lahic, Spinach-Yogurt, 45
  Georgian Lobio from Gori, 34
  Jermuk Cucumber-Yogurt, 42
  Mtskheta Eggplant Caviar, 32
  Pickled Mushrooms, 47
  Pickles and Relishes, 46
  Red Caviar Spread, 30
  Rice-Stuffed Grape Leaves, 43
  Salted Almonds, 27
  Sesame-Almond, 35
Apple-Horseradish Sauce, Fish with, 103

Apsheron Chicken with Okra, 147
Apricot (s)
  Armenian Baked, 231
  -Raisin Confection, 232
Armenia (n)
  Baked Apricots, 231
  Barley-Yogurt Soup, 60
  Bulgur Pilaf, 182
    with Fruit, 193
    -Vegetable Dip, 39
  Fish Plaki, 105
  Ground Meat Kebabs, 138
  Küfte, 134
  Lamb Stew with Spinach, 127
  Lentils and Bulgur, 183
  Stuffed Mussels, 118
  Thin Bread, 203
Azerbaijan (i)
  Baked Eggs with Vegetables, 86
  Herbed Lamb Patties, 133
  Rice with Fruit, 191
  Spinach-Veal Stew, 130

B

Baked Mackerel with Yogurt Sauce, 116
Baked Quinces, 239
Baklava, 241
Balkar Lamb Pilaf, 126
Barley
  -Mushroom Casserole, 181
  -Mushroom Soup, Nazran, 68
  -Yogurt Soup, Armenian, 60
Bass with Tomatoes, 115
Batumi Fisherman's Omelet, 82

Bean(s)
  and Eggs, Green, 79
  Eugenia's Cold White, 40
  Georgian Green, 161
  Lobio from Gori, Georgian, 34
  Pie, Georgian Green, 87
  Salad, Seda Gelenian's, 170
Beef
  Armenian Ground Meat Kebabs, 138
  Armenian *Küfte*, 134
  Kebabs, 13
  Kotlety, 123
  Meatballs with Egg-Lemon Sauce, 139
  Mint *Köftas*, 135
Beet
  Borshch, 51
  Soup with Sour Cream, Cold, 53
  -Yogurt Salad, 173
Beverages, Drinks and Wines, 249
Black Sea Olive-Stuffed Carp, 108
Bliny, 200
Boereks, 220
Borshch, 51
Braised
  Carrots with Yogurt, 162
  Quail with Pilaf, 150
Bread (s)
  Armenian Thin, 203
  Georgian Cheese, 204
  from Kuba, Onion, 202
  Kutashi Corn, 207
  Pastas, and Savory Pastries, 197
Bulgur
  Armenian Lentils and, 183
  Pilaf,
    Armenian, 182

  with Fruit, Armenian, 193
  with Yogurt, Minted, 184

C

Cabbage (s)
  "Rose," A Pink, 41
  Salad, Winter, 169
  Soup, Russian, 71
Cake (s)
  Lemon-Yogurt, 243
  Walnut, 242
Carrot (s)
  Salad, Sauerkraut-, 176
  with Yogurt, Braised, 162
Caspian Sea Caviar, 28
Cauliflower Salad, Garnished, 171
Caviar
  Caspian Sea, 28
  Mtskheta Eggplant, 32
  Spread, Red, 30
Chechen Mushroom-Pepper
  Medley, 163
Cheese (s)
  Balls, Yogurt, 95
  Bread, Georgian, 204
  -Filled Pasta, 209
  -Filled Pastry, 220
  -Garlic Spread, 93
  Georgian
    Fried, 90
    Grits with, 194
  with Olives, Fried, 90
  Pancakes, 91
  Spread, Walnut, 92
  Yogurt, 95
  Yogurt Dressing, Cottage, 97
Chicken
  Chakhokhbili, 144

Circassian, 141
with Okra, Apsheron, 147
with Plum Sauce, Georgian
Spitted, 14
Rice-Nut Stuffed, 143
Salad Olivier, 148
Soup,
Georgian Lemony, 54
Kislovodsk Yogurt, 59
Tabaka, 146
Chickpea Medley, 196
Cinnamon Cookies, 245
Circassian Chicken, 141
Coffee, 255
Cold
Beet Soup with Sour Cream, 53
Meat-Vegetable Soup, 56
Yogurt Drink, 256
Soups, 62, 63
Cookies
Cinnamon, 245
Twigs, 244
Corn Bread, Kutashi, 207
Cottage Cheese Yogurt Dressing,
97
Cucumber
Pickles, 46
-Radish Salad, 175
-Yogurt Appetizer, Jermuk, 42

D

Dairy Dishes, 73
Dates, Nut-Stuffed, 248
Derbent Fish Soup, 66
Desserts and Sweets, 225
Apricot-Raisin Confection, 232
Armenian Baked Apricots, 231
Baked Quinces, 239

Baklava, 241
Cinnamon Cookies, 245
Easter *Paskha*, 229
Figs
in Wine, 235
Nut-Stuffed, 236
Fruit Compote, 238
Georgian Walnut Sweet, 246
Honey Mousse, 228
Kissel, 227
Lemon Yogurt Cake, 243
Mount Ararat Pudding, 233
Mount Kazbek Honey Walnuts,
247
Nut-Filled Shredded Pastry, 237
Nut-Stuffed Dates, 248
Pistachio Milk Pudding, 230
Pumpkin-Nut Pudding, 234
Twigs, 244
Walnut Cake, 242
Yogurt Fritters in Syrup, 240
Drink(s)
Coffee, 255
Cold Yogurt, 256
Mint Tea, 256
and Wines, Beverages, 249
Dumplings, Filled, 212

E

Easter *Paskha*, 229
Echmiadzin Rice-Filled Tomatoes,
165
Egg (s)
Batumi Fisherman's Omelet, 83
Gardener's Omelet, 85
Garnished, 77
Georgian Green Bean Pie, 87
Green Beans and, 79

and Lemon Soup from Gyumri, 55

Pancakes, Potato-, 84

à la Russe, 7

Sour Cream Stuffed, 78

in Spinach, Poached, 82

from Tarki, Spiced, 76

with Vegetables, Azerbaijan Baked, 86

with White Cheese, Scrambled, 81

in Yogurt, Poached, 80

Eggplant

  Caviar, Mtskheta, 32

  Chips, 156

  Dishes, 156

  Fried, 157

  in Olive Oil, 158

  Pasta with, 214

  -Vegetable Stew, 159

  with Walnut Sauce, 38

  -Yogurt Salad, 172

Eugenia's Cold White Beans, 40

Herbed Grilled Trout, 107

Kebabs, Mount Aragats Skewered, 112

Kobuleti Bream Stuffed with Kasha, 104

Lake Sevan Trout, 106

Makhachkala Herring Salad, 101

Plaki, Armenian, 105

Rice-Nut Stuffed, 113

Soup, Derbent, 66

Stepanakert Baked, 109

Stew, 117

Sturgeon Baked in Sour Cream, 102

Fresh Mint Yogurt Dressing, 96

Fried

  Cheese with Olives, 90

  Fish with Caper Sauce, 114

Fritters in Syrup, Yogurt, 240

Fruit,

  Armenian Bulgur Pilaf with, 193

  Azerbaijani Rice with, 191

  Compote, 238

F

Fig (s)

  Nut-Stuffed, 236

  in Wine, 235

Filled Dumplings, 212

Fish, 99

  with Apple-Horseradish Sauce, 103

  Baked Mackerel with Yogurt Sauce, 116

  Bass with Tomatoes, 115

  Black Sea Olive-Stuffed Carp, 108

  with Caper Sauce, Fried, 114

  Cooked in Paper, 111

G

Gardener's

  Omelet, 85

  Stew, 160

Garlic Spread, Cheese-, 93

Garnished

  Cauliflower Salad, 171

  Cold Yogurt Soup, 63

  Eggs, 77

Georgia (n)

  Cheese Bread, 204

  Fried Cheese, 90

  Green Bean (s), 161

  Pie, 87

  Grits with Cheese, 194

Holiday Pilaf, 187
Lemony Chicken Soup, 54
Lobio from Gori, 34
Meat-Rice Soup, 57
Pheasant, 149
Spitted Chicken with Plum
    Sauce, 140
Walnut Sweet, 246
Ghivetch, 128
Grains and Legumes, 177
Grape Leaves, Rice-Stuffed, 43
Green Bean (s)
    and Eggs, 79
    Pie, Georgian, 87
Grits with Cheese, Georgian, 194

H
Herb (s, ed)
    A Centerpiece of Fresh, 25
    Basmati Rice *Plov*, 190
    Grilled Trout, 107
    Soup from Tusheti, Mushroom-,
    69
Herring
    Platter, A Garnished, 31
    Salad, Makhachkala, 101
Honey
    Millet Porridge, 195
    Mousse, 228
    Walnuts, Mount Kazbek, 247
Horseradish Sauce, Fish with
    Apple, 103

J
Jermuk Cucumber-Yogurt
    Appetizer, 42

K
Kasha
    Kobuleti Bream Stuffed with, 104
    Pilaf, 180
    Russian, 179
Kebab(s), 136
    Armenian Ground Meat, 138
    with Yogurt Sauce, Shish, 137
Kislovodsk Yogurt-Chicken Soup,
    59
Kizlyar Rice with Mushrooms, 189
Kissel, 227
Kobuleti Bream Stuffed with
    Kasha, 104
Kobustan Zucchini Cake, 88
Kulebiaka, Salmon, 218
Kutashi Corn Bread, 207

L
Lake Sevan Trout, 106
Lak Winter Vegetable Soup, 70
Lamb
    Armenian
        Kebab, 136
        Küfte, 134
    -Filled Noodle Crescents, 222
    Ghivetch, 128
    Kebabs, 136
    -Lentil Pot, 65
    Mint *Köftas*, 135
    Musaka, Rice-, 132
    Patties, Azerbaijani Herbed, 133
    Pilaf, Balkar, 126
    Shashlyk, 124
    Shish Kebab with Yogurt Sauce,
    137
    Stew with Spinach, 127
    -Stuffed Vegetables, 131

Legumes, Grains and, 177
Lemon
    Sauce, Meatballs with Egg-, 139
    Soup from Gyumri, Egg and, 55
    Yogurt Cake, 243
Lentil (s)
    and Bulgur, Armenian, 183
    Pot, Lamb-, 65
    -Spinach Soup, 64
Lobio from Gori, Georgian, 34

M

Makhachkala Herring Salad, 101
Meatball (s)
    with Egg-Lemon Sauce, 139
    Koftas, Mint, 135
    Soup, Yogurt, 61
Meat, Poultry, and Game, 121
Millet Porridge, Honey-, 195
Mint (ed)
    Bulgur with Yogurt, 184
    Köftas, 135
    Tea, 256
    Yogurt Dressing, Fresh, 96
Mount Aragats Skewered Fish
    Kebabs, 112
Mount Ararat Pudding, 233
Mount Elbrus Tomato Pilaf, 186
Mount Kazbek Honey Walnuts, 247
Mtskheta Eggplant Caviar, 32
Mushroom
    Casserole, Barley-, 181
    -Filled *Pirozhki*, 216
    -Herb Soup from Tusheti, 69
    Kizlyar Rice with, 189
    Patties, Potato-, 153
    -Pepper Medley, Chechen, 163
    Pickled, 47

Soup, Nazran Barley, 68
Mussels, Armenian Stuffed, 118

N

Nazran Barley-Mushroom Soup, 68
Noodle (s)
    Crescents, Lamb-Filled, 222
    Pilaf with, 188
    with Sour Cream, 211
    with Yogurt Sauce, 215
Nut
    -Filled Shredded Pastry, 237
    -Stuffed Dates, 248
    -Stuffed Figs, 236

O

Okra, Apsheron Chicken with, 147
Olive (s)
    Fried Cheese with, 90
    -Stuffed Carp, Black Sea, 108
Onion Bread from Kuba, 202

P

Pancakes
    Bliny, 200
    Potato-Egg, 84
    Yogurt, 208
Pashka, Easter, 229
Pasta (s)
    Cheese-Filled, 209
    with Eggplant, 214
    and Savory Pastries, Breads, 197
Pastries, Breads, Pastas and Savory,
    197
Pepper(s)
    Medley, Chechen Mushroom-, 163
    Vegetable Stuffed Green, 166
Pheasant, Georgian, 149

Pickle (s, ed)
  Cucumbers, 46
  Mushrooms, 47
  and Relishes, 46
Pilaf (s), 185
  Armenian Bulgur, 182
  Balkan Lamb, 126
  Braised Quail with, 150
  with Fruit, Armenian Bulgur, 193
  Georgian Holiday, 187
  Kasha, 180
  with Noodles, 188
  Mount Elbrus Tomato, 186
Pistachio Milk Pudding, 230
Pirozhki, Mushroom-Filled, 216
Pita Pockets, 206
Plov, Herbed Basmati Rice, 190
Plum Sauce, Georgian Spitted
  Chicken with, 140
Poached Eggs in Spinach, 82
Poached Eggs in Yogurt, 80
Porridge, Honey Millet, 195
Potato (es)
  Anchovy Flavored, 155
  -Egg Pancakes, 84
  -Mushroom Patties, 153
Pudding
  Mount Ararat, 233
  Pistachio-Milk, 230
  Pumpkin-Nut, 234

Q

Quail with Pilaf, Braised, 150
Quinces, Baked, 239

R

Radish (es)
  Salad, Cucumber-, 175
  in Sour Cream, 174
Red Caviar Spread, 30
Relishes, Pickles and, 46
Rice
  -Filled Tomatoes, Echmiadzin,
  165
  with Fruit, Azerbaijan, 191
  Lamb *Musaka*, 132
  with Mushrooms, Kizlyar, 189
  -Nut Stuffed Chicken, 143
  -Nut Stuffed Fish, 113
  Pilaf (s), 185
  Plov, Herbed Basmati Rice, 190
  Soup, Georgian Meat-, 57
  -Stuffed Grape Leaves, 43
  Stuffing, 192
Russian
  Cabbage Soup, 71
  Kasha, 179

S

Salad (s)
  Beet-Yogurt, 173
  Cucumber-Radish, 175
  Eggplant-Yogurt, 172
  Garnished Cauliflower, 171
  Makhachkala Herring, 101
  Olivier, 148
  Sauerkraut-Carrot, 176
  Seda Gelenian's Bean, 170
  Vegetables and, 151
  Vegetable-Walnut, 168
  Winter Cabbage, 169
Salmon *Kulebiaka*, 218
Salted Almonds, 27

Sauerkraut-Carrot Salad, 176
Scrambled Eggs with White
   Cheese, 81
Seda Gelenian's Bean Salad, 170
Sesame-Almond Appetizer, 35
Shashlyk, 124
Shish Kebab with Yogurt sauce, 137
Soup (s), 49
   Armenian Barley-Yogurt, 60
   Borshch, 51
   Cold Meat-Vegetable, 56
   Cold Yogurt
      Garnished, 63
      Zaqatala Walnut, 62
   Derbent Fish, 66
   Georgian Lemony Chicken, 54
   Georgian Meat-rice, 57
   from Gyumri, Egg and Lemon, 55
   Kislovodsk Yogurt-Chicken, 59
   Lak Winter Vegetable, 70
   Lamb-Lentil Pot, 65
   Lentil-Spinach, 64
   Nazran Barley-Mushroom, 68
   Russian Cabbage, 71
   with Sour Cream, Cold Beet, 53
   from Tusheti, Mushroom-Herb, 69
   Yogurt-Meatball, 61
   Zaqatala Walnut-Yogurt, 62
Sour Cream
   Cold Beet Soup with, 53
   Noodles with, 211
   Radishes in, 174
   Stuffed Eggs, 78
   Sturgeon Baked in, 102
   Vegetables in, 154
Spiced Eggs from Tarki, 76
Spinach
   Armenian Lamb Stew with, 127

-Lentil Soup, 64
   Poached Eggs in, 82
   -Veal Stew, Azerbaijan, 130
   -Yogurt Appetizer from Lahic, 45
Stepanakert Baked Fish, 109
Stuffed Vegetables, 164
Stuffing, Rice, 192
Sturgeon Baked in Sour Cream,
   102
Sweets, Desserts and, 225

T

Tabaka, Chicken, 146
Tea, Mint, 256
Tomato (es)
   Bass with, 115
   Echmiadzin Rice-Filled, 165
   Pilaf, Mount Elbrus, 186
Trout,
   Herbed Grilled, 107
   Lake Sevan, 106
Twigs, 244

V

Veal Stew, Azerbaijan Spinach-, 130
Vegetable (s)
   Azerbaijan Baked Eggs with, 86
   Dip, Armenian Bulgur-, 39
   Lamb-Stuffed, 131
   and Salads, 151
   Soup,
      Cold Meat, 156
      Lak Winter, 70
   in Sour Cream, 154
   Stew, Eggplant, 159
   -Stuffed, 164
   -Stuffed Green Peppers, 166
   -Walnut Salad, 168

W

Walnut (s)
  Cake, 242
  -Cheese Spread, 92
  Mount Kazbek Honey, 247
  Salad, Vegetable-, 168
  Sauce, Eggplant with, 38
  Sweet, Georgian, 246
  Yogurt Soup, Zaqatala, 62
Wine (s), Beverages, Drinks and, 249
Winter Cabbage Salad, 169

Y

Yogurt
  Appetizer
    from Lahic, Spinach-, 45
    Jermuk Cucumber-, 42
  Braised Carrots with, 162
  Cake, Lemon, 243
  Cheese, 95
  Cheese Balls, 95
  Chicken Soup, Kislovodsk, 59
  Dressing
    Cottage Cheese, 97
    Fresh Mint, 96
  Drink, Cold, 256
  Fritters in Syrup, 240
  Minted Bulgur with, 184
  Pancakes, 208
  Poached Eggs in, 80
  Raw Vegetable Dip, 94
  Salad
    Beet, 173
    Eggplant, 172
  Sauce
    Baked Mackerel with, 116
    Noodles with, 215
    Shish Kebab with, 137

Soup,
  Armenian-Barley, 60
  Cold, 62
  Garnished Cold, 63
  -Meatball, 61
  Zaqatala Walnut-, 62

Z

Zaqatala Walnut-Yogurt Soup, 62
Zakuska (i), 21, 22, 251.
Zucchini Cake, Kobustan, 88

SUBJECT INDEX

A

Abkhazia (ns), 4, 9, 10
Abu al-Fida, 3
Adzharia (ns), 1, 10, 83, 104
Alazani River, 252
Apsheron Peninsula, 2, 12, 13, 147
Aras River, 7, 12
Areni, 254
Armenia (ians), xi, 2, 4-8, 11-15,
    22, 39, 42, 43, 50, 55, 60, 74,
    75, 99, 105, 106, 118,127, 231,
    254
Armenian Apostolic Orthodox
    faith, 6
Asia Minor, 251
Azeri(s), 3, 12, 13, 14
Azerbaijan (ians), xi, 2, 4, 11-15,
    22, 37, 45, 50, 62, 74, 75, 86,
    88, 130, 133, 202, 248

B

Baku, 12-14, 147
Balkar (s), 126
Batonistsikhe Castle, 252
Batumi, xi, 10, 83, 104
Black Sea, xi, 1, 2, 6, 9, 10, 83,
    99, 104, 108, 155
Blanch, Lesley, 124
Borzhomi, xii

C

Cappadocia, 251
Caspian Sea, xi, 1, 2, 6, 11-13, 28,
    66, 99, 101, 147
Caucasian Mountains, xi, xii, xiv,
    1, 2, 3, 5, 8, 15, 249, 252

Caviar, 28, 29
Central Asia, 13, 14
Chechnya, 1, 8, 18, 163
Chavchavadze
    Ilia, 9, 252
    Prince Alexander, 252
Circassians, 3, 141
Colchis, xi, 2, 9, 149, 251
Cressey, Dr. George B., 15

D

Dagestan, 1, 3, 12, 69, 70, 76, 101
Dagomis, Tea Farm, 249
Derbent, 66

E

Echmiadzin, 165

F

Fuzuli, 14

G

Garden Of Eden, xi, xvi
Gelenian, Seda, 176
Georgia (ians), xi-xvi, 2, 8-11, 22,
    32, 34, 50, 54, 57, 74, 75, 87,
    99, 124, 140, 149, 251, 253
Georgian Military Highway, xii,
    15, 247
Georgian Orthodox Church, 9
Golden Fleece, xi, 9
Goldstein, Darra, 199
Gori, 34
Grozy, 161
Gyumri, 55

H

Hadji Murad, 37
Homer, 251

I

Iberia, 9
Imerti, 207
Ingushetia, 1, 8, 68
Iran (Persia), 2, 6, 12, 13, 38
Istanbul, Turkey, xvi, 40
Iveria, xi

J

Jermuk, 42

K

Kabardino-Balkaria, 1, 126
Karachay-Cherkessia, 1
Kakheti (ans), xi, xiv, 18, 251-53
Kaplan, Robert D., 8
Karny, Yo'av, 3
Kartli, 34
Kartilian Plain, 9
Kazbegi, 247
Khevsureti, 11
Kislovodsk, 17, 59
Kizlyar, 18, 189
Kobuleti, 104
Kobustan, 88
Kolkhida, 2, 9
Krasnodar, 2
Krasnodarsky Tea, 250
Kuba, 202
Kura-Aras Plain, 2
Kura River, xii, 2, 3, 12, 13
Kurds, 4
Kutashi, 207
Kvareli, 9, 252

L

Lahic, 45
Laks, 70
Lake Sevan, 3, 99, 106, 254
Lake Van, 6
Learmont, George, 16
Leningrad (St. Petersburg), xi, xiv, 16
Lenkoran lowlands, 13
Lermonton, Mikhail Yurievich, 16-18

M

Maclean, Sir Fitzroy, 18, 19
Maiden's Tower, 14
Makhachkala, 76, 101
Margvelashvili, Julianne, 204
Maxwell School of Citizenship, Syracuse University, 15
Mongols, 249
Moses, xv
Mount (Mt.)
    Aragats, 2, 6, 112
    Ararat, 2, 8, 186, 233, 251
    Bazar-dyuzi, 12
    Blanc, 2
    Dykh-Tau, 2
    Elbrus, 2, 186
    Kazbek, 2, 247
    Shkara, 2
    Ushba, 2
Mtskheta, xii, 32

N

Nagorno-Karabakh, 4, 12, 109
Nakhichevan, 4, 12
National Carpet Museum, Baku, 14
National Press Club, xi

Nazran, 68
Nizami, 14
Noah, 6, 233, 251

O

Ossetia (n), 3, 4
  North, 1, 8, 18
  South, 10

P

Pasanauri, 199
Polo, Marco, 12
Prometheus, xi, 247
Pshavi, 11
Pushkin, Alexander S., 16
Pyatigorsk, 17, 18

R

Rioni River, 3, 149, 207
Ritchie, Elisavietta, 253-4
Russia (n), Federation, 1, 3, 12,
  51, 250
Rustaveli, Shota, xii, 9

S

Saint Nino, 251
Saniore, 18
Scythians, 3
Sea of Azov, 1
Shekki, 37
Sochi, 249
Stavropol, 2
Stepanakert, 109
St. Petersburg (Leningrad), xi, xiv
Sukumi, xii, 10
Supra, xiv, 253
Surami Range, 3, 8
Svanti, 11

Syracuse University, xi, 15

T

Taman Peninsula, 2
Tarki, 76
Tbilisi (Tiflis), xi, xii, xiv, 11, 16, 18
Telavi, xi, 251, 252
Terek River, 189
Tolstoy, Leo, 18, 37, 71
Transcaucasia (Transcaucasus), 2,
  5, 6
Tsinandali Winery, 252
Tskhinvali, 10
Turgenev, Ivan, 123
Turkey, xi, 2, 6
Turks (Turkish), 250
Tusheti, 7, 8, 11, 69

V

Vodka, 250, 251

W

Wines, Beverages, Drinks And,
  251-255

Y

Yerevan (Ervean), 7, 8, 112, 165,
  254
Yessentuki, 17
Yogurt, 74, 95

Z

Zanga River, 7
Zaqatala, 62
Zheleznovodsk, 17

Also by Kay Shaw Nelson . . .

ALL ALONG THE RHINE
RECIPES, WINES AND LORE FROM GERMANY, FRANCE, SWITZERLAND, AUSTRIA, LIECHTENSTEIN AND HOLLAND

This wonderful collection of over 130 recipes spans the range of home cooking, from Appetizers, Soups, Main Courses, and Side Dishes, to Desserts and Beverages. Among the recipes included are traditional favorites and signature dishes from the six countries: "Cheese Fondue," "Balzers Split Pea-Sausage Stew," "Alpine Sauerkraut Soup," "Bratwurst in Beer," and "Pears in Red Wine."

Each chapter covers the culinary history and winemaking tradition of a different Rhine country. The literary excerpts, legends and lore throughout the book will enchant the reader-chef on this culinary cruise down one of the world's most famous rivers.

230 PAGES • 5 ½ X 8 ½ • B/W PHOTOS • 0-7818-0830-8 • $24.95HC • (89)

THE SCOTTISH-IRISH PUB & HEARTH COOKBOOK

From hearty, wholesome recipes for family dinners, to more sophisticated and exotic dishes for entertaining with flair, this book is the perfect source for dining the Celtic way! In this collection of 170 recipes of the best of Scottish and Irish pub fare and home cooking, you'll find old classics like Corn Beef 'N Cabbage, Cock-A-Leekie, Avalon Apple Pie, and Fish and Chips, and new recipes as well: Tobermory Smoked Salmon Pâté, Raisin Walnut Porridge, and Skibbereen Scallop-Mushroom Pie. Each chapter begins with entertaining stories, legends, and lore about Celtic peoples, traditions, customs, and history.

260 PAGES • 5 ½ X 8 ½ • B/W PHOTOS/ILLUSTRATIONS • 0-7818-0741-7 • $24.95HC • (164)

Prices subject to change without prior notice. To purchase Hippocrene Books contact your local bookstore, call (718) 454-2366, or write to: **HIPPOCRENE BOOKS**, 171 Madison Avenue, New York, NY 10016. Please enclose check or money order, adding $5.00 shipping (UPS) for the first book, and $.50 for each additional book.